D1563380

Elliott Sharp

IrRational Music

Terra Nova Press
NEWARK   CALLICOON   MATSALU

2019

© 2019 by Elliott Sharp
all rights reserved
ISBN: 978-1-949597-00-4

Published by

in collaboration with

Terra Nova Press
NEWARK   CALLICOON   MATSALU

found sound nation

Publisher: David Rothenberg
Editor-in-Chief: Evan Eisenberg
Designer: Martin Pedanik
Development: Kyla-Rose Smith and Christopher Marianetti, *Found Sound Nation*
Copy editor: Tyran Grillo
Cover photo by Andreas Sterzing

set in Giovanni and Gotham
printed by Tallinn Book Printers, Tallinn, Estonia
on Munken Lynx paper, flexibound

Library of Congress Control Number: 2018957964

1 2 3 4 5 6 7 8 9 10

www.terranovapress.com

Distributed to the trade by the MIT Press

IrRational Music:
Sixteen Pieces in the Shape of a Memoir

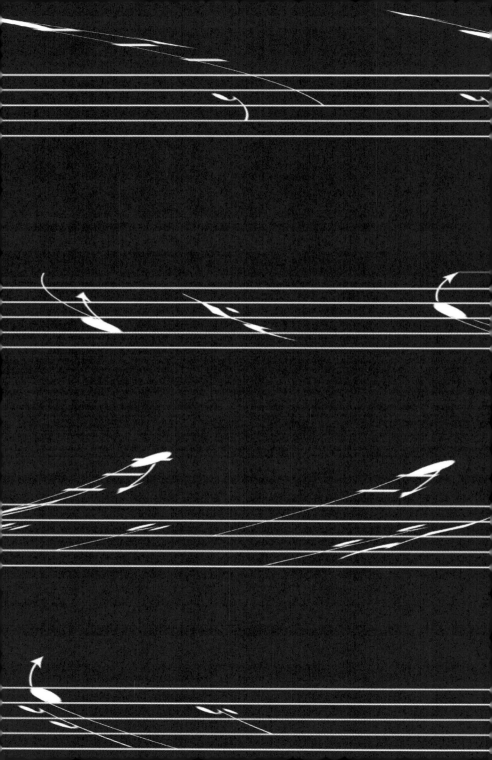

Preface

Found Sound Nation (FSN) is an artists' collective that uses music-making to connect people across cultural divides. We believe that collaborative music creation is a deeply effective way to become aware of the beauty, trauma, and hidden potential in our communities. Our aim is to enliven a global conversation about how creative collaboration in music can address issues we face locally and collectively, while making the world a funkier and more harmonious place.

When we began Found Sound Nation, we started with with two seemingly disparate questions: how can we be the most creative musicians that we can be? And how can our music be relevant to the greater world? We found that at the confluence of these two questions was a fraught and intriguing slice of artistry that some call art as social practice, and others (perhaps Eliott Sharp included) might prefer to call "art as life itself."

Over the years we've had countless inspiring encounters with musically luminous souls, from greats like Pauline Oliveros to incarcerated teenagers to third-graders just discovering the endless joys of noise-making. We wish to support books and media in which musicians share their creative processes so that readers can be inspired to make things in new ways—in solo contexts, in collaboration, and within our neighborhoods and nation-states.

We are very honored to take this maiden voyage into publishing under the wide sails of Elliott Sharp. His dedication to listening to the minutiae of the Inner Ear is both relentlessly abstract and deeply rooted in morality, linked with the mass movements of humanity and even the grinding of tectonic plates. *IrRational Music* is part memoir, part philosophical treatise, and part manifesto. We hope that upon reading it you, dear reader, will listen to the wildest tones within your imagination, and explore the sonic potential of all the resonant objects within your grasp.

Jeremy Thal
Kyla-Rose Smith
Christopher Marianetti

Introduction:
Portal to Sound
and Silence

I enter the factory. Its dark space looms over me, dominated by three towering punch presses, their black iron cut by the gleaming shafts of pistons. The presses make a visceral impact—a deep thud accompanied by a crunch, then a muted ring—as a raw metal speaker basket is stamped out. There's movement in the air with each cycle, a slight breeze to accompany the distortion and cutting of steel.

Stamped steel has a smell, a tang of iron and chill, tempered here by lubricating oil. As the machines are hardly ever in sync, there's a continuous asymmetrical dance, a groove of seemingly infinite variations that never resolves. It's monstrous, terrifying, seductive. I don't think of it as music, though it reminds me of the dinosaur segment in Disney's *Fantasia* (which I will later learn was Stravinsky's *The Rite of Spring*). I've never heard a clatter like that before. I love it.

A few steps away, a door leads to an office. Quiet and fluorescent-lit, it glows against the dark of factory. Then another door. I enter the anechoic chamber, amber tiles absorbing and dissipating all reflection. It's eerily quiet. When I say "Hello," my voice feels disembodied. The hearing part of my brain feels like it's been transported outside of my skull.

It's 1958, and I'm seven years old. This is my first visit to "the plant," the office and factory of University Loudspeakers where my father has recently become a design engineer. With that initiation, doors open to sound, and from there to music.

I'd never imagined that music would become my life. But the exhilaration I feel being in the plant for a few short minutes is like escaping from my familiar world to an alien universe that I can't even begin to describe, only replay again and again. That night I dream about the punch presses, about the silent chamber. More than just the sensations or their organization, sound has become a mapping of the physical to the metaphysical, what I hear in the world translated to what I hear in my Inner Ear and back again. I can immerse myself in the memory of the sound. The Inner Ear is now a place to both reflect on the perceptions of the world and invent what sound could possibly be: a soundtrack to the utopian.

I.

IrRational Music and the Inner Ear

Feedback: something for nothing. Generation of sound and light, structures growing from a seed, the tiniest impulse. Feedback loop: returning information from output to source. The Inner Ear could not exist without it. IrRational Music is my name for the manifestation of that which I hear in my Inner Ear.

In grade school I became fascinated by number patterns, such as the Fibonacci Sequence and the irrational numbers, both for their nature and for their appearance. Their presence, I felt, infuses the infinite into all that we perceive and act upon. Most of the music I was experiencing was all too concrete: songs, short classical pieces, television music. I wondered how music could be infinite, but I couldn't then move beyond the finite limits of my thinking. As math and science pulled me into a working relationship with the Void, the concept of the irrational number became a symbol for how a simple equation or set of operations could result in a process that was complex and unpredictable, endless and non-repeating, an elegant synergy of form and function.

The need to capture this essence and apply it to sound drove me as I began diving into the process of making music outside prescribed borders. I would imagine wonderful music—hear arcs of pure sound unfolding, with no way of bringing them into the outer world. These sounds inhabited a place I began to refer to as my Inner Ear. The prime question was how to manifest this inner world as physical sound so that both I and others could hear it.

At first, there was the obstacle of everyday noise, both internal and external, always interrupting the beauty unless I took it in and made it mine. Observation, reflection, self-discipline, practice—all techniques to quiet the noise. The quest seemed asymptotic: how to strip away everything but unfettered sonic manifestation. Came the realization: this is a process, not an arrival.

It continued. Music didn't appear fully realized, but required work. In a positive feedback loop, I obtained skills in the techniques of various musical styles while exploring sounds and their production. Eventually, I came to codify my strategies, constructing a music drawn from the abstract locus of the Inner Ear yet based on the results of research, informed both by history and by real-world experimentation. Each approach amplified and transformed the other.

Initially applying these strategies to my own explorations of guitars, saxophones, synthesizers, and electronics, I later tried them in improvisatory ensemble meetings, in rock and jazz groups, and in written compositions, whether fully notated, algorithmic, or graphic. The resulting music would be equally grounded in intentional acts and in something more evanescent: the very nature of sound and psychoacoustic phenomena.

I sought to create music that, when improvised, had the inevitability of a well-constructed composition and, when composed, had the spontaneous excitement and mutability of an improvisation. Such music wouldn't be trapped in temporal anchoring, but rather exist in the ever-present *now*: one foot in the past, one in the future.

When I began to perform this music in public, I would invariably be asked: "Just what kind of music is this?" The question might just as often be posed after I'd played as before. Preparing to move to New York City in 1979, I began to think about how to explain my work. Should I proclaim the indivisible totality of the music, or define it by breaking it down into the elements from which it was composed? Should I invoke the mystery of improvisation, or allow myself to be pinned and placed in the taxonomy of a vast and diverse musical scene?

While clarifying my analysis of what the music was, I began using a process of elimination to define what it wasn't. Despite often working with formal systems, I felt little resonance with the academics. Though I'd cut my teeth playing in dozens of odd electric bands between 1968 and 1979, used electric instruments and loud dynamics, and often performed in rock clubs, most who heard my music didn't consider it rock. It definitely wasn't jazz, though suffused with improvisation and fashioned, in part, of raw materials shaped by years of playing jazz of all styles. I sometimes made use of motoric repetition and simple motifs inspired by non-Western music, mimicry of natural processes, and acoustic phenomena, yet the music had no place in the sociocultural milieu of Minimalism—which, inextricably tied to its origins in New York City's Downtown music scene of the 1970s, was meant less for engagement than for zoning out or as sonic wallpaper. Neither did I have any desire to bury the muse in politics or social realism, so I dumped any baggage from those realms. While in a few works I'd flirted with the ironic stance of postmodernism, I never resonated fully with it. As someone not nostalgic by nature, I had no desire to recreate any past era or to reinvent a flat tire. I scanned the list of "isms" only to cross them off.

I return again to the Inner Ear, a metaphoric device but as real as anything in my life. With no instrument at hand, I could hear forms and processes in their ideal state. Working with a physical instrument revealed certain spectra through correspondences between sound and the physics of nerves, muscles, bone, wood, metal, and moving air. The feedback loop was everything. My solo pieces were always the most concentrated representations of this ethos. Now that I was a New Yorker, I performed as often as possible, playing gigs in basements, lofts, bars, galleries, parties, and museums, solo or with other musicians or dancers. In December 1980, I decided to release on my zOaR label a cassette of excerpts of solo concerts from the previous year and decided on the title *IrRational Music*—a phrase that would serve as a general description of the underlying sonic strategies of my compositions:

Ir: the acoustics of sound in a space and in the ear, and its connection to the perceptual engine of difference tones, feedback, volume effects, dynamic definitions of melody, groove, and vertical simultaneity (a.k.a. harmony).

Rational: denoting structure and order, algorithms of use and process, systems of organization, and social context.

IrRational: chaos, intuition, emotion, and the tangential.

Improvisation—nonlinear and tied to no specific genre—is an essential part of IrRational Music. Improvisation brings the music to life. It transforms the static into the dynamic, is the individual effector in the sonic flux. Forces revealed by improvisation are embodied in the fixed construction—they feed each other.

Like any creative act, the manifestation of music is a translation from one frequency band in the spectrum of consciousness to another. The creative impulse appears; our job, then, is to decode it and find the proper mode of presentation. This output may be of any form that remains true to the impulse. The impulse creates tension, questions, disturbance, elevation, excitement—in stark contrast to the everyday noise that engulfs us. It may also welcome the noise and interference and build from them. Ultimately, the signal must rise above all-that-is-not-the-signal to be heard. Actualization is the process by which we reach one of the many paths to inevitability. It may mean picking up an instrument, making a score or painting, cooking a meal, or taking a walk with eyes and ears open. Inspiration is recognition of the impulse; creation, translation of the spectrum.

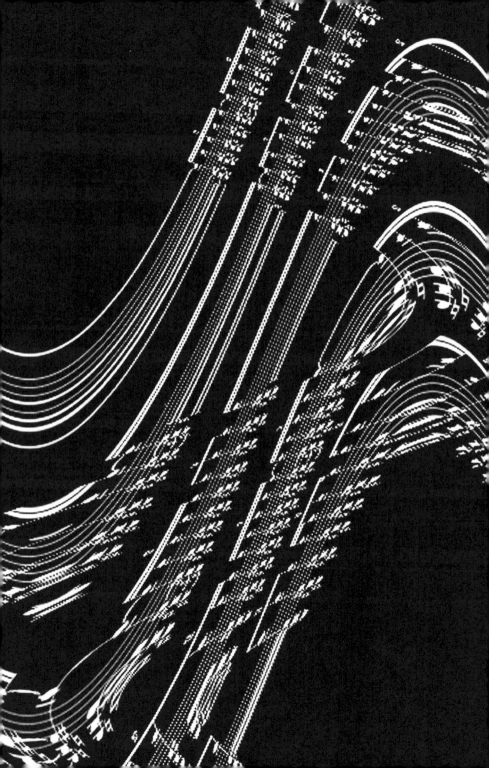

II.

Vibrations

Mea culpa: I was an electronics geek and amateur radio operator during my late childhood in the early 1960s. I loved the smell of solder and would build kits and circuits from scratch using parts purchased from Lafayette or Allied Electronics. These distributors carried items appealing to hobbyists and professionals, including musicians, and the pages in the catalogs devoted to electric guitars drew me in with a heavy magnetic force. I'd gaze at images of beautifully garish made-in-Japan mutants laden with chrome and studded with banks of mysterious switches and knobs, and imagine myself generating Godzilla-sized waves of sound. So much of that early appeal of the electric guitar was visual: it looked like the sound of the future.

In 1956, our family moved from Cleveland, Ohio to White Plains, New York when my father, Bernard Charles Sharp, took a position at University Loudspeakers. Cleveland left its mark on me, or rather a cloud of murk: memories of being packed off to nursery school in a dark car plowing through heavy snow; the Terminal Tower, a huge edifice that haunted my nightmares; waiting on the railroad platform just after sunset to board an overnight train to New York State. In White Plains, we first lived in a small apartment before moving to a newly built middle-class housing development that allowed Jews. Our new home was filled with books on acoustics, electronics, and art history. My father was an accomplished visual artist who painted and sculpted in his spare time with great skill, vision, and joy, and his artworks covered our walls: landscapes, portraits, abstractions, nudes. I loved hanging out in the basement with him, working on my own little projects while he invented or painted. His balancing act between inspiration and systematic methodology was a fine model for my operations. I didn't have a lot of toys. If I wanted a model airplane or spaceship, my father would say "Make one," and would show me how to choose materials and use the proper tools.

My mother, Eugenie Hoffman Sharp, a Holocaust survivor, was born in Pont-à-Mousson, France, near the city of Nancy, and spent much of World War II hidden, together with her mother, by farmers in the Lorraine region while her two sisters and brother were hidden elsewhere by local partisans. She could never know when she would be confronted on the farm by German soldiers suspecting that this pretty little French "farm girl" might actually be a *Jüdin*. Needless to say, she had some thrilling tales. My grandmother, however, looked very "Jewish" and was always kept well away from view, hidden in a barn loft or even in the trunk of a car. My grandfather was imprisoned in the Drancy internment camp for most of the war and then deported in January 1945 to a camp in Poland, which he survived. With amazing luck, compounded by the kindness and bravery of local farmers, my mother and her immediate family survived the war and came to the United States in 1948, invited by cousins in Philadelphia and in Cleveland, where she met my father. She loved to regale us with stories of her close calls with the German occupiers. This, I believe, imbued in me a sense of defiance, along with the notion of having an escape route at hand for any situation. My sister Denise was born with Down syndrome, and much of my mother's energy was taken up with her care, as well as crusading for schools for Down children. Later, two more brothers were born into the family, Howard and Kenneth, who would become, respectively, an educator and a computer scientist.

Art was part of my daily life. I'd spend hours drawing and painting dinosaurs, outer-space scenes, monsters and horror characters, and post-nuclear-apocalypse scenarios, fueled in no small part by the tenor of the times, with widespread instructions for making a fallout shelter in the basement and duck-and-cover drills at school. Walking to school on the morning of the denouement of the Cuban Missile Crisis, I nervously scanned the sky.

Home life was a contradictory mix: stifling and overprotective, yet highly encouraging for academic and artistic endeavors. Piano studies began at age six and were drudgery, an affliction of banal ditties and Czerny exercises that I had to play over and over until perfect. Despite my deep aversion to this routine, I managed to develop a fair amount of proficiency and greatly enjoyed attempting to play dark, fast music such as Liszt's *Hungarian Rhapsody No. 2*, which I performed at Carnegie Recital Hall at age seven as a student of Ms. Jean Mayer—my first NYC gig, though I had to play it dressed by my mother in a red blazer and bow tie. Shortly thereafter, I was hospitalized for asthma and nearly left this earthly plane. When I emerged from the hospital after nearly two weeks' stay, my arms, thighs, and buttocks were black and blue from round-the-clock injections of adrenalin and penicillin. Though I suffered from allergies, I still believe that the pressure of piano practice was the major exacerbating factor in my illness. Recovery process in the works, I was freed from the piano and, now in the fourth grade, took up the clarinet, as I liked the sound and it was therapeutic for my lungs. I practiced somewhat dutifully and skills developed.

Electronics had become a major obsession and I obtained an advanced amateur radio license, call letters WA2CLX. By fourteen, I'd become a huge fan of any music with intense electric guitar. The sound resonated deep within my soul and I wanted to hear more and more of it: the medicine that healed my ills, the missing chemical that restored my metabolism to balance, the philosopher's stone of sound. Was it the attack, the whine of a bent string, the pulse of a tremoloed chord? Perhaps the saturated sound of even harmonics over the fundamental frequency? I could never break it down into components. The Yardbirds, The Rolling Stones, and the Paul Butterfield Blues Band opened the door. Thanks to them, I found my way to the masters of electric blues: Howlin' Wolf, Muddy Waters, Otis Rush, and so many more. The Beatles' psychedelic masterpiece *Revolver* was a revelation and inspiration, and Bob Dylan's electric records were the musical equivalent of a trepanation, as vivid verbal imagery framed by megawatts of guitar from Mike Bloomfield and Robbie Robertson opened my skull to a previously unimagined cosmos of sounds, punnery, and the possibility of revelation. Watching television, I might also take in twangy cowboy music, Les Paul and Mary Ford, Elvis Presley with Scotty Moore, the "talking steel guitar" of Alvino Rey, fat-box jazz guitar, James Burton with Ricky Nelson, fancy picking from Chet Atkins, and even Lawrence Welk's hot guitarist Buddy Merrill.

I enjoyed it all, but it didn't change my chemistry in the way the simple fuzz lick in "(I Can't Get No) Satisfaction" or one of Jeff Beck's chaotic extrapolations could. In 1966, some friends and I formed a rock 'n' roll band that we called The Last Words, with a set list comprised of our favorite tunes of the day. I taped a cheap crystal microphone into the bell of my clarinet and ran it through a homemade fuzz box in an attempt to emulate Beck's solos, carefully learned from Yardbirds records. Guitar was what I most wanted to play, but the closest I could get to it was randomly plunking on my father's unplayable Harmony with nylon strings and impossibly high action. When The Jimi Hendrix Experience was unleashed on the world via the debut album *Are You Experienced*, I was beautifully devastated, my ears and conception of the guitar irrevocably altered. Hendrix had redefined the instrument so completely as to create an onomatopoeic, incomprehensible, alien entity. I couldn't even imagine that the sounds he was making were findable anywhere on a normal guitar fingerboard. Pulled into this parallel reality by Hendrix's music, I felt my neurons following new pathways to a place that was utopian, ecstatic.

Jazz was an unknown world. On July 17, 1967, I saw notice of the death of John Coltrane on the front page of the *New York Times*. His name meant nothing to me, but after reading the detailed obituary I was very curious to hear his music. Calling up my buddy Steve Cohan, I mentioned Coltrane's death; Steve thought that his father, a jazz fan, had some of his LPs. Later that day, we spun *Coltrane "Live" at the Village Vanguard*, starting with Side 2's "Chasin' the Trane," then advancing in reverse to Side 1's "Spiritual." Again, I was absolutely and joyously destroyed by the passion, power, and virtuosity of the music and became, at that moment, a true believer. The next day, I found a copy of Charles Mingus' magnificent *Oh Yeah* in the bargain bin of a local department store for $.99 and began to check out other jazz records from the town library. The cutout bins yielded more treasures: John Coltrane's and Don Cherry's *The Avant-Garde*; Cecil Taylor's *Unit Structures*; Archie Shepp's *Three For A Quarter, One For A Dime*; Sonny Rollins' *East Broadway Run Down*; and Thelonious Monk's *Solo Monk*. I didn't always understand what I was hearing, but I understood the commitment and discipline that went into making music of such glorious abandon. I needed to find out more.

The guitar beckoned again, but my first attempts on that wretched Harmony guitar bore little connection to the fluid soliloquies I could imagine myself playing and only created frustration. Finally, in April of

1968, with money saved from various after-school jobs and inspired by visions of Jimi Hendrix, B.B. King, Buddy Guy, Jeff Beck, Otis Rush, Albert King, and Mike Bloomfield, I purchased a Hagstrom III electric guitar and small Fender amplifier from a friend. That June, guitar in hand, I headed off to Carnegie Mellon University in Pittsburgh where, as the winner of a Ford Future Scientists of America fellowship, I would be working as a scientist's assistant before returning to White Plains to finish my senior year of high school. My head was filled with more than science and guitar. The assassinations of Bobby Kennedy and Dr. Martin Luther King, Jr., along with the ever-widening war in Vietnam, brought despair and anger. Yet I was strangely optimistic, giddy with excitement from the Free Speech Movement, the huge protest marches at the Pentagon, and the student-led strikes in Paris.

Once in Pittsburgh, in addition to fulfilling my responsibilities in the lab under the terms of the fellowship, I devoted a healthy portion of my time to finding ever-better ways to modify the sound of my guitar through the design and construction of fuzz boxes, ring modulators, and other distortion circuits, as well as by experimenting with an Ampex seven-head tape deck used for time studies. Hooking up my guitar to an oscilloscope allowed me to view the waveforms created by exciting the strings in various ways. I found out how to make Lissajous figures on the scope by electronically combining an oscillator's output with audio from a guitar or other source. Mutually perpendicular waveforms tracing curves on the screen: this visualization of sound became a provocative stimulation, a personal light show, a concrete correspondence between the realms of sound and vision.

The campus radio station at Carnegie Mellon, WRCT, seemed a good place to mix technology and music, and I was able to score a midnight-to-4 a.m. broadcast slot twice a week, along with additional time for studying the engineering mysteries of the station's equipment and wiring. The WRCT library was stocked with obscure wonders, and with these I filled my ears: free jazz from ESP-Disk and BYG Actuel; extreme psychedelia from independent underground rock labels like Imperial Records; exotic music from all over the globe provided by the Nonesuch Explorer series, Folkways Records, and the UNESCO Collection; "American primitive" guitar from John Fahey and Robbie Basho on Takoma Records; and contemporary music from Deutsche Grammophon's Avantgarde series, Erato, Columbia's Music of Our Time series, RCA Odyssey, and Nonesuch proper. *The World of Harry Partch* on

Columbia was an immediate favorite. I also borrowed his book *Genesis of a Music* from the library and dug into it deeply, trying to parse the nature of Utonalities and Otonalities. His invented instruments overwhelmed me with their visual beauty and unique sounds. Partch called himself "a philosophic music man seduced into carpentry," a line that I've since appropriated, replacing "carpentry" with "engineering."

Digging into Partch and the guitar itself inevitably led to investigating its history, international sources, and relatives such as the oud (*al'oud* = lute). I began to view the guitar as a collection of six monochords, each capable of generating a full spectrum of sound. If only my fingers had the same independence! Finding *On the Sensations of Tone* by Hermann Helmholtz in the library, I devoured it and made a quick leap to the notion of the guitar as set of oscillators and a resonator, an idea that has stayed with me to the present. This view also parallels the mapping of sonic processes to thought processes, a translation of music to realms of mind. As listening to music could stimulate images and thoughts, so thoughts and images could generate music that I could almost physically sense as sound. I learned about the Fourier transforms, by which any complex sound can be deconstructed into its component sine waves—a concept that later became the basis of modern digital music. Could all creativity be reduced to the vibrations of cellular oscillators stimulating the resonator that is the Inner Ear?

I reveled in the electronic and electroacoustic music of Iannis Xenakis, Tod Dockstader, Morton Subotnick, and Karlheinz Stockhausen—sounds that provoked and surprised, irritated and aroused. The radio programs I constructed might concentrate on a single artist or style, or might be devoted to presenting as much varied music as I could pack in. I might also do mixes, freely blending genres and styles. The process consumed me; I was immersed in sound and music. My days and nights were packed with exciting research and delightful work—for three weeks.

Whereupon the new station director at WRCT, Fred Braun, decided that, between my program and those of my psychedelic fellow travelers, things at the station had gotten out of hand. He decreed that strict formatting would be imposed. All WRCT DJs were forced to hew to a rigid Top-40 playlist, with the "freedom" once per hour to play a track from an "alternative" list that was really just the nether reaches of the Top 40. Some DJs quit immediately. I decided to push the limit and ended up being fired on the air by Fred himself, who burst into the control room with the microphones open and the station broadcasting. There was a crack in one of the lenses of my glasses, and Fred's immortal words still ring in my ears: "You one-eyed freak, you're finished!"

Longhaired and bearded, I returned to my shocked parents' home at the end of the summer to face the reality of my final year of high school and crucial decisions about the immediate future: college, employment and, with the Vietnam war raging, the draft. Guitar became the focus of my intensities, and I continued to experiment and practice. My amateur radio activities were now transformed into freeform late-night listening sessions, as the normal practice of using Morse code to compare equipment with fellow geeks began to seem fairly vacuous. The shortwave spectrum, however, was filled with mysterious sonic processes and textures: shipping communications, "spy" stations broadcasting chains of numbers in strange accents, Afghan orchestras, Italian rock 'n' roll, teletypes, Indian classical music, and propaganda emitted by Communists, capitalists, and Bible-Belt right-wingers. When the family was asleep, I would don my headphones and, atmospheric conditions permitting, partake of an incomprehensibly vast array of sounds suspended on a black velvet cushion of complete silence and seemingly infinite depth, as if staring into the limitless reaches of the night sky. I would lose myself in this timeless and pixilated cloud of otherworldly sound, unconcerned that just a few hours later I would have to rise and go to school.

My studies held no great interest, and the more I immersed myself in the guitar, the less I practiced my clarinet. Throughout the first semester of senior year, I rapidly slipped from first clarinet, first seat, to third and third. When football season commenced, and marching band rehearsals with it, I was bounced: while long hair could be hidden inside the tiger-festooned cap, a full beard could not. It was all for the best, as there was no music I liked less than marches, with their mechanical, militaristic rhythms and rah-rah melodies. Ironically, the band and orchestra director, Al Renino, was a fan of what he called "aleatoric" music and developed a conducting technique for wind ensemble—composing music in real time—remarkably similar to the such contemporary methods as Butch Morris' Conduction and Walter Thompson's Soundpainting. Renino might have the brass players tap on the bells of their horns or blow white noise while we clarinetists hummed into our instruments or took off the mouthpieces and blew into them to elicit high-pitched squeals. String players were also subject to his creative whims, and I found many of the textures exciting. But when I suggested bringing my electric guitar to one of these sessions, Renino reacted with absolute horror, admonishing me that it was not a "real instrument." The saxophone, too, he considered a "bastard" that had no place in the orchestra.

The public library in White Plains had a comprehensive collection of music books, which I systematically attacked. I read texts by Cage, Cowell, Xenakis, and Stockhausen, as well as Robert Craft's interviews with Stravinsky. Cage's philosophical correlations and Xenakis' use of stochastic processes and set theory got my blood running. In the realm of jazz, there were such titles as *Black Music* and *Blues People* by LeRoi Jones (a.k.a. Amiri Baraka); *Urban Blues* by Charles Keil; and Frank Kofsky's *Black Nationalism and the Revolution in Music*, a text that explicitly drew the lines between this exhortatory music and the political movements calling for an end to racist structures and capitalist-fueled wars. On the list as well were *The Autobiography Of Malcolm X*, *Another Country* by James Baldwin, and *The Wretched of the Earth* by Frantz Fanon. There was fiction by Pynchon, Joyce, and Burroughs; books on Zen Buddhism, anarchism, and Gandhi's satyagraha; poetry by Blake, Eliot, Pound, Hughes, Snyder, Corso, Creeley, Williams, and Ginsberg; and tons of sci-fi by the likes of Philip K. Dick, Cordwainer Smith, Arthur C. Clarke, Ray Bradbury, Samuel Delany, Theodore Sturgeon, C. S. Lewis, Isaac Asimov, and Richard Matheson. This literary stew nourished the growth of streamers and tendrils, connections between radical political thought and radical music—consciousness fertilized and expanding in all directions.

I delved into preparing the guitar with pieces of wood and metal hardware from my father's workshop and continued to experiment with distortion, feedback, and tapping the fretboard with the fingers of both hands. Early one evening in December 1968, I had an epiphany: after patching the guitar through some of my homemade pedals, I was overcome by the sound pouring out of that little amplifier, its waves of undefinable beauty and exotic texture pulling me into a deeply strange, wondrous parallel reality… only to be brought back to Earth by my parents yelling to "turn it down." Improvising music on guitar, I had glimpsed a small slice of the Void and wished to return there as often as possible.

The electric manifestations were only one portion of the picture: I was equally consumed by acoustic country blues. Each artist heard on old recordings led me to others, and I was soon devouring the sounds of Robert Johnson, Lightnin' Hopkins, Robert Pete Williams, Blind Willie Johnson, Charley Patton, Blind Willie McTell, Son House, Bukka White, and more. Bending notes by use of slide or bottleneck, country blues musicians transformed the guitar from an Apollonian, precise, well-tempered instrument into one that was Dionysian, vocalized, passionate, non-tempered, and non-Western. Using a test tube from my chemistry set (there being a shortage of wine bottles at my parents' house) allowed me to approximate the sounds I was hearing. Since the Harmony was long gone from our house, I purchased an eight-buck wreck of a steel-string guitar at a pawn shop in town, raised the nut and, laying it in my lap, attempted to imitate the melismatic wailing of the blues masters. With my buddies Steve Cohan and Joel Eckhaus, a wide-ranging "folk" group, IzzyDaSplit, was aggregated to play traditional string band music from the 1920s and '30s, both black and white, as filtered down to us via the Holy Modal Rounders and Even Dozen Jug Band with touches of The Fugs, Beat poetry, aleatoric weirdness, Julius Lester, William S. Burroughs, and Mimi and Richard Fariña. I doubled on plastic recorder and occasional banjo. The more we played, the more my guitar skills began to improve. We were a rowdy bunch—especially when expanded to "jug orchestra" forces with two beautiful cellists, a washtub bass played by David Pollock, jug, washboard, and additional guitarists, including the brilliant Mark Slifstein—and were banned from coffeehouses across Westchester County. The electric guitar was now used only for solitary ruminations at my parents' house, and at a much lower volume.

Early one morning in July of 1969, I hitchhiked down to the City to wander around. These journeys would usually include a visit to Sam Goody's bargain outlet, where I could score an amazing selection of hard-to-find and out-of-print blues, jazz, and classical LPs for $0.99 each. I would then make my way to Manny's Music on 48th Street to gawk at the latest guitars, all way beyond my miserable personal economy, and occasionally try out a more modest one. On this particular morning, I was auditioning another cheapo acoustic guitar, the least expensive Gibson to be found. Though already deep into the theory and practice of extreme guitar noise, as far as traditional guitar technique went I considered myself a rank novice. I certainly knew the chords to G-L-O-R-I-A though and was pounding them out when I noticed directly in front of me a pair of gold boots and brilliant turquoise pants. I looked up. Standing there, smiling down at me, was Jimi. I looked up and stuttered: "Uh, hi." He smiled and answered: "Uh, hi." I put the guitar down *very* quickly while Jimi tried out fuzz boxes for the next hour, absorbed in his task. He might reject one pedal or another, but for me it all sounded equally glorious. Infinitely curling blues lines pealed from his fingertips as casually as the guys in the store sipped their deli coffee. Jimi finished and with my ears and brain overflowing, I floated out to the avenue.

III.

Former Postal Worker

Spring of 1969. Outside: Vietnam War and the coming of the Revolution. Inside, typical teenage turmoil: battles with parents, the demands of high school, my upcoming graduation and ejection into the real world, losing my girlfriend to a creep, money woes both immediate and looming. Realistically, the only element on this list that I could attempt to tackle with any hope of success was the final one. I obtained a job at Alexander's department store, which was unaccountably willing to hire this long-haired, bearded youth to undertake an unlikely assignment: selling incredibly ugly and cheaply made imported men's shoes to the lumpensuburbatariat six days per week, 3:30 p.m. to 9:30 p.m., for the minimum wage of $1.60 per hour.

After school on weekdays and all day on Saturday, I'd stoke up on NoDoz or the occasional hit of speed and punch in for my shift. The job was torture in almost every way. I had to muster fake enthusiasm for hawking crappy but colorful golf shoes and shiny tasseled loafers to suburban guys with smelly feet. My immediate superior was Manny, a Vietnam vet discharged from the Marine Corps with a Purple Heart thanks to a bullet that passed through his buttocks. Though he seemed a gentle soul, he liked to reminisce about getting wasted on weed and firing machine guns randomly into the jungle. When we received a shipment of cheap Mexican sandals with soles made of truck tires, Manny waxed nostalgic about his squad going into a Vietnamese village, blowing everybody away, and taking the authentic, handmade, B-52-tire-soled sandals of the villagers as souvenirs.

The saving grace of my gig was Jim in the camera department. We would repair to his girlfriend's nearby apartment on breaks to smoke and listen to Coltrane's *Om* and Miles' *Kind of Blue*. The job was depressing and stultifying but necessary. Still wired when I'd punch out at 9:30 p.m., I'd take a two- or three-mile run through the darkened streets to clear my head. Home again, I'd blast through any homework, then put on my headphones and zone out, whether to music on FM or weirdness on the shortwave bands. NYC was at the peak of the progressive FM era, with DJs William Mercer and Alison Steele (a.k.a. Rosko and The Nightbird) on WNEW; Bob Fass and Larry Josephson on WBAI; and African-American gospel, blues, and Caribbean music on WLIB. Relief was at hand. Any spare money was spent on LPs or tickets to shows at the Fillmore East in the East Village, where I would see Albert King, Paul Butterfield, Jefferson Airplane, Santana, In Cold Blood, Slim Harpo, John Mayall, the Grateful Dead, B.B. King, the Youngbloods, Savoy Brown, and more.

Needless to say, I wasn't contemplating the retirement benefits that might accrue from a lifelong career at Alexander's. Steve Cohan suggested that we take civil service exams and get jobs at the local post office. After all, Charles Mingus and Charles Bukowski both worked at the post office, so why not us? We aced the tests and soon received notices of our assignment. Arriving at the orientation meeting, we were met with horrified stares from the presiding officials. They couldn't *not* give us the jobs since, legally speaking, hiring was based strictly on score and there were no guidelines about appearance. And so, on June 23 at 5 a.m., we reported to the North White Plains Post Office, where supervisor William Rutherford greeted us with instant disdain and pointed insults regarding our hair and clothes. He then put us to work unloading 40-foot trailers filled with parcel post: boxes of books, magazines, 60-pound sacks of bulk mailings, sundry commercial detritus, and tubular cardboard containers from local funeral homes and crematoria marked with someone's name under "CONTENTS." We would pile the sacks on large iron carts, wheel them into a huge shed, and empty them onto a conveyor belt for sorting.

Because of our matching beards, we were christened The Smith Brothers by the P.O. crew and were the butt of many jokes in those first few days. The only functional response was to master the subtle art of wisecrackery, a form of humorous retort that was lost on Rutherford and most of the workers but not on Ken, a 40-year-old African-American gentleman who'd been employed in the post office for twenty years while moonlighting as a soul and jazz DJ at the local radio station, WFAS. Having decided we were worth befriending, he took it upon himself to educate us: "Okay guys, now what's soul food?" Since we'd been listening to lots of Lightnin' Hopkins, Charlie Patton, and Howlin' Wolf, we figured that was an easy one. "Chitlins, fried chicken, grits, collard greens," we answered. Wrong! Ken opened his lunch bag and pulled out a tuna salad with mayo on white bread and a can of grape soda. "*This* is soul food, and do you know why? 'Cuz I'm eating it!"

The postal workers were unionized and subject to a strictly monitored schedule with a fixed daily routine, which Steve and I adapted to the demands of our particular jobs: punch in at 5, pile up mailbags, and go to sleep until 5:50, when Rutherford and the other workers would show up. Bust chops unloading the truck until 7, then break for 30 minutes. More heave-ho until 9, followed by another 30-minute break. Work until 11 and break for lunch. Work until 1, break until 1:30. Punch out, go home. Back-breaking labor, to be sure, but not the worst job in the world, especially as our pay, at $3.25 an hour, was over twice the minimum wage.

After the first week, Rutherford decided that Steve and I, not being union lifers, should not be indulged in this luxurious schedule. We were ordered to work through the breaks, stopping only for lunch. On the first day of our "new order," we had an especially full trailer. We cranked, processing the entire load and dumping its contents on the conveyor by 7:30. When the mail handlers returned from their break, they faced a 6-foot-high, 30-foot-long pile of parcels. We had the rest of the day to lounge around. Sure enough, the next day we were returned to scheduled breaks with the rest of the crew.

There was a general air of insanity around the post office. Ours was a small facility but I can imagine that this current was greatly amplified in the sectional centers and larger stations. Intermittent bursts of gibberish or hostility from a worker, directed either singly or to the group, might spontaneously fill the room. One of the sorters would whistle demented bird calls every ten or fifteen minutes. At any moment, Rutherford might storm through the shed and single out someone for abuse, deserved or not.

One of the many banes of our existence was Cheerful House, a mail-order company that sold unutterably wretched kitsch, mostly statuettes made from porcelain: little black-and-white Scottie dogs romping, Hansel and Gretel walking hand in hand, Boy Scouts in uniform shorts saluting, fully functional miniature ceramic cuckoo clocks. Such beauty was too fragile to exist in this world, and the air was often punctuated by the sounds of a Cheerful House box being reduced to crumpled cardboard filled with pleasantly-rattling ceramic shards, thus cementing the popular image of the post office's sociopathic incompetency. This also happened to be the summer that humans first landed on la Luna. Our P.O. crew was evenly divided along racial lines as to whether or not it actually happened, with our African-American colleagues not buying it. Especially heavy sacks of mail were called "moon rocks." There was an exceptional amount of rain that summer. It was blamed on the moon trip.

Every afternoon after punching out, I'd go home and head straight to my room, crank up the air conditioner, blast *Electric Ladyland*, *Miles Smiles*, *The Rite of Spring*, Coltrane's *A Love Supreme*, Ornette's *Free Jazz*, Subotnick's *The Wild Bull*, Xenakis' *Metastasis*, Captain Beefheart's *Trout Mask Replica*, Ali Akbar Khan, Velvet Underground, Jajouka, Albert Ayler, Neil Young & Crazy Horse, Rahsaan Roland Kirk, or Charles Mingus and go comatose for two or three blissful hours. After a tense and sullen dinner with my family, during which I'd endure commentary about my hirsute appearance and uncertain future, I'd head over to Steve's house, where we'd listen to our latest vinyl acquisitions—Archie Shepp, Frank Zappa, Reverend Gary Davis, Art Ensemble of Chicago, Spirit, The Fugs—or perhaps rendezvous with various friends for more of the same. I'd haunt the often-replenished 99-cent bargain bin at Alexander's and one day came upon Sonny Sharrock's *Monkey-Pockie-Boo* on BYG Actuel. I knew nothing about Sonny's playing, but the back cover showed him drenched in sweat while obviously riding an intense wave of sound on his electric guitar. I tore the cellophane off, anxious to hear the disc. Side 1 featured Sonny playing slide whistle with Linda Sharrock's moans and shrieks over free-jazz bass and drums. I checked to see if the wrong record was in the sleeve, but no, it seemed to be correct. Things heated up somewhat later on that same side with Sonny switching to guitar and playing his trademark high-intensity sputtering slides and crashes. I'd never heard anything like it, and I loved it immediately. Side 2 was the vindication and the redemption: full immersion in the seething glisses, slashing chordal washes, and skittering lines bathed in chaos for which Sonny was famous. My conversion was complete.

That September, now in my freshman year at Cornell, I saw notice of a concert featuring flutist Herbie Mann and his band in the not-too-distant town of Elmira. A friend and I hitchhiked there, arriving just in time to enter the auditorium where Herbie's set was about to begin. He had a band of incredible musicians: Miroslav Vitous on bass, Roy Ayers on vibraphone, Bruno Carr on drums, and Sonny himself on guitar. Hearing Sonny on record was one thing, but to experience his tsunami of sound in person was quite another. The set included Herbie's popular "Memphis Underground" but otherwise was mostly cover tunes. On The Beatles' "Come Together," Sonny's solo was like a high-rise office tower exploding into shards of glass.

Steve and I lasted at the post office until August 14, when we packed up with Joel Eckhaus and some female friends and headed to Woodstock for "three days of peace and music." Sorry to say, we didn't even get close to the climax with Hendrix. Thanks to our lack of proper preparation, we were soaked, tired, wasted, and hungry. After the second night, we called it quits. We returned to suburbia and prepared to face the mythical beast that loomed before us: college. I was almost sad to see the post office job end. I had grown comparatively muscular, squirreled away enough money to cover the living expenses for my upcoming first year at Cornell, and learned a few things about the real world. After the United States Postal Service was reduced from a cabinet-level agency and given bureaucratic independence in 1971, there was a growth in violent outlets to worker psychosis—"going postal"—giving birth to the popular notion of the "former postal worker."

IV.

In and Out
of Place

Before departing for Ithaca, New York in September of 1969 to begin my studies at Cornell University with a focus on anthropology—a discipline I thought of as my portal into realms outside of my limited life experience—I traded in my electric guitar and amp for a 1964 Gibson L48 archtop acoustic guitar, easy-playing and with a thin, bright sound. During this first year in Ithaca, my academic pursuits were leavened with music, anti-war activities, expansion of consciousness, and more music. In my cultural anthropology studies, a common dictum was that researchers must not allow themselves to "go native," but must preserve their Western objectivity when interfacing with a foreign culture. The panorama of musical activities I found around Ithaca was as exotic as anything I could imagine, and I desired to lose myself in it, to shed my skin and molt, to go native ASAP.

I attempted to play with as many musicians as I could and in as many possible zones: blues, acoustic improvisation, free jazz, original songs, drone explorations. The Gibson was sold and a Yamaha dreadnought acoustic acquired, a guitar with better sound and feel for most of the music I was playing. I began to focus on long-form improvisations in open tunings. Because of my interest in slide and country blues, I concentrated on Vastopol (open D) and G tunings, but also devised my own, sometimes using theory but more often making them up on the fly, randomly twisting the pegs until I arrived at a set of pitches that would ring with unusual overtones, beat frequencies, or implied melodies. Many friends played in electric bands, and I found myself displaying the telltale symptoms of that wonderful virus, an inexorable urge to play electric whenever possible on borrowed guitars. This was exacerbated by the presence of Robert Moog, who taught a class in "sound synthesis" through the College of Engineering. Although the class wasn't open to me as a freshman, I visited just to listen in. Moog mentored both Mother Mallard's Portable Masterpiece Company, a pioneering synthesizer ensemble helmed by David Borden, and The Creative Act, a rock and jazz band with synthesizers led by Linda Fisher. I would try to catch them both whenever they played. I also enjoyed performances by my friends, the psychedelic explorers of Death & Taxes. There was a convivial openness between the psychedelic rock, modern songwriter, and contemporary electronic music scenes at the time, with frequent gigs of all sorts happening at the campus coffee houses, in the student union, in bars, even at fraternity houses. This cross-fertilization was exciting and inspired me to write songs, each of which served as a blueprint for future directions.

With freshman year drawing to a close, I felt that my time in academia had not quite measured up to my musical endeavors. Our cultural anthropology professor (named Sharp!) had been outed as a CIA agent during his field work in Vietnam in the 1950s. The bombing of Cambodia caused major uprisings at Cornell, as elsewhere. Our campus was occupied by the National Guard and a strict curfew imposed (though generally ignored). With these disruptions, classes ended early and most of our professors gave us pro forma "good grades." Cohan and I decided to take that summer of 1970 to hitchhike to California via Colorado, as we both had friends to see Out West and were still under the sway of the Beat writers and the glorious myth of The Road. Despite the serious limitations of Kerouac's writing, his spirit and ideas changed the way many people thought about life. How many backpacked odysseys were launched under the aura of On the Road or The Dharma Bums? How many contemplations of the possibility of satori? Banjo and guitar in hand, we set off from Ithaca for points West, first stop being Cincinnati to visit a high school buddy.

We made good time until early the next morning, when we stalled at the outskirts of our destination, standing for over three hours while enduring epithets, threats, and the thrown remains of a cheeseburger. After a brief respite in the Land of Five-Way Chili, we continued on toward the sunset. Whenever we found ourselves stuck in a rest area, we'd pull out our instruments, both to entertain ourselves and to invite potential rides with our sweet sounds. Late one afternoon, somewhere around Abilene, Kansas, we were eating freshly baked pie à la mode served by a friendly and freckle-faced young blonde waitress. One a.m. on that moonless night found us stuck at a rest area west of Wakeeney for two hours, the air hot and sticky and thick with flies and moths. Even the picnic table that was our temporary base was covered with crawling beetles. Suddenly, a ride appeared in the form of two guys driving a dingy brown Chevy Nova, all looking a bit worse for wear. Near Colby, they decided to pull into a truck stop as the car was beginning to shudder and spit up hairballs.

It was 3 a.m. but the joint was jumping, the parking lot filled with dudes in cowboy drag and girls sporting beehive hairdos and white go-go boots. Twangy country guitar was blasting from an open car window. We stop near a pump, and the throng gather 'round to greet us. Everybody's smiling as the spokesman announces with glee: "We're gonna kill those two hairy hippies in the back and we're gonna beat you guys up for drivin' 'em." Mustering up some survival instincts, the guys start up the car and head back to the interstate where they tell us to get out, then putt-putt off.

It's pitch-black and the air is thick with heat and the buzzing of insects. There are strange animal sounds surrounding us, not too loud but with a deep resonance implying a certain heft to their source. Being city kids, we have no idea which creatures might be producing this sound. After a few minutes, pickup trucks begin to slowly cruise by. One stops and we run toward it, thinking we're being offered an escape. We see flashes, then hear the unmistakable whoosh and zing of bullets rushing by our heads, just like on television. We grab our things and jump into a drainage ditch by the side of the road, cowering and shaking as we await the inevitable coup de grâce. The ditch is filled with little creatures that can't resist nibbling on our ankles. The burning and itching is agonizing but we know we can't get up or even make a sound for fear of revealing ourselves. Finally, after what seems like way too many hours, the rising sun cracks the horizon and we decide to brave it, emerging cramped and sore from the ditch. The menacing animal noises turn out to be the intermittent snores and grunts of dozing cattle.

We walked to a rest area a few miles up the road and took stock of our situation. We were feeling pretty wretched but we were alive. Around 9 a.m., the equipment crew of the Paul Winter Consort picked us up in their truck and drove us all the way to a ghost-town Boulder, deserted for the holidays. The address of our destination, a school friend of Steve's, didn't seem to exist so we set up in a little park and played some tunes, attracting a friendly local who advised us to get out of town immediately as "some freaks burned a flag and there's going to be vigilantes." Our original plan was to head north to Cody, Wyoming and from there west to San Francisco, but we were dissuaded by a driver who told us that we'd certainly get killed in Cody after being given haircuts. She suggested that we head to Los Angeles, already an important part of our itinerary, and drove us to the southern border of town where we soon got a ride down to Colorado Springs and from there just over the border to Raton, New Mexico (named for its large population of the eponymous rodents), arriving around 6 p.m. We were surrounded by buttes stretching out to the horizon, accompanied by the whistling of the wind. The otherworldly sight was dramatic and mesmerizing, and as day turned to night and then morning again, we were treated to incredible transformations of the landscape through light and shadow. I could hear the music in the air and in my Inner Ear, though my fingers were unable to make it happen.

Our trip continued on legendary Route 66. Night scenes or hallucinations: deserted stretches of flatlands bearing only spidery trees, their trunks permanently bent to the east from the relentless wind. Collared lizards dash across the road on their hind legs. Somewhere in Arizona at a gas station at 4 a.m.: the attendant gives me and Steve the once-over and in a drawling voice, more curious than hostile, asks: "Are you *Jewwws?*" As we drive through the blistering Mojave Desert at midnight, my hand out the window feels like it's being trawled through hot soup. The rest area at 3 a.m. is populated with a hint of California's human abundance: surfers, cowboys, soldiers in uniform, Mexican families, party animals, a group of young Asian men in athletic wear. We arrive in LA at dawn and drop in on one of my college friends, home for the summer. We spend a day of recovery from our trip eating peaches and plums right off the tree and dozing in the sun. That night, Richard drives us into Hollywood, where we cruise the Strip and take in the technicolor scene. Steve decides to return to New York by Greyhound while I spend a few days crashing in a low-key commune in Temescal Canyon, entertaining the troops with my droning modalities and slide blues. More interested in the psychedelic culture of the north, I hitchhike up to the Bay Area where, after spending a few hours in the Haight, agog at the drugged-out squalor, I head over to Berkeley and a crash pad whose address was given to me by my LA friends. My meager funds nearly depleted, I take my guitar to the university's Sproul Plaza. My playing over the next few days nets me interesting conversations, some shared meals, and a little cash. A big presence in the Plaza is Street Preacher, an evangelist who has taken upon himself the task of saving the lost souls who congregate there; he holds frequent theological debates with a nattily dressed and goateed gent who calls himself The Devil. Preacher offers me $1 (a princely sum in 1970) to play "Down by the Riverside" with him. I do so readily, though I assure The Devil that this implies no agreement on my part with Preacher's theological positions.

I'm consumed by an ongoing internal debate as to whether I should return to Ithaca by September for my studies or continue the journey, albeit one with no real goal or destination. I feel blank. I head north, planning to visit Vancouver, a welcoming city from all I've heard and, of course, a safe haven from the draft in case I decide to stay. My draft number is 14, so I'm likely to be called up for service if I leave college. Early one evening, on the interstate outside Eugene, Oregon, a cherry-top pulls over to me, the trooper gesturing with his thumb to get in back. Arrested! As we pull out, he asks me about my guitar and what kind of music I play and listen to, then drops me off at a coffeehouse where he says I'll meet some people I'll like who will hook me up with a place to stay. Shocking as it seems, this greeting from the law feels oddly in keeping with the verdant setting.

Directed to a self-styled agricultural cooperative, I paint signs for their ancient pickup truck in exchange for a piece of floor in the living room. To bring some money in, I pick beans. This entails getting up at 5 a.m. and assembling at a pickup point downtown, where we pile into the back of trucks to be transported to farms in the surrounding Willamette Valley. We're handed bushel sacks, placed at the ends of rows and told to go forth and harvest. The pay is 75 cents a bushel. By the end of the first day my hands are raw, my back is aching, and I've picked $1.34 worth of beans. The little Mexican kids are having a great time; being the perfect height for this gig, they're each bringing in three or four bucks a day with very little effort, singing and laughing amongst the rows. At night I play guitar in the house. Somehow bottleneck seems to be just the right sound, especially as my fingers are too sore to try anything fancy.

After a week of this, I'm wishing for a more urban ambience and, it now being early August, decide to head back down to LA to contemplate further action. My journey southward is somewhat easier, though I do spend a chilly night standing on I-5 north of Sacramento. I have a brief reunion with my Los Angeles friends then head out towards San Bernardino and the beckoning East. By 4 a.m. that night, with fourteen hours passed, I'm barely 70 miles out of LA. Finally, a 1956 Ford convertible stops, driven by a blond-haired youth in a Marines t-shirt. Just returned from a tour of duty in Vietnam, he's put all his severance pay into this boss car equipped with an eight-track player and two tapes: The Supremes' *Greatest Hits* and Creedence Clearwater Revival's *Cosmo's Factory*. There's also a very shady-looking character named Paul in the back seat who says he's from Brooklyn. The driver is heading to his family home in St. Louis and has a large supply of white crosses to facilitate our round-the-clock journey. I happily share the driving. The soundtrack is a continuous loop of the two aforementioned albums, neither of which I have ever been able to hear again without being transported back in time and space to that '56 Ford.

We're east of Albuquerque on I-40 when Paul takes the wheel while our host falls into a deep sleep on the rear seat. Paul floors it, and after ten miles the engine begins to emit thick clouds of black smoke, the car grinding to a halt by the side of the road. Adding to the tension, the sky is rapidly filling with ominous dark clouds.

Soon, though, a pink 1959 Cadillac convertible pulls over and all three of us get in. The Marine will get dropped off at the next gas station; Paul and I will continue in the Caddy as the driver is heading home to Michigan and needs us to drive. Seconds after we get in, the skies open up, immersing us in a flash flood, the water halfway up the door. Fortunately, the seals hold and we remain dry. We make good time by spelling each other with the driving, Paul now a little more careful with the weight of his foot. We get a flat, just before we've reached the interchange in Jefferson City, Missouri, where the driver had planned to drop us.

We cross the border into Ohio that night and, having been warned about an aggressive state trooper presence on the interstate, debate whether we should wait until morning or try and hitch through the night. Paul tells me that whatever we do will be cool, as he has "protection." He pulls a .38 Special out of his shirt. I am not at all happy to see this, imagining us on the losing end of a shootout with the troopers. Around 3 a.m., Paul dozes off, so I sneak away and about a mile up the road catch a ride all the way to Cleveland. By 7 the next night I'm back in Ithaca, my odyssey complete.

Returning to school that September was the path of least resistance and the one that would keep me away from an undesired sojourn in Vietnam. Some friends and I moved into a dump of an apartment on Eddy Street by the university gate and it became Action Central, a 24-hour gathering place for musicians, poets, transients, weirdos, street people, and most likely a few undercover cops. Four bands rehearsed there and you never knew whom you might run into crashed out in the living room: an LA session guitarist, The Blues Project organist John-John McDuffy on the lam from some altercation in NYC, AWOL GI's and draft resisters heading to Canada, the cousin of a friend of a friend's sister. Al Kaatz was an esteemed housemate, a fantastic guitarist who played a wide variety of American and psychedelic styles. He gave me the sage advice, "Listen to B.B. King." I did.

Taken with the keening, vocal sound of the pedal steel guitar as heard in classic country music, I'd bought an old, inexpensive, and unreliable Fender 1000 from a Pennysaver listing and, having been gifted a battered cowboy hat by a girlfriend, learned just enough technique to gather some friends together and begin playing acid-tinged country rock in a band that we called Colonel Bleep. Our set was a mix of traditional songs old and new by Hank Williams, Johnny Cash, Lead Belly, Bob Dylan, and Big Bill Broonzy, with a smattering of originals in the same vein. Frustrated with my particular steel's inadequacies, I then purchased my first Telecaster, a 1968 rosewood-neck model with the paint stripped off and a Dearmond "toaster-top" pickup in the neck position. Taking my cue from Clarence White's work with the Byrds, I worked on emulating the sound of the pedal steel on the Tele, as well as the stylings of Memphis great Reggie Young and Don Rich of Buck Owens' band. A fair amount of my time was also spent exploring the more abstract zones of the spectrum, trying to get my fingers to reach the realms of Jimi, Hubert Sumlin, and the "three Kings" (B.B., Albert, Freddie). My guitar signal was passed through an Arbiter FuzzFace and Maestro Boomerang wah-wah pedal and an occasional borrowed Echoplex.

As far as school went, I took an incoherent array of courses: French poetry of the 19th century, structural anthropology, Chinese philosophy, harmony and counterpoint. Depressed and unsatisfied, I took a leave of absence in the middle of the second semester of my sophomore year. Within two weeks, I received a notice to report for a pre-induction physical on Whitehall Street in NYC. As I pondered undertaking an acid and amphetamine fast to prepare myself for the examination, a better option presented itself: through the Ithaca War Resisters League, I met a girl who was distributing computer cards she'd lifted from the Cornell bursar's office that indicated a student was registered. To the Selective Service, I was now back in school and therefore exempt.

Relieved of this anxiety, I dove into music. Any free moment was spent with guitar in hand or reading music texts and examining scores. I set out to build a technique from which I could jump into the music that I was beginning to hear with more clarity.

A matrix of pitches was constructed, beginning with the diatonic major scales and all of the resultant modes. Next up were symmetric scales of equal intervals: chromatic, whole tone, dimished, augmented. Patterns followed: whole step-half step diminished, jagged up-and-down, wide leaps. Now visual frames were introduced and superimposed on the fretboard to guide my fingers into movements outside of tonality or mode. My fingers and ears built connections. Doubled intervals based on diatonic verticalities and parallel intervals twisted my digits into new mudras. I began to think of harmony not so much as a set of rules for voice leading, tension and release, and dominant-tonic resolution, but as simultaneities in time. Solo explorations deepened as I focused more on the sound properties of the guitar itself, especially as modified with distortion devices, preparations, and slides. The borderline between music and noise began to dissolve.

Augmenting the abstraction, I built a vocabulary referencing my blues, swing, and bebop heroes but imagining new extrapolations. I was still building and modifying equipment for myself and others, a way to both make a small living and create sounds that might prove useful. Playing along with recordings was a good way to develop technique and grasp its application to specific styles, and during 1970 to '71 I focused hard on *Trout Mask Replica*, Miles Davis' *Bitches Brew* (with John McLaughlin), Jimi Hendrix' *Band Of Gypsies*, Ornette Coleman's *Friends and Neighbors*, Coltrane's *Meditations*, and Cecil Taylor's *Unit Structures*. Having inherited my younger brother's abandoned alto saxophone, I began work on transferring my clarinet technique to this horn (which aligned more closely with my favored listening) as well as on translating breath-oriented saxophone phrasing and timbre to the guitar.

Deciding to give Cornell another shot, I enrolled in music theory and history courses, but my heart wasn't in it. The music department was incredibly conservative and between the distractions of my own practice regimen and the political turmoil on campus, I barely squeaked through with passing grades.

Colonel Bleep would play our odd mix of country, psychedelia, Wilson Pickett, shuffles, Bob Dylan, boogie, and originals at coffeehouses in the college as well as dorm and fraternity parties. By January of 1971, the band's sound had metamorphosed into something darker, with extended dronal jams, all original songs, and a new name, St. Elmo's Fire. The highlight of our run was performing at the Sunshine Festival, a marathon concert event held on the lawn at Cornell that May with an array of bands that included Death & Taxes and headliners Boffalongo, who had a regional hit with *Dancing In The Moonlight*.

On a Friday afternoon in September of 1971, we decide to celebrate the equinox with a party on Eddy Street. Foregoing permits, we drag the equipment down from the living room, set up amps and drums and a small PA, and call the extended gang to come jam. Within minutes of the first pealing notes, the Ithaca police are out in force to shut us down. Having restored the street to its normal less-than-pristine state, two friends and I head to campus to sit in one of the gorges, lick our wounds, and contemplate existence. As we walk up the main drag, a cherry-top follows us, stops, and through the loudspeaker we hear: "You longhaired scum, get off the campus!" Cop turns and drives off and we salute him with middle fingers upraised. A hundred yards away, he makes a U-turn. Pulling up next to us, he singles me out and throws me against the side of the cruiser.

It's the notorious Officer Pupperweg (not his real name), rumored to have shot a black child who had broken into a cigarette machine. I'm spreadeagled and searched, then told to get in the car. I ask if I'm being arrested. "The charge," he says, "is harassment of an officer." My friends go pale. We drive to the station downtown, the Memphis Jug Band version of "We're in the Jailhouse Now" playing on a loop in my head.

The cops on duty are none too happy to see Officer Pupperweg and less than thrilled at the prospect of spending their weekend here at the station on round-the-clock shifts, with me as sole prisoner. Telling them he'll write me up later, Pupperweg leaves. They ask me what happened and seem amused at the tale. I have no ID or wallet on me and they suggest that I go home, get $25 for bail and return.

My pre-trial hearing is set for mid-October. In the crowded courtroom (crowded thanks to its caseload, not my notoriety) the judge calls me up and begins to read Pupperweg's report in a stentorian voice: "He did willfully raise his right hand with the middle finger upraised, signifying..." Here he breaks off, pauses, and finally holds up the paper while pointing to the offensive terms. The assembled multitudes break out in laughter. Gavel bangs: "Order in the court!" I'm asked for my plea and I answer: "Innocent." On what grounds? "I'm left-handed, and if the officer couldn't tell my left arm from my right, how could he tell if it was my middle finger?" Justice prevails and I'm given an ACD: Action in Contemplation of Dismissal. If I can avoid being arrested for the next six months, the charges will be eliminated and my record cleared.

By the end of September, St. Elmo's Fire had disintegrated because of personality issues and divergent goals. At the same time, we were evicted from Action Central on Eddy Street and new digs had to be found. Without the band, my income had greatly diminished and I was forced to room in a dank basement. This isolation had its benefits, though, and I spent the larger portion of the 24-hour cycle with guitar in hand. Left to my own self-constructed discipline, I felt my guitar work taking a quantum leap upward in skills and sonic understanding and, inversely, my interest in rock diminishing. When I wasn't playing or thinking about music, I was depressed and lonely and couldn't come up with any good reason to stay in Ithaca.

Back at my parents': go to jail, do not pass Go.

In those weeks after leaving Ithaca I was reliant for employment on a temp agency called Manpower, which would send me on ill-paid assignments that might last anywhere from half a day to three or four. The work might involve dismantling and clearing out an abandoned warehouse, laying asphalt on a stretch of county road, cleaning trays in the IBM cafeteria, or (oddest of all my odd jobs) a stint as a porter in the Maybelline cosmetics factory, where I would schlep around 30-gallon cans of dye and other chemicals in a room filled with 200 women from all over the world, none of whom spoke English.

Just when things looked bleakest, a visit with Joel Eckhaus revealed to me that composer and trombonist Roswell Rudd would be teaching jazz and ethnomusicology at Bard College. Roswell's arrangements for Archie Shepp's seminal album *Four for Trane* were an inspiring landmark. Excited, I decided to look into Bard and, thanks to a meeting with composer and department chair Elie Yarden, felt that it could be an encouraging environment in which to develop as both composer and player. Once again, my electronics skills netted me a job on campus, this time maintaining equipment for the music department and language lab and thereby knocking off the greater part of my tuition.

Back to the insulated world of academia! Guitar explorations made room for studies in theory and composition. My saxophone practice progressed and was bolstered by the acquisition of a bass clarinet (paid for by my work as a shipping clerk and quality-control inspector at the Emergency Beacon factory, which made electronic devices for aircraft that would automatically signal the location of a crash). The most direct connection between my Inner Ear and its sonic manifestation was now equally split between guitar and saxophone, each informing the other.

Saxophone practice involved scales, patterns, work on jazz standards, and—inspired by Rahsaan Roland Kirk, Roscoe Mitchell, and Evan Parker—development of such extended techniques as circular breathing, multiphonics, and the altissimo register. The purchase of a Fender electric bass brought me work as an accompanist to singers and horn players; it also allowed me to share the low-end duties in Roswell Rudd's jazz composition workshop, which already had a plethora of guitarists. Roswell had a royal presence, enhanced by his curly hair and full but well-trimmed beard. He embodied cool, with hip threads telegraphing the era's NYC jazz mystique: big shades, clogs, cotton bell-bottoms, a thick woven sweater of Andean origin. His obvious intelligence and New England reserve were balanced by the warmth of his personality and overall funky vibe. His passion for music was infectious and he drew an expansive line connecting Ellington and Monk, Pygmies and Tibetan monks, New Orleans heterophony and space-age funk. He would urge us to "tell a story" when soloing. While his classes were informative, the real transmission of information happened after hours at Adolph's, the bar of the Annandale Hotel, a.k.a. "Down The Road." Ros might reminisce about playing with Herbie Nichols and Steve Lacy or describe how he'd lived in a tent in his Chambers Street loft because it was too expensive to heat.

Life at Bard was close to idyllic for me; even goofing off seemed enlightening. Between classes, practicing guitar and reeds, and solitary explorations, there would be long conversations about anything and everything with fellow students Steve Piccolo, Paul Diamond, Fiona Kelley, brothers Paul and Andrew Weinstein, Rhonda Postrel, Dorothy Lifka, Bob Reselman, and Stewart Gilbert. I would take long walks with my dog Buffy down to the Hudson River or in the surrounding wilds. Reverend Sun Myung Moon, leader of the notorious Unification Church, owned property adjacent to Bard and on more than one occasion I encountered Moon, barefoot and in full tuxedo and tails, walking through the woods with four companions similarly attired.

Our jazz club would put on a few concerts each semester. The Revolutionary Ensemble (Leroy Jenkins, Sirone, Jerome Cooper) was one of our first events in 1972 and I was amazed at how they balanced the screaming fire of Jimi Hendrix with the crystalline intensity of a Webern string quartet. The same year, we booked Cecil Taylor for a solo recital at Bard Hall. I picked him and his manager up at the Rhinebeck train station but he said not a word throughout the drive back to campus, made all the longer by the manager's injunction against driving above fifteen miles per hour. At 5:30 p.m. the two-lane highway was jammed with cars in both directions, unable to pass and honking their disapproval. I enjoyed the massive horn chorus, a majestic salute to this great musician.

The hall was packed and I had a seat just off of the uppermost keys of the piano. It was like being immersed in molten magma, flowing prominences of solar flares, choirs of angelic bailophones. I couldn't possibly imagine that one day I'd be sitting in Cecil's Brooklyn apartment while he spun tales of seeing Billie Holiday perform, or that we would work on a recording project together.

Bard also had an active film department, recently founded by the antic experimentalist Adolfas Mekas. Screenings were held almost nightly at Sottery Hall, with programs ranging from the earliest films of Meliès and Vertov, Expressionist classics, Italian neo-realism, French New Wave, and early animations to the activities of current faculty member Bruce Baillie, the wildness of George and Mike Kuchar, and the iconic work of Stan Brakhage. *Dog Star Man Parts I-IV* was at the top of the charts. I made my way to Sottery as often as possible as it fed the sound in my Ear. I imagined making music as a form of experimental film, full of stark contrasts, absurdist non sequiturs, Minimalist reductions, jump cuts, and extended neurotic and erotic reveries.

Improvising sessions would happen in off hours and odd spaces and though sometimes very enjoyable, they often fell prey to individual egos who would hijack the ensembles as accompaniment for their marathon solos. To try and add a touch of organization to these open music sessions, I was creating both graphic and algorithmic scores such as *Noise Floor* and *Spectral Shift,* making use of my love of painting and the quantified presentation of information. It seemed like an obvious tack to use colors and textures to transmit musical instructions. I was finally beginning to get a clearer sense of how to communicate my ideas, and developing a systemic approach took priority. This top-down, cerebral outlook affected my playing and hearing, that old feedback loop working its magic. The Inner Ear stretched and added a few coils to its infinite spiral.

After graduating from Bard, I decided to stay in the immediate area as I still had my employment on campus and a loose band called The Music Collective with Steve Piccolo on bass, keyboardist Bruce Wolosoff, percussionist Steve Pouchie, and drummers Harvey Nosowitz or Alan Kirschenbaum. I was sharing a small house in Germantown on the Hudson River with Steve and his wife Wendy, saxophonist John Lurie, pianist Evan Lurie, three dogs, and seven cats. Many surreal conversations were had, and little sleep. At the time, John was a hirsute hippie emitting such words of wisdom as "There's nothing like apples, peanut butter, and John Coltrane." For amusement at 2 a.m., we might pack into my Dodge and head for the newly-opened 24-hour supermarket in Hudson. We'd fill our shopping cart while munching on the free donuts and coffee provided to lure in customers, eventually buying just a jar of peanut butter or some eggs. Once we spotted local resident Sonny Rollins in the store but were too awestruck to even think of greeting him. Another night we mounted an after-hours excursion to Olana, the exotic Victorian-meets-Middle-Eastern mansion of Hudson River School painter Frederic Church. There was no nightime security and we wandered both the lush grounds and the interior of the house for hours, until the first hints of dawn.

Back at the shack in Germantown, much time was spent on the porch watching the myriad fireflies with the expectation that at any second they would spell out words or cohere into pictures. This, I thought, could be a score. Down by the Hudson, I would find secluded places to practice soprano sax. Sunrise on the river—which might be witnessed from either end of the day—would reveal thousands of birds taking off at once, the air so thick that foreground and background were reversed, a living Escher drawing, the sound symphonic and granulated. Another score. I had a favorite spot on a hill overlooking the Germantown cemetery, where I could witness an incredible audio panorama at sunrise, insects and birds creating a pixillated cloud of sparkling sounds, hocketed crosstalk of pure abstraction, Miró sonified.

There were occasional forays into civilization for gigs. Pouchie, who was working as a music teacher at Matawan State Hospital for the Criminally Insane in Beacon, about an hour away, arranged for The Music Collective to perform a concert there. Arriving as directed a few hours early, we went through an elaborate check-in procedure where our persons and our equipment were thoroughly searched. An assembly room had a stage where we set up and at the sound of a bell, the prisoners were ushered in according to a strictly ordered protocol. We faced a sea of gray coveralls and mostly African-American faces. I knew from the stories told by Pouchie, and by another friend who worked there as an art therapist, that the inmates ranged across the full spectrum of violent behavior and many were heavily medicated. Still, the air crackled with anticipation, and many other emotions, as we picked up our instruments.

Our funkier numbers were much better received than the jazz tunes, and Pouchie's solos on vibes and congas were met with loud cheers. We took a break and I was approached by a long-haired, bearded young man in a prison jumpsuit who asked very politely if we could play any songs by the Doors. I found out later that he had murdered his parents. One of the counselors asked if the prisoners could use our instruments to play two or three songs, as they had a band but little opportunity to play on good equipment. We welcomed this, and the volcanic intensity with which they played their doo-wop songs was absolutely stupefying. We returned to the stage to finish our performance and the commitment and energy of the prisoners' set helped focus our own.

After the show, bells rang and the prisoners were led from the assembly, again in quite an orderly fashion. We packed and had moved our equipment to the loading dock when more bells rang and guards began scurrying around. A lockdown was announced over the public address system and everything came to a standstill. At one point, two guards took off the front head of the bass drum and began unscrewing the back panels of the larger amplifier cabinets. Apparently a prisoner was missing in the head count and they had to make sure that he was not attempting to smuggle himself out in our gear. After about fifteen minutes, he was located and we were allowed to complete our packing and depart.

In May of '72, The Music Collective went down to New York City to play the "Spring Dance" at an SRO welfare hotel on the Upper West Side at the invitation of Mitchell Korn, who was working as a counselor there. Though by now I fancied myself somewhat worldly, this event—a Big Apple remix of Fellini's *Satyricon* with Jack Smith's *Flaming Creatures*—was fairly shocking to my narrow range of reality. Playing to a group of intoxicated dancers of many genders was its own reward, though, and I felt that the band never sounded better.

Back in the rarefied atmosphere of my life on the river, I was developing sonic strategies involving natural forms and processes. These were manifested as the *Hudson River Compositions*, a set of simple instructions and condensed reflections, neither "heads" to spark improvisation nor an ordered sequence of musical notes. Any of the lines could be combined in a musical action or used individually. Using a copy machine, I took images from books and magazines and superimposed them on music manuscript paper to illustrate 1, 4, and 6:

1. *Play the fireflies.*

2. *Play as fast as possible in rhythmic unison.*

3. *Hocket! Play pointillistically to build a groove - never play at the same time as any other player.*

4. *Birds flock: Chop -> space*

5. *Max density -> space*

6. *Emulate the river: music streams - never play the same thing twice while maintaining a continuous single identity*

7. *Play and record a monophonic line slowed to half-speed. Repeating the process. And again...*

8. *Branching: go tangential but maintain the initial impulse*

9. *Octave overtones - map speed to range*

10. *Hemiola: each player chooses a different time signature and repeats a simple figure in that time. Pop out.*

11. *Play the opposite*

It was music that I could both see and hear and even feel coursing through my neurons, music that would be infinitely variable yet always itself, the IrRational, music from and for my Inner Ear.

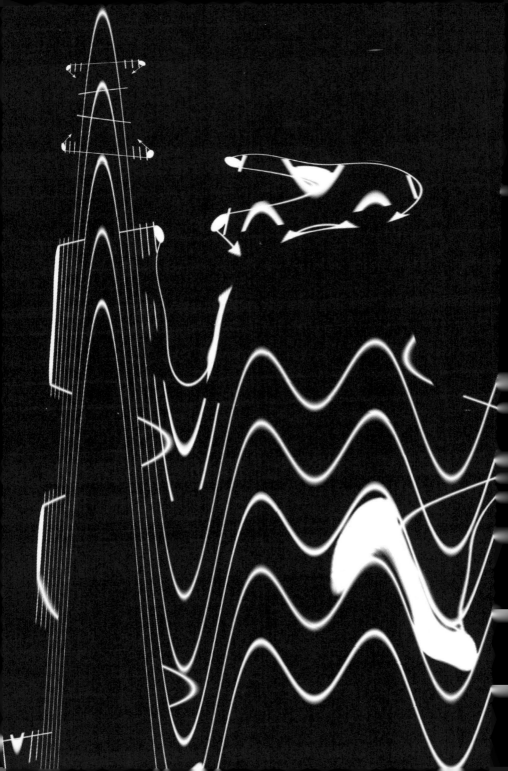

V.

June in Buffalo
(December Too)

During my stint at WRCT in Pittsburgh, I came upon Lajaren Hiller's *HPSCHD*, a long-form work composed in collaboration with John Cage and heard on the eponymous Nonesuch LP. It was a sonic overload of great beauty, its massive sound field resonating with me in the same way that Xenakis' work did. Hiller's use of the computer to create the *Illiac Suite* in 1958 especially piqued my interest and I sought out recordings and any writings either by him or about his music. Post-Bard, Elie Yarden and Benjamin Boretz had encouraged me to look into continuing my studies at either the State University in Buffalo or the University of California in Davis. After some investigation, Buffalo looked distinctly better, especially as I couldn't imagine moving my whole existence to now-distant California. And given that both Hiller and Morton Feldman, another inspirational composer, were teaching in Buffalo, it seemed quite an attractive solution to the problem of the immediate future.

In July of 1974, I cold-called Hiller to arrange a meeting and a few days later drove to Buffalo. Jerry had the air of a mad but genial scientist: a thin man, bright-eyed, skinny tie. He was incredibly gracious and receptive as I described my musical work to date and showed him some of my scores. He was especially interested in the fact that I had experience in designing, building, and repairing electronic circuits. On the spot, he offered me a place as a part-time graduate student for the fall semester and, equally important, a job as the assistant to George Ritscher, the maintenance director for the music department.

The moment the meeting concluded, I picked up a newspaper and a map and found myself an inexpensive apartment on Buffalo's East Side. With lease signed, I drove back to the Hudson, arriving home in the wee hours. Being more used to rural than urban geography, little did I realize that a one-mile radius from the University might encompass strange and hostile territory. When I moved into my new apartment a month later, an afternoon walk in the neighborhood revealed the White Power Bookstore just around the corner on Bailey Avenue, complete with swastika-adorned thugs lounging on the porch yelling "Death to Jews" as I walked by. I flipped them a peace sign with one hand and the bird with the other.

Besides providing me with a small income and tuition-free admission to my two classes at the University—composition with Jerry and Computer Music with John Myhill—my job and its set of keys allowed me 24-hour access to the electronic-music studio. George Ritscher was a fantastic boss who let me know that as long as I fulfilled my responsibilities within certain very open windows, I could spend as much time in the studio as I wished. Balding, with a fringe of long hair and severe horn-rimmed glasses, George loved to tell stories about the legendary composers and musicians who had walked these hallowed halls. He could be cryptic, as when he intoned solemnly: "One day you will meet a woman named Maryanne Amacher. You won't forget it." At the time I found little documentation about her. When we finally met in 1985, I had learned much about her work but not so much that I wasn't knocked for a loop by her blunt style.

The studio was equipped with a pair of Ampex 440 tape decks and racks of early Moog and Bode equipment, including a prototype Vocoder. Hiller enthusiastically discussed the principles behind this device and his plans to exploit its transformational potential in a composition titled *Metamorphoses*, based on Ovid's classic. I would lock myself in the studio on a Friday afternoon and emerge on Monday, having immersed myself in manuals and systematic experimentation with the synthesizers. I learned to take apart and rebuild Ampex and Revox decks and keep them aligned, to do the necessary routine maintenance on the synth modules and mixing desk, and to build up my own repertoire of patches and sonic techniques. I dreamed of putting microphones in each of the cell-like practice rooms and recording and mixing the results, an idle fantasy.

With one ear to the ground and the other facing upward, I could luxuriate in the snap and crackle of creative musical energy bubbling through the general noise of football and business administration chatter. Baird Hall buzzed with esteemed guests and frequent concerts. I would also attend lectures and screenings in the film department by such notable faculty as Paul Sharits, Hollis Frampton, Steina and Woody Vasulka, and Tony Conrad (whom I met bagging raisins together at the local food coop.) There was a system of colleges within the university that included Women's Studies, American Studies, and Tolstoy College, all hotbeds of provocative ideas that extended well beyond the campus. I connected with various other aspiring composers, players, and musical thinkers, including Bobby Previte, Mark Steven Brooks, Greg Ketchum, and Charlie Kaufman. We had endless discussions, sessions of improvisation, and experiments with graphic scores, game pieces, and philosophical approaches to composition.

In my weekly meetings with Jerry I came to appreciate the breadth of his music and accomplishments, evidence of a boundless curiosity, not to mention a great sense of mischief. (He told me that as a child he liked to place pennies on the railroad tracks near his house to see if they would derail the train.) In *Three Rituals for Two Percussion, Projections and Lights*, disco balls and strobe lights illuminated a stage encrusted with percussion instruments; the second movement was the orchestrated demolition of the setup of the first movement (including some very noisy accidents) and the build of the second. In contrast, his fifth and sixth string quartets, austere and beautiful, each presented unique sound worlds, one in microtones, the other in overtones. His ensemble works *Algorithms* encouraged a view of composition in which the musical piece might be considered an operating system, a piece of software, rather than a fixed sequence of pitches in time—an idea that, for me, resonated deeply.

Because of my commitment to improvisation, I would often discuss scoring with Jerry, why it was necessary and how I might best approach it. In academic circles there was generally a deep suspicion of improvisation, as if it were somehow cheating. Hiller felt no such thing and believed that whatever was necessary to manifest the music was the proper score, even if that meant no score at all. We compared the positive and negative qualities of algorithms and instruction sets, graphics, game pieces, time lines, even conventional notation—which, at times, might be the best solution. Jerry favored clarity of intent and execution. As I was developing the score to *Attica Brothers/Life Cycle*, he offered astute suggestions, always in the form of questions: "Why do you have this particular rhythm? Do you hear it or is it a construction? Why is there a conductor?" Thinking back upon my meetings with Hiller, I continue to find material for inspiration and reflection, as well as matters I wish I'd had the presence of mind to raise with him. The Ostrava Music Days festival in 2009 gave me the opportunity to hear intense performances of a number of Jerry's compositions by Joe Kubera and Conrad Harris; with the objectivity of decades passed, I found that the writing remained unique and free of cliché, angular and passionate.

As part of my employment, I would set up sound reinforcement and playback for the concerts produced by the Center For Creative And Performing Arts, founded by Hiller and Renée Levine. Through the Center, I first met and worked with Julius Eastman, Richard Teitelbaum, Frances-Marie Uitti, Joseph Kubera, Petr Kotik, Joelle Leandre, Eberhard Blum, Don Knaack, Ralph Jones, Yvar Mikhashoff, Benjamin Hudson, the Grateful Dead's Tom Constanten, and many others—an incredible panorama of incandescent talent. Professor of percussion Jan Williams was an integral part of the Center and a positive presence in the department, constantly performing and organizing events and encouraging the young composers. Most of my work was as a technician or engineer, but on occasion also as a musician. Julius asked me to play soprano saxophone for his piece *Masculine* in a group he was putting together with bassist Sabu Adeyola. Julius was impish and often smiling but absolutely exacting and dead serious about his music and how it had to be performed. We had two rehearsals but it was extremely difficult for us to transform the skeletal score into what he was hearing, which was clear to the composer but not necessarily to the players. Doing tech for an SEM Ensemble performance of *Femenine* at Albright-Knox Art Gallery was much more direct and the results extremely gratifying, with Julius' lyrical, futuristic Afro-Minimalist sounds floating on a grooving bed of mechanically excited sleighbells. I was deeply saddened to witness Julius' drug-related deterioration after he left Buffalo for NYC. My apartment in the city was adjacent to Tompkins Square Park and in the mid-to-late 80s I would often run into him when, homeless, he was crashing there. When I had money I'd give him some or get him a meal. He had the peculiar glow that emanates from certain addicts and his conversation veered unpredictably from brilliant to incoherent. In those last days he was still smiling and optimistic, but there was no hiding from the inevitable tragedy.

The Composer's Forum was a slightly formal seminar within the music department, meeting on Friday afternoons and planning a concert for each semester. Morton Feldman held court. A large man with a big belly, usually dressed in a white shirt and suit pants, he presented an imposing figure with his horn-rims, pompadour, and ever-present Camel, an inch of ash perpetually ready to drop. When he was the center of attention, he would relax and be generous with his thoughts and digressions: waxing philosophical, reminiscing about the good old days of avant-garde music in the 1950s, issuing pronouncements about what should and should not be done in the composition of music, and intimidating the generally fearful and insecure students—except those anointed by him to carry the torch via pale imitation of his own work, who thereby felt entitled to pass judgment on everyone else. If there was any challenge, self-righteous anger would take over. I recall one contentious concert—planning session in which one of the anointed declared himself to be an "aristocrat," not subject to the considerations that applied to the other composers. Feldman acquiesced with his silence. A rare exception among Feldman's students in the Forum was composer and pianist Nils Vigeland, whose luminous and well-balanced music and genial presence transmitted clarity and a personal approach outside of any agenda. Feldman's music certainly had been an influence on me; indeed, his and Jerry's presence was the reason I was in Buffalo. To hear him expound, in his thick Queens accent, on *teppich*, painting, and poetry was always stimulating and often startling. Morty's office was next door to my base in the electronic-music studio and there would often be friendly greetings and queries into my work. I had very mixed feelings about Morty and I began to understand that the artist and their art could be very different entities.

For the October Composers' Forum concert, I decided to present a realization for soprano sax and tape of the algorithmic piece *Hudson River #7*. On one channel of the tape was a 90-minute through-composed melody that I had played on the soprano through a ring modulator. This track was slowed down to half-speed and another ring-modulated sax track improvised and overdubbed to the remaining channel together with the now-180-minute line. For the performance, this tape was then slowed down to half-speed again, yielding a 360-minute heterophonic background over which I improvised a third sax part through a ring modulator pedal I'd built. Morty called me into his office the next morning. "Sit down," he commanded, and quickly dismissed me: "Ya know, improvisation... I don't buy it."

In November of 1974, inspired by political activities that would have a dramatic effect on my Buffalo career, I began work on *Attica Brothers/Life Cycle* for presentation at the March 1975 concert. Composed for violin, cello, both double bass and electric bass, orchestral percussionist Don Knaack, Bobby Previte playing a rock drum kit, conga drummer, and my own electric guitar, the piece was structured in two parts over a continuous pulse played by the conga. A conductor with time cards cued the various entries and transitions. The first section featured a through-composed seven-note pentatonic melody for the strings, stretched over five minutes and harmonized microtonally to produce an angry bluesy buzzing while the drummers exchanged terse intense blasts notated graphically and placed on the timeline. In the second section, three minutes in length, drums and bass played a through-composed angular groove in 21/8, while the strings and guitar wailed like sirens with glissandi read from a graphic score and the percussionist generated earthquakes. As we prepared to commence the performance, Feldman rose from his seat in the packed house and, pointing at the conga drummer, shouted: "Where's his music stand?" I replied that he didn't need one because his entrance and exit were cued by the conductor. (I didn't want to have to explain then and there, but the lack of a music stand was intended to make a point about the role of the congas.) Feldman's answer was to climb on stage, grab a music stand from the wings, bang it down in front of the conga player (jaw dropped, eyes glazed with fear) and announce, "Now you can play the piece." As before, Morty called me into his office the next morning. "Ya know," he raged, "you put too much sociology in your music. Music should be listened to sitting in red plush seats, but your music, you have to sit on the floor."

Early one morning in April of 1975, I took part in a campus demonstration in support of amnesty for those prisoners who had participated in the 1970 Attica Prison riots against inhumane conditions, but had not committed violence in doing so. I did not consider myself to be an activist and was certainly not one of the organizers, just a student-citizen who wished to attend and bear witness. That morning, I found myself on the receiving end of a police attack. The security forces had assembled inside the president's office and at a certain point burst out upon us, grabbing people and indiscriminately bashing them with nightsticks, their dogs snarling and snapping all the while. Ten of us were arrested; in the local newspapers we would be dubbed "the UB10." I had been pulled into the office by my hair and beaten with telephone books, a weapon favored by Buffalo police because it apparently didn't leave bruises. My arms were trussed behind my back with my belt and I was then handcuffed so tightly that my wrists bled. Carried by two cops to the paddy wagon, I was hit on each kneecap with a nightstick by a third grinning and obese representative of "the law." The wagon, which usually transported the K-9 Korps, was filthy with dog feces. I spent the day in a cell, denied both telephone calls and treatment for my injuries. My glasses and shoelaces were confiscated along with my driver's license.

When we were brought to the courthouse at 4 that afternoon, I was shocked to learn that I was being charged with stabbing the chief of campus security and would, if convicted, face a sentence of 35 years to life. My bail was set at $50,000. Being a graduate student, I was painted as a ringleader of the demonstration, which was far from the reality. Fortunately, an ad hoc group of activists and lawyers, including Attica defense attorneys Lenny Klaif and Barbara Handschu, engaged a bail bondsman and we were all released that evening. Among the first things Lenny said to me were the all-too-true words: "You're lucky that you're white—if you were black, they would have killed you."

Needless to say, I was not guilty of the charge and after a seemingly interminable series of depositions and hearings in city court over the next eighteen months, all criminal charges were dropped in exchange for my not suing for false arrest and police brutality. On campus, a hearing in July 1975 cleared me of all charges except refusing to leave the building. This, however, was followed by a unilateral and despotic ruling by the university president, Robert Ketter, rejecting their decision. Suspended from school and banned from campus for six months, I lost my electronics maintenance position. I also found myself estranged from the music department, where most of the teachers and students seemed unsympathetic. The exceptions were some of my fellow student composers, who offered their moral support, and among the faculty Julius Eastman, Jan Williams, and especially Jerry Hiller, who was horrified by the violent and and thuggish behavior of the authorities and wrote letters in my defense to both the court and the administration. I found support, too, among the faculty of the American studies department, in particular Charles Hayney and Charles and Angelika Keil.

I had avidly read Charles Keil's *Urban Blues* while in high school and his course Music in Culture was on my shortlist of classes to take. Charlie led an open-ended band called Outer Circle Orchestra and called the forces into motion to raise money for the defense of the UB10 at a benefit concert at a local pub. He contacted me and asked if I would play with them for this event. Tall with a trim mustache, Charlie led the ensemble standing at his double bass, the picture of seriousness except when his frown of concentration flickered into a wicked grin. Mark Dickey on Fender Rhodes ran down the *montunos* and Bob Nowak laid down claves and conga drums. I brought my tenor sax and we had a fantastic time jamming on rumbas, highlife, boogaloo, and funk grooves. Later, when Charlie asked me to join the group, I readily agreed. We dug into tunes by Mongo Santamaria, Eddie Palmieri, Manu Dibango, Willie Bobo, Tito Puente and more.

After my minor exile from campus was complete, I re-entered the university, but now in the American studies department with Charlie as my advisor. Upon learning that Roswell Rudd had been my teacher at Bard, he told me that they were first cousins and talked about their playing on cruise ships with Steve Lacy and Steve Swallow. Discussions in class might lead to hanging out at the home of Charlie and Angelika, a professor of women's studies who would happily whip up little pots of potent Greek coffee to spike our sessions. Charlie liked to call me "F" (the enharmonic equivalent of E#). I'd play recordings of some of my synthesizer experiments to him and he'd say, "Y'know, F, that sounds like a clucking grandmother. Why do you want to mess with those electronics?" Charlie turned me on to a different branch of the electric guitar family tree, the realm of highlife and jújù where (metaphorically) Wes Montgomery returns to Africa to render a free-running counterpoint to interlocked vocals and percussion.

Music in Culture was a series of lectures with a "lab." To put it simply, the lectures covered the relationship between people's lives and the music they make. The course could be seen as an introduction to ethnomusicology, but Charlie's sociological and economic interpretations gave it a depth that far surpassed the usual "survey of the exotic" that most such courses presented. We delved into African pop music from highlife to *kwela* and its relationship to Banda polyphony, M'buti Pygmy hocketed singing, or James Brown and Cuban *son*. We analyzed the acoustic principles in Tibetan ritual music and in the essential Macedonian power trio of a pair of *zurnas* with *daouli*. Greek *rembetika* and Blind Willie Johnson shared the tape player with John Coltrane and Mongo Santamaria. In the lab, we learned the mysterious ways of what

Charlie dubbed "The 12/8 Path": claves and bell beats from Afro-Cuban music, *shekere* technique, and how to hit a conga drum while generating difference tones from saxophones, flutes, zurna, and even electric guitar. When the gods demanded, Charlie and I might climb up to the roof of the American Studies building with two zurnas and send out piercing waves of close-interval melodic extrapolation into the surrounding North Buffalo neighborhood. One of Charlie's favorite tunes for this was John Denver's "I'm Sorry."

Charlie was also a huge fan of polka, which he viewed as one of the few cultural musics in the United States untainted by commercial exploitation. With a large Polish population, Buffalo was an epicenter of modern polka, with a variety of clubs and social halls where bands would play for dancers and drinkers. Once, Charlie booked Outer Circle to perform at a polka festival at a hall out in Cheektowaga headlined by Wanda and Stephanie, a mother and daughter team of singing accordionists who represented the more traditional side of modern polka. The Dynatones, an exciting young band that leavened their polkas with funk and disco, had the audience out on the floor, stomping and line-dancing. The show was completely foot-powered and Charlie explained to us after our set fell flat that people liked to dance to songs that they knew, not to an abstract groove, no matter how funky. When we played, we saw a few people moving but mostly they listened politely. Charlie invited Wanda and Stephanie to do a number with us but, unsurprisingly, they declined.

When Charlie went on sabbatical for a year, Outer Circle Orchestra became more of an electric band with the addition of vocalist Ellen Greenberg, Bill Nowak on Fender bass, and a variety of guest musicians. The repertoire comprised James Brown and P-Funk riffs, some reggae, and a number of original songs. Ellen had been the curator of the Patti Smith collection at Gotham Books and was very much in tune with the NYC rock underground. In that fall of 1975, she brought me to see the Ramones play in the cafeteria of Buffalo State College and it was a life-altering experience. Though the manic music, reduced to three chords, was not intrinsically interesting, the vibe they created was unlike anything I'd witnessed and absolutely changed the air. I'd heard them on records and wasn't impressed but this was exhilarating, transformative. Our Outer Circle rehearsals might now be punctuated with a shouted "ONE-TWO-THREE-FOUR" leading to a burst of high-speed sonic hilarity.

Before my ban from campus went into effect in August of 1975, I was able to attend the "June in Buffalo" seminar, hosted by Feldman and Hiller, where my first encounter with John Cage took place. He was one of the guest artists that year, along with Christian Wolff, Earle Brown, and Steve Reich, each there for a few days of lectures and performances of their works. Reich's presentation was clear and appealing. He played a recording of *Music for 18 Musicians*, which had just been premiered at NYU's Loeb Student Center. It was lush and hypnotic, though perhaps a bit smooth. I was a little suspicious of a sound world seemingly appropriated from African and Indonesian music. At Reich's concert that evening, acoustical science stole the show. *Piano Phase* had seemed flat and mechanical on record, but live in Baird Hall the phasing created unpredictable and rich psychoacoustic phenomena, making for a riveting performance. Previte and I kept turning to each other: "Are you hearing that?"

John Cage's legend preceded him and expectations were high for all of us overeager young composers, who somehow felt that we were being ushered into an audience with the Dalai Lama. There was the blue chambray workshirt, the big smile. His presence in the packed and stifling classroom was luminous. Before that first session began, I witnessed a very disturbing example of bullying behavior from Feldman. He spotted Mark Brooks, who couldn't afford the tuition for June in Buffalo, sitting quietly on the floor in a corner hoping to hear Cage speak. Ordering Mark to stand up, Feldman berated, humiliated, then ejected him in front of the gathered composers and students. Mark left Buffalo the next day.

After a long and uncomfortable silence, Cage began his lecture—though his demeanor hinted to me that he might, at that moment, have preferred to be doing almost anything else. This first talk reiterated themes found in his writings, after which he entertained questions with patience. For those of us familiar with his books, there were no surprises. But that first night saw the performance of Cage's *Songbooks* at the Albright-Knox Gallery by Petr Kotik's SEM Ensemble, and Julius Eastman's portion of the performance created a major scandal.

At the score's instruction "Give a lecture," Julius undressed a boyfriend, then attempted the same with a woman volunteer. As I recall, they were asked to walk towards each other. At the seminar the next morning, Cage was absolutely furious. He devoted his talk to the notion of ego and the interpreter's responsibility—a question that some of those present have continued to ponder. When there is a personal relationship overriding any aesthetic or political differences, liberties may be freely given, and they may enable powerful and surprising realizations. But the composer opens a potential can of worms when offering liberties in an unpredictable situation. The solution perhaps is to share with the performer a context, not just the sonic intentions—at the very least, an additional sentence in the instruction set—and thereby share responsibility. This might be consider a utopian approach; it would fall within classic definitions of anarchism, which I'd always thought a viable model for open musical interaction without predetermined strictures—a self-organizing system. From his writings, I had thought this was central to Cage's work as well.

I was to meet Cage again some years later under much more relaxed circumstances. "Mondays at Diane Brown Gallery" was a series organized by Petr Kotik, taking place in April of 1986, that would include John Cage performing *Muoyce*, Petr's SEM Ensemble, and my solo performance *Cochlear Medley*. Preparing publicity for the concert, Petr arranged for us to meet at Cage's loft on 18th Street to be photographed by Felipe Orrego. It was a chilly, rainy afternoon in February: John made tea and we all made polite chit-chat, everyone quite reserved. I asked if the tea we were drinking (black, caffeinated) was considered an acceptable part of a macrobiotic diet. John brightened up. "Well," he said, "I usually start the day very good but finish it very bad." Grinning proudly, he pulled out a bottle of single malt, enlivening the proceedings greatly. Since I had the use of a friend's car, I would on occasion be pressed into service by Petr to pick John up for events or drop him off at his loft in Chelsea. It was a bit terrifying to be navigating Saturday night traffic in all its hyperaggressive unpredictability knowing that the one-and-only John Cage was in the back seat.

Buffalo had an insular jazz scene centered around swing and some bop, with just a few clubs, such as the Sheraton Hotel, the Anchor Bar (famous for the invention of "Buffalo wings"), and the legendary Revilot on East Ferry, which was in decline by the time I moved to town. Bookers, venues, and even the majority of musicians were quite conservative. There was an open session on Monday nights at the Central Park Grill in North Buffalo hosted by James Clark, a knowledgeable and highly skilled bop guitarist. Composed almost entirely of straight-ahead playing, the sessions featured only rare forays into light weirdness, but as there was not much else to do in Buffalo in the evenings they became a regular hang for me and my friends, among them Bobby Previte, bassist Peter Piccirilli, and guitarist Stew Cutler. A big jazz town in the first half of the 20th century, Buffalo had been a major industrial city as well. Though in decline, the industries—as evidenced by air horribly polluted with exhaust from steel mills and auto plants—had not disappeared. Of the three Trico windshield wiper factories in Buffalo running 24-hour shifts, Nr. 2 sat just around the corner from the Central Park Grill. When we tired of the endless ii-V-I of the CPG, my friends and I would spend a fair amount hanging out in front of Trico Nr. 2, listening to the industrial-strength phasing of the multiple punch presses while discussing the state of music and the world.

The music of Trico—which brought me back to the punch presses of my father's speaker factory—may have been a factor in our formation of an electric improvising ensemble, rock-oriented but open to all sounds, grooves, and directions. In 1977, with the addition of percussionist Greg Ketchum, the NTVC Group was born, the name an acronym for Neuron-To-Voltage-Conversion. (Greg and I also performed in a trio with bassist Joëlle Léandre.) Peter had designed and built from scratch a large modular analog synthesizer and it became our mascot. The sounds from any one of our instruments might be routed into his filters and ring modulator. We had a few structures, written collaboratively, but mostly we improvised. It was trance-oriented and sonic, with overlapping narratives pouring out, jagged and reticulated lines forming saturated textures rather than functioning like jazz solos. We would bring oscilloscopes to our shows, the screens displaying Lissajous figures.

There were very few places in town where we could perform. We were too weird for the hard-rock club McVan's or any of the boogie bars on Elmwood Avenue. Our main outlet was the Cold Spring Warehouse, a chaotic anarchist/hippie/punk loft on the edge of the ghetto. We experimented with shows at the local vegetarian restaurant, where our two events were packed well over capacity. Unfortunately, we were banned from further gigs as the staff considered our music "inappropriate to their vibe," despite unprecedented sales of munchies to our stoner audience. We were asked to perform at the legendary Hallwalls Gallery for a big free public event and we set up on the loading dock. Midway through our first set, the director of the gallery asked if we could play some rock 'n' roll because "people want to boogie." Previte, incensed, asked him why they weren't showing paintings of bowls of fruit.

It was also in 1977 in Buffalo that zOaR Records came into being. I had continued to stay in touch with Bard buddy David Fulton, a mathematician and frequent musical collaborator. Any time we'd meet, our conversations would be extended on guitars with duo improvisations ranging from warped versions of jazz standards to the outer reaches of sound. When I visited him in NYC in January of 1977, we decided to try and book some gigs for our duo but found that without a record release it was a tough sell. Fortunately, the New Music Distribution Service/Jazz Composer's Orchestra illuminated the way for the DIY movement with generous instructions and references for self-publishing an album. We were able to record gratis at the studio of SUNY Buffalo's radio station WBFO thanks to the help of saxophonist Steve Rosenthal of the Amherst Saxophone Quartet, an engineer and producer at the station. We edited and mastered the tapes at the music department studio in Baird Hall and a cover was designed by Deb DeStaffan. The results were sent off to a one-stop aggregator that would press the vinyl, print the sleeves, assemble the package and, finally, shrinkwrap it. I plucked the label name both from nearby Zoar Valley, a sprawling and twisty canyon filled with wildlife about 60 miles south of Buffalo—a fantastic place for hiking, and historically a sacred site for the native tribes of the region—and from the foundational Kabbalistic work the *Zohar*. It seemed inevitable to draw a correspondence between an enigmatic, apocryphal work of mysticism and a vessel for the propagation of obscure and challenging music. Though only a casual student of the Kabbala, I had a deep appreciation for its intersections with nonrational modes of thought across various cultures, its numerological analyses and constructions, and its promotion of altered states of consciousness. As poetic myth, it provided yet another matrix for the translation of the Void into our conscious realm.

Our initial release, zOaR 1, *Hara*, was finally out in the world but the gigs were slow in coming. Our record-release party at Hallwalls was a lonely event attended by just a handful of friends.

During Charlie Keil's sabbatical beginning in the fall of 1977, I was hired to teach Music in Culture, continuing the format of two nights of lectures plus a lab. The course was cross-listed by the music and American studies departments and was required for those pursuing a degree in music education. The great majority of the 60-plus registered students were commuters from the Buffalo suburbs, for the most part incurious and ignorant of the world at large and only concerned with what they needed to do to achieve a passing grade. Most approached the class as a lowest-common-denominator introduction to ethnomusicology, a basic guide to the weird and out-of-tune music played by primitive peoples. I followed Charlie's curriculum with its focus on how and why people made music within a matrix of social and economic factors, both in the United States and elsewhere. We examined blues, polka, free jazz, ritual music from Tibet and both north and sub-Saharan Africa, as well as Carnatic and Bengali Indian music and Afro-Cuban music. The role of improvisation was stressed and correlated with the musics under examination. There were a few reading assignments, photocopied essays from Cage, Colin Turnbull (author of *The Forest People*), Amiri Baraka, Wilhelm Reich, Karl Marx, Laozi, Walter Benjamin, and Charlie Keil himself.

I attempted to make the lectures informative and open-ended, with lots of listening to recorded music. Believing that education was not the pouring of quantified knowledge into a student's brain, but rather a feedback process whereby the student finds the knowledge through her own questions and explorations, I encouraged discussion. General response to my strategies was limited at best: only the handful of students from American studies took an active role in class, while the music department students were mostly indifferent and even hostile. The lab portion of the class fared slightly better with learning of claves and bell beats, expository storytelling on instruments, and hocketed groove-making. There were neither tests nor homework, just one requirement: a 1000-word essay on a topic of one's choice relevant to the class, or else a musical autobiography. This met with much confusion, leading to a mid-semester Q&A session that climaxed with one student whining, "But Mr. Sharp, just what do you want from us?" I had thought the course requirements and goals both modest and clear but apparently they were not clear enough. At the end of the semester, I received a letter from the dean of the music department terminating my employment and cancelling my course. The letter presented various complaints from the students, including the suspicion that I was disseminating Communist propaganda. Fortunately, the American studies department was quite pleased with what I was doing and renewed Music In Culture for the following semester, though with decreased pay for a reduced format of two seminar/labs each week. These turned out to be extremely enjoyable sessions filled with freewheeling discussion, listening, and lots of musical interaction in the form of group improvisations that might last well past the class time and spill over into sonic orgies in Delaware Park.

Since my teaching salary was a pittance, survival meant taking whatever odd low-paying gigs came my way. I had met a bassist named Marvin who led a band called NEWS. I became the guitarist for a few months with a regular Friday gig at the Derby Lounge, a long narrow room adjacent to the Off-Track Betting joint in a strip mall in the ghetto. Marvin had excellent time but little knowledge of the intricacies of harmonic movement. He kept nylon-tape strings on his Fender and with the tone on his amp turned down, no one could ever tell what notes or chords he was playing—it was just "bottom." We played light jazz-funk for the partying winners and anesthetizing losers spilling over from the betting parlor.

Getting by encompassed intermittent gigs at bars, parties, lofts, or coffeehouses; private guitar and saxophone students; and, at a certain crucial point of desperation in July 1978, a job as a short-order cook/counterman on the graveyard shift at For Pete's Sake, a tiny Greek diner near the corner of Main Street and Fillmore specializing in chili dogs, burgers, and breakfast 24/7. The bulk of the clientele was from the huge industrial bakery next door but there were cops, firefighters, and truck drivers galore, as well as more than a fair number of drunks. Sharing my shift was an amateur bodybuilder and Elvis impersonator who told me that once he had learned "all 1200 guitar licks in the world" he would be primed for stardom. He liked to tell me how he would thwart any would-be robbers with his judo expertise. I told him that I'd rather give them the money in the register and a free hot dog to boot if they didn't kill us.

Just across Main Street and visible from Pete's was Buffalo's main jazz club, Tralfamadore. It was a pleasant place to hang and I saw some great shows there, including Elvin Jones, Joe Henderson, and the Willem Breuker Kollektif. The trio of Muhal Richard Abrams, Leroy Jenkins, and Andrew Cyrille performed one night to an audience of Bobby Previte, Peter Piccirilli, and myself. The musicians had a realistically cynical view of the music biz which they explained to us after their incandescent set. Leroy (whom I'd met when we brought the Revolutionary Ensemble to Bard) said not to worry that we couldn't get a gig in Buffalo—we should probably move elsewhere if we were planning to be serious musicians. Tralfamadore seemed to be packed only when hometown heroes Spyro Gyra performed there ("Shaker Song" was on every radio station all the time). On the night I was fired from For Pete's Sake (the owner could clearly see that I was not committed to devoting my life to his culinary crusade) there were lines down the block of the Tralf for a Spyro Gyra show. It was inspiring in the sense that it clarified my plans to leave Buffalo, a nagging undercurrent in my life thoughts. Fulton was down with the program and suggested that, as part of recovery from Buffalo, we head to verdant and tranquil Western Massachusetts, where further musical strategies could be hatched in more pleasant surroundings.

This idea was enhanced when Previte told us of a crew of great musicians he'd met while attending a workshop in Washington, DC. Mostly based in the Pioneer Valley but with activities extending from Southern Vermont down through New Haven to the City, they included Michael Gregory Jackson, Pheeroan akLaff, and Marty Ehrlich. A bonus was the fact that Marion Brown was living in the Hamp and Archie Shepp was teaching at the University of Massachusetts in nearby Amherst. The ancient Volvo wagon was loaded to the gills with my dog Buffy, sundry instruments and amps, and boxes of clothes and books strapped to the roof. On August 1, we headed off to the Berkshire Mountains town of Cummington, Massachusetts and a house and recording studio owned by Al Shackman, an old friend of David's who'd been an Atlantic Records staff guitarist and musical director for Nina Simone. Al regaled us with tales of jamming with Bird and Trane and playing on R&B dates. The house was surrounded by bogs lush with wild blueberries and the air was incredibly sweet, especially after four years of Buffalo's steel mills and auto plants. The month in Cummington was a most welcome period of transition ahead of the move to the college-town hubbub of Northampton, Amherst, and environs.

VI.

Down in the Valley

Marion Brown, a warm and funny man, was a haunting presence walking up and down Main Street in Northampton. His solo on Coltrane's *Ascension* was a landmark for me, as was his album *Three For Shepp* on Impulse! and a later one on ECM, *Afternoon of a Georgia Faun*. It was always a great hang at his sparsely furnished apartment, where there would usually be a covered pot boiling on the stove. We would speak about music, politics, or food: "You guys eat fruit but I'm a stringy little guy and I need my meat." He would concertize infrequently in the area but when he did, especially solo, the playing was epic, with spiraling lines of coiled fractal intensity and seemingly infinite length. He might fall into loops and cycles that, instead of remaining static, would increase the total energy of the system to the point where it seemed ready to explode—then begin building again from this last plateau, a visceral lesson in accessing the Void.

In addition to those from the jazz realm, residing in the Valley were Indian and African musicians, folkies, New Agers, and a growing number of punk-rockers. There were improvisers to play with in the area, but they tended to be somewhat conservative. More interesting for me was an entertaining and sonically adventurous band on the punk end of the spectrum called the Scientific Americans. Their synthesist, Jim Whittemore, and I formed a project called Human Error to record and perform big-beat electroacoustic weirdness, sometimes augmented by guitarist Chris Vine, percussionist Greg Ketchum, and other guests. I would also play tenor sax with the Scientific Americans and we opened for Pere Ubu, DNA, and Pylon, which led to ongoing friendships.

Life in the Valley was pleasant enough but far more expensive than Buffalo, and in my first five months there I experienced mostly famine and only very occasionally, meager feast. I survived on oatmeal, lentils, peanut butter, and coffee. Food for Buffy was always the priority. Gigs were rare and ill paid and my guitar and saxophone students unreliable. I shared a house ten miles west of Northampton with three others. It was too expensive to heat, so to stay warm I'd practice tenor sax obsessively and drink vast amounts of coffee brewed in a Mr. Coffee machine by a housemate, painter Andy Hammerstein. When I had enough money for gas, I'd drive into town, working on my *khoomei* and *kargyraa* throat singing as I tore around the bends on Route 9. Usually, hitchhiking was the preferred mode of travel.

In January of 1978, I sold some equipment that I no longer needed and used the money to record a solo album, *Resonance*, at a tiny studio in nearby Vermont. This was a collection of pieces for various instruments alone: fretless and twelve-string electric guitar, soprano and tenor saxophones, prepared acoustic guitar. Each work concentrated on a specific aspect of sonic vocabulary or gesture from my extended techniques. No electronics were used. The pieces were mixed in an ascetic fashion, with scant reverb, yielding a detailed and hyperreal sound.

Resonance was released on zOaR that March and a copy given by a friend to a Boston critic, resulting in an invitation to appear at the Planet Gong festival for two nights in April at the Modern Theatre in Boston. There were local Boston bands in the afternoon but the curator, Michael Bloom, placed me in the evening program along with NY Gong. This edition of Gong was Daevid Allen and Gilli Smyth backed by Zu Band, soon to be renamed Material and led by bassist Bill Laswell and keyboardist Michael Beinhorn, with guitarist Cliff Cultreri and drummers Bill Bacon and Fred Maher. The festival was created and directed by Giorgio Gomelsky, the legendary producer of the Yardbirds, the Rolling Stones, John McLaughlin, and Magma. Despite his iconic status, Giorgio was unpretentious and joyful, incredibly enthusiastic about the music, and encouraging of spontaneity. He was the picture of a Russian aristocrat gone to seed, elegant and a bit Mephistophelean with his goatee and pomaded hair. When saxophonist Yochk'o Seffer failed to appear for his scheduled slot, Giorgio drafted me and Kramer (playing trombone with Zu Band) for an impromptu duet: "Go play something beautiful!" After our freewheeling set, Kramer gave me numbers for various musicians I should contact if I moved to NYC. I also connected with Mark Dagley and David Hild of the maniacal rock band The Girls.

Summer in the Valley was extremely pleasant but I was frustrated by the tiny and ingrown music scene. I had moved from the country to a loft space in an empty factory in Florence, across the street from the Miss Florence Diner, famed for its squash pie and New England clam chowder. Having accumulated a more reliable set of students, I found life more comfortable but unsatisfying. Thoughts turned to moving on and I began preparations to relocate to New York City, the magnetic pole for so much of the music I currently resonated with: Ornette Coleman's electric Prime Time, James Blood Ulmer's harmolodic funk, the No Wave of the Contortions and DNA. The music boiling up inside me, I felt, could interface easily with that scene. Only essential instruments and pedals were retained, the rest sold to fund my move.

One of the last gigs I played before moving to NYC was on a marathon produced by WCUW, a community radio station in Worcester. I performed solo on the first day; on the second, Human Error was booked on a bill of punk and metal bands at a local rock bar, the Union Jack. In 1979, the realm of American metal seemed to be inhabited mostly by mullet-sporting jocks with a reactionary bent. After three sets of exceedingly loud, dull, cliché-ridden bands, Human Error commenced with Jim Whittemore playing a random sequence of bass tones in a parody of a jazz walk, punctuated with gruesome noises, while Greg Ketchum fractured the groove on his drum set. I riffed and screeched on tenor sax, wandering through the crowd and making my way to the stage, where I channeled my horn through a delay and distortion unit. We dug in, I closed my eyes, and we entered the zone. Five minutes into our set, I was confused by a sound that I didn't recognize as being generated by any of us, a vast wave of murk that could only have been produced by a thousand cows on acid. Opening my eyes revealed the entire audience, hundreds of metalheads, booing and gesticulating angrily with middle fingers or clenched fists. Our hosts from the radio station were leaning against the bar near the stage, huge grins plastered across their faces. The sets were supposed to be short and after about five more minutes we dissolved into double-time high-density abrasiveness while I shredded my guitar, then suddenly cut it short. Amid drunken cries of "We'll get you after," we swept our gear off the stage and into Greg's waiting van. We gunned it out of the parking lot just in time. NYC was calling.

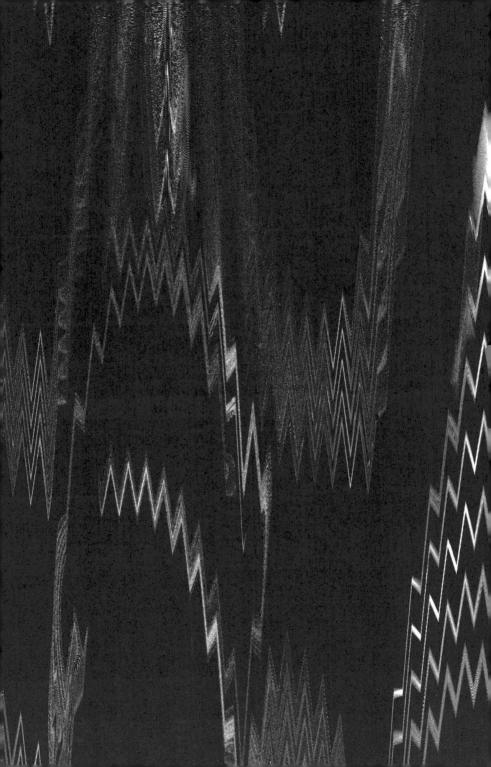

VII.

From the Hudson to the Donau

In October of 1979, I stepped onto a Greyhound in Northampton and arrived five hours later in New York's Port Authority packing a few clothes, a soprano sax, and an electric guitar. I'd passed through that bus station enough times to be unsurprised by the stench and sleaze and air of chaos. Weaving through the mess, I found the subway and headed down to the Fulton Street station in lower Manhattan, emerging around 9 p.m. onto a deserted avenue illuminated with magnesium riot lights and populated only by Con Ed ventilation tubes spouting steam. On John Street I nearly stumbled over an inert figure nestled against a wall, seemingly more dead than alive.

With a promise from a friend of a place to stay at her "loft" in the business district (a 200-square-foot office with a public bathroom down the hallway), I had decided to finally throw caution to the winds and brave NYC. Buzzed into the building, I encountered a leather-jacketed man in shades with an electric bass slung over his shoulder, also waiting for the elevator: my first meeting with David Hofstra, journeyman bassist and multi-instrumentalist. His terse greeting—"Who are you?"— blossomed into a conversation in which he revealed that he was playing with the Contortions. I took this as an omen: I was in the right place and this was the right time. Dave and his partner, the author Lynne Tillman, occupied the loft one floor above my new temporary home. Greeting me at the door, Deb DeStaffan looked at me and said, "That beard has to go." And so, later that evening, it went. I hadn't seen my naked face since 1968. It seemed a stranger's.

My first morning as a New Yorker I hit the ground running. I needed to contact old friends and colleagues and put mechanisms in place to meet new ones. My dream was to sustain myself with music and to live without having to take a day job, a lofty and perhaps unrealistic goal. Before leaving Massachusetts, Jim Whittemore and I had made demo packages of our Human Error project that we sent to A&R people at labels we thought might be sympathetic. Cold-calling Island Records at 10 a.m. on that first morning, I was shunted over to A&R honcho Mark Kamins, who shocked me by saying that he liked the tape and wanted to hear more. Over the next few weeks, I began to meet with him, bringing him cassette demos that I would record by overdubbing from one wretched machine to another.

A month later I was renting the living-room floor of another relocated Buffalo friend's Fourth Street apartment in the heart of the East Village. I had managed to put together about $600 before hitting the City, an amount that might last six months in Buffalo but very much less in NYC, even living frugally. Daily survival rations were a Ukrainian breakfast special from Leshko's on Avenue A for 55 cents, including endless coffee, and a 35-cent slice of pizza for dinner. My money was burning up; I had no apartment to call my own, and no gigs. But I was in New York.

Thanks to a referral from percussionist Greg Ketchum, I met with the Improvisational Dance Ensemble, a trio of multitasking dancers, thinkers, and talkers based in a loft on Warren Street and led by Richard Bull, a visionary choreographer and excellent pianist out of the Lennie Tristano "cool school." Brilliant and beautiful, Cynthia Novack and Peentz Dubble were the perfect balance for Bull's headstrong ways and with their free-running use of improvised texts along with outrageous movement, the three created work that was provocative, energetic, deeply witty, and unlike anything else going on then in dance. They needed a full-time musician, and after an afternoon improvising together I was signed on, agreeing to work with them until the following June. There would be concerts one weekend per month on Friday and Saturday evenings, plus a Sunday matinee. Each concert had a theme and structure but the internal detail would play out differently in each iteration, an approach that mirrored how I was thinking about organizing spontaneous music. Through the IDE I met a number of artists, including pianist Borah Bergman, choreographer Susan Foster, saxophonist Jane Ira Bloom, and polymath vocalist Meredith Monk. Borah and I began rehearsing together, as he had a plan for a rock band in which he could play electronic organ with his right hand and piano with his left. In between bouts of improvising, Borah would harangue me with semi-coherent soliloquies on music and masturbation.

Work with the IDE gave my life a touch of welcome order and a tiny bit of cash, also most welcome. Our collaboration culminated in an interpretation of Italo Calvino's *Invisible Cities* at Chelsea's Dance Theater Workshop in the spring of 1980. It was a dark and moody piece with movement, text, and sound enhanced by lighting effects: saturated, strobed, black-lit. For *Invisible Cities*, bursting out of the Inner Ear was a rapidly developing language based on rhythmic use of harmonics and noise and realized on fretless electric guitar and soprano sax.

During my first days in town, Steve Piccolo, bassist for the extremely popular Lounge Lizards, the "fake jazz" group founded by John Lurie with his brother Evan, Steve, guitarist Arto Lindsay, and drummer Anton Fier, brought me around to all the hot spots, introducing me to the door people at Tier 3, the Mudd Club, Danceteria, Club 57, and CBGB. Endowed with hip cred by Steve, I could now get into all of them for free and they all became favorite haunts. Going out to hear music was a nightly activity, often extending until dawn. Some of what I heard was great, some not; the point was to check out everything. In fact, everybody in the scene was checking out everything and each other and this meant painters, filmmakers, musicians, dancers, poets. We made the rounds of the clubs almost every night in hopes of hearing music heretofore unheard, the opportunity to have our brains rewired in sound. The club bookers would put together evenings seemingly designed to mix constituencies that might never have otherwise intersected. I reconnected with John and Evan, Bill Laswell, and Art Baron, the wonderful trombonist who would come to Bard to hang out in Roswell's class and had played with Duke Ellington's band as well as with Stevie Wonder. On my first visit to Tier 3, I met drummer Phillip Wilson playing in a band with Lurie on a double bill with Jean-Michel Basquiat's band Gray. I had thrilled to Phillip's deep groove when catching him live with the Paul Butterfield Blues Band between 1968 and 1970, as well as on his recordings with the Art Ensemble of Chicago.

That November, seeing a handmade notice on a bulletin board in a record store led to meeting pianist Robin Holcomb at Studio Henry, a dingy basement underneath the Exotic Aquatics pet store in the West Village. My first question to her was "How do I get a gig here?" The second was "Do you know of any apartments for rent?" Quite graciously, she put me in touch with drummer Mark E. Miller and I began to meet the "New York free improvisers scene" based around Studio Henry, including Charles K. Noyes, Wayne Horvitz, John Zorn, Polly Bradfield, Bill Horvitz, Jim Katzin, Carolyn Romberg, Dave Sewelson, and Bob Ostertag. Though the level of musicianship was high and some of the concerts enjoyable, I found the scene somewhat uptight and insular, conforming slavishly to what I termed "The Rules of Free Improvisation" as derived from the English axis of Derek Bailey, Evan Parker, and their associates. These proscribed the use of grooves, explicit rhythms, or any audible melodic material, no matter how abstracted. Rock dynamics were also *verboten* and timbres were to be kept dry. Much as I loved Derek's playing, he'd indicated in conversation and later in writing that one should never listen to other musicians while improvising with them. Ironically, improvising in duo with Derek during his 1981 visit to NYC, I found that despite his pronouncements he was an acute listener and thoroughly engaged.

Though the sound was foremost, improvising for me was very much a social activity. It was about the interaction and the metalanguage of sonic conversation as much as the output itself. While I could enjoy playing in the overly defined style of Studio Henry's "free music," I was more focused on working toward the sound in my head. Certainly it would be improvisational, but not alien to rhythm and melody. There would be juicier timbres employing the electric guitar in all its noisy saturated chaotic glory. I found that Miller was a kindred spirit. Because of its ingrown nature, he referred to the improvising scene as "The Toenail." He wanted to rock or at least hang out in some less insular surroundings. We became frequent improvising partners and played wild and raucous duos, or as a trio with bassist Laswell under the name Surds (including a show at Inroads the night of Reagan's election with guests Noyes, Henry Kaiser on guitar, and trombonist Masahiko Kono). Miller and Noyes had a wonderfully excruciating duo called Toy Killers, with performances akin to a demolition derby as scripted by Samuel Beckett. Shows at Studio Henry could be challenging as the environment was somewhat sketchy, with rats in the stairwell around the garbage cans and sundry other vermin. The equipment was ragtag and there were hums and buzzes aplenty. One night, Miller opened a bass drum case and hundreds of giant water bugs poured out, streaming across the floor in great waves and disappearing into the crevices. As the venue was under a pet store, we might be treated to the sight of an escaped lizard or tarantula making its way across the floor. When the sound revved up, crickets used for feeding larger critters would sing their little hearts out.

Daily, I marveled at New York's musical universe, players operating at extreme poles in jazz, electronic music, and rock and attempting to make unheard music real. The anthropologist in me wanted to examine the subcultures, kinship structures, rituals and rites of passage. At clubs and record stores, at coffee shops and on the street, I was meeting musicians anytime and everywhere. Sonny Sharrock, Butch Morris, Ned Rothenberg, Diedre Murray, Takehisa Kosugi, Don Cherry, Adele Bertei, Henry Threadgill, Jody Harris, Bob Ostertag, Bern Nix, Anthony Coleman, Charles Bobo Shaw, Pat Place, Arthur Russell, Vernon Reid, Thurston Moore, Frank Lowe, David Van Tieghem, Cynthia Sley, Baird Hersey, Jamaaladeen Tacuma, Jeffrey Lohn, Fred Frith, Jim Pepper, George Scott, Clarence "C" Sharpe, D. Sharpe, Denardo Coleman, Marc Bingham, Grachan Moncur III, Melvin Gibbs, George Cartwright, Rhys Chatham, Peter Stampfel, Joe Bowie, Ikue Mori, Nic Collins, Fred Hopkins, Don Christensen, Kelvyn Bell, Scott Johnson, Jay Oliver, Tim Wright, James Blood Ulmer, Robert Quine, David Wojnarowicz, Michael Lytle, Dougie Bowne, Robert Sietsema, Billy Ficca, A.C. Chubb, Michael Gira, William Parker, Billy Bang, Percy Jones, Willie Klein, Jim Matus, Chris Nelson, Susie Timmons, Rick Brown, Roberta Baum, Sue Hanel, and Ann Rupel… to name just a few.

There were collaborations of all sorts, some impromptu, others organized around gigs or recording sessions. I began playing guitar in the band of singer Roberta Baum and through her met Ornette Coleman, who said nothing to me but shook my hand warmly, looking directly into my eyes. Roberta was determined that I should wear a dress onstage for our first show at CBGB but I declined. In between gigs and other responsibilities, there was lots of free-form hanging out—arguably one of the most important aspects of a vital scene, and the best way to build unpredictably branching creative networks.

After two months on East 4th Street, in January of 1980 I moved into the loft of my old Bard buddy Andrew Zev Weinstein in the downtown business district near City Hall. Andrew was a tireless raconteur and a great cook and I was always hungry. The loft had a small music studio with a drum kit and I was able to practice when I wanted and record on a Dokorder four-track tape deck, refining my demos. Andrew introduced me to a friend, Alan Peller, wired and sarcastic, who worked at the nascent J&R Music World and I soon had a job in the returns department. After the suicide of Phil Ochs, there was a run on his albums and the J&R stock was soon depleted. When customers would complain, Alan would answer, "If you had bought his records when he was still alive, he might not have killed himself."

Introduced to one of my new colleagues, I must have had a shocked look on my face. He was grinning, and a day later he told me he knew what I was thinking: "What's Danny Davis, world-famous Sun Ra saxophonist, doing schlepping boxes of records in a store?" Danny nailed it. I soon learned that what we saw from afar as the glorious lives of heroic innovators were sometimes less than glorious in the service of "getting by." He filled me in on Sun Ra history and loved telling stories about freakish times at the Arkestra house in Philly.

Miller and a number of other musicians from the scene lived in apartments in Alphabet City on East 7th Street between Avenues B and C in a building that was, thanks to the city's Tenant Interim Lease program, being slowly transformed from a decayed slum into a nearly liveable tenement cooperative. TIL was being used to raise up neighborhoods that were just one step up (or down) from demolition into viable habitations by using artists as the advance guard of gentrification. Artists would take a marginal area and improve it enough for people to survive in relative comfort, thereby attracting cafés and galleries that would then bring in further development. Finally, the "pioneers" would be priced out of a now desirable neighborhood, which would instead be populated by young professionals, students, and trendoids. This was the formula and it was repeated time and time again.

Our building, for instance, had first been settled in the previous year by Polly Bradfield, Carolyn Romberg, actor Joe Casalini, and others, and was in a transitional state between the "old" population of elderly Ukrainians, junkies, prostitutes, and minor drug lords and the new line of musicians, actors, painters, and self-proclaimed socialists. I certainly was hoping to get in, as the monthly maintenance was only $55 and one "bought" the apartment and a membership share in the coop for a one-time payment of only $250. Truth be told, you got what you paid for: there was no heat, just a trickle of hot water for twenty minutes a day, the hallways stank, and one never knew what or whom one would find lurking under a stairwell when returning home, day or night. Alphabet City east of Avenue A resembled Dresden after the bombing, with rubble-filled lots vacant but for the usual feral inhabitants: rats, packs of wild dogs, and youthful street gangs. Rivington and Stanton streets south of Houston were a scene from Hieronymus Bosch, with gutters filled with syringes like autumn leaves and zombie-like characters squatting in puddles injecting drugs, while around them the street people hustled, groaned, moaned, fought, and fornicated. East 7th Street was slightly better.

The first time I visited Miller on 7th Street was an edifying and terrifying experience for this greenhorn hick. The ominous block had only one other occupied building and my destination was overseen from the top of the outside stairway by Frankie, a surly thug who headed a drug gang known by their headquarters: "Laundromat." He lorded over his turf, his weapon of choice a fishing rod that he brandished menacingly. There were hostile lookouts stationed along the street and the overall feeling was one of imminent violence—and this at 1 p.m. on a sunny afternoon. I could only imagine what the scene would be like in darkness.

Miller met me in front of the building and introduced me to another gentleman hanging out: Dennis Charles. I was awestruck. From listening to Cecil Taylor's early quartet albums, Dennis' drumming was deep in my ears; his life story, too, was imprinted from reading A.B. Spellman's seminal work *Four Lives in the Bebop Business*. Dennis lived across the street and within a few months we became buddies and musical collaborators, forming a trio with bassist Jay Oliver and playing at Club 57 or Rashied Ali's joint Ali's Alley. When Jay moved to Berlin, Steve Piccolo became the bassist.

The 7th Street building had a history of artistic occupants extending back to the 1950s. In Ann Charters' biography of Jack Kerouac, there's a picture of Jack on one of its fire escapes. Allen Ginsberg and William Burroughs had apartments there, as did the poet Jesse Bernstein. By June of 1980, I was honored to finally be a member of the coop and full-time resident.

Alphabet City, referred to by its Hispanic residents as Loisaida, was called home now by older Eastern Europeans, free jazzers, hardcore punks and New Wavers, Hare Krishnas, bohemians and artists, junkie burnouts, actors and poets, and, thanks to a few men's shelters, a large number of overcoat-clad homeless men known in those days as "winos." Junkies on methadone would form strange human statues balanced in a perpetual fall that never quite happened. Among the legendary neighborhood characters was the poet Irving Stettner, who would walk the beat of the various East Village coffee shops and hawk his self-published volumes. Tree Man was a wino who would roam the 'hood with a leafy branch strapped to his shoulders, not begging, just a presence. Bag Man was always perched near the corner of 7th Street and Avenue A in an overcoat and a fur hat wrapped in a brown paper bag, no matter the weather. He never spoke but quietly acknowledged contributions placed in his blue paper coffee cup from Ray's newsstand. Though I was letting my hair grow then, I'd get it trimmed at Pete's Barber Shop on 7th merely to converse with Pete, a longtime anarchist who'd served with the Lincoln Brigade in the Spanish Civil War. He had tales aplenty and one time told me about Bag Man arriving from the Ukraine in 1947 with his family, only to have his wife leave him shortly thereafter. This instigated his move to the streets—never to look back, never to complain or cry, always silent, witnessing the daily joys and horrors of street life in the East Village.

Survival meant taking any gig that came along and while I still hoped to get a band together that would play what I was hearing inside, that plan was mostly put on hold. My time was split between accompanying singers at bars, playing jazz standards on pickup gigs, and occasional improvising gigs at Studio Henry or 626 Broadway or A's, the loft of Arlene Schloss, an epicenter for performance art where, in her "Wednesdays at A's" series, one might see Stuart Sherman's shifting objects, Glenn Branca's thrashing guitar, and Phoebe Legere's vocal and keyboard prowess and rotating yoni. By 1981, I was also gigging fairly regularly with art/hardcore bands such as Crazy Hearts and the punk/blues Hi Sheriffs of Blue led by Mark Dagley, with Lydia Lunch as occasional guest vocalist. Each of these odd shows might net me $10 or $15, but by playing four or five in the course of a long day and night I could survive almost comfortably, though sleep-deprived. It was an incredibly exciting time, fueled by our artistic obsessions and by stimulants of all stripes, including plenty of adrenalin. A quiet but constant fear of assault and mugging, usually deep in the background noise, emerged at odd times. Once, as I returned from a grocery run to Chinatown at 2 p.m., a young man stepped in front of me on Essex just below Stanton and pushed a .38 into my ribs. He stares at me—I'm frozen as is all time—then bursts out laughing and walks away.

The art scene was a more genial escape, which also provided free wine and cheese. Audiences dared the artists to hit them with something they'd never experienced. We performed for fellow musicians and visual artists, dancers and poets, tourists from Europe and Japan, all hungry for some version of a soon-to-be legendary New York underground. Adding another jolt of cortisol was the all-pervasive feeling of impending doom ushered in with Ronald Reagan's presidency. It lurked at the edge of every daily act, nagging with the notion that the sky might explode with atomic fire at any moment. In some ways it brought me back to my childhood.

Some of my New York City shows were seamless and fun, others torturous from start to finish, the seconds dragging like hours. The only thing I could be sure of was that anything could happen. Now with a toehold in the city, I continued to send solicitations to various venues to present my own solo or band projects, but there were no takers—not surprising considering my subterranean profile. It was a shock when the Ear Inn, on the shores of the Hudson in the far-western reaches of Soho, answered my letter and cassette with the offer of a Saturday night gig in February of 1980. Having perused their listings in the *Village Voice* and *Soho Weekly News*, I knew the Ear Inn presented a wide range of notable artists across the realms of jazz and the avant garde. Thrilled to have this opportunity, I imagined a dignified scene with a sophisticated and knowledgeable audience listening intently and respectfully.

My high school buddy Joel Eckhaus was visiting from Vermont on the weekend of my gig and I was grateful for his company and his assistance in moving my equipment: fretted and fretless electric guitars, bass clarinet, soprano sax, Polytone amp. Besides being a fantastic mandolinist and ukulele player who'd studied with and accompanied the legendary Roy Smeck, Joel was also 6'6"—a fact whose importance will shortly become clear.

Setup was quick: guitars into amp, assemble and check the horns. Just before the concert, R.I.P. Hayman, the Ear Inn's music director, invited me upstairs to run down the biz and protocol for the show. He also described the Ocarina Orchestra, which he co-led. I was regaled with excerpts from cassettes as well as a view of the arsenal itself: over the fireplace were displayed perhaps two dozen ocarinas of all sizes, closely resembling phalli—not the symbols but the real thing. Had I stumbled into some sort of cult? No matter, it was time to play. Returning downstairs, I found the joint hopping: boisterous conversations, plenty of clinking glasses and kitchen clatter, smell of burgers cooking, shouts, laughter.

I opened with a soprano sax solo, figuring it might cut through the din: microtonal, multiphonic, circular-breathing, extended techniques, the works. When I finished, the sounds of scattered clapping, giggles, and a "Boo!" emerged like distant buoys in the sea of sound. Switching to electric guitar for a lyrical piece closer to jazz in feel and based on melodic extrapolation, I received even less response. The seconds began to crawl as, distracted from the music, I became more and more concerned with my immediate surroundings. At a nearby table was a portly middle-aged man in a wide-collar suit, accompanied by a chic young lady with too much makeup. They're happily drinking, smoking, gazing into each other's eyes, and shouting to each other over the ambient murk. Since I perceive that my job is to subdue and dominate the maelstrom, I pick up the bass clarinet for the final piece of the set. As I run down the lines of the piece, honking and overblowing in counterpoint, their voices rise in volume to match mine. I play louder. They yell louder. Finally, I move directly in front of them, take the horn out of my mouth, and holler: "I hope I'm not disturbing you!" They're completely oblivious and ignore me. I return to my playing, now striking a somewhat cynical tone—contemplative but spiky, a touch of blues—then finish up and head to the bar.

Joel has been greatly enjoying all aspects of this show and greets me with a big grin. To his left at the bar is a gentleman covered with tattoos on muscular arms issuing from a cut-off blue-jean vest, accompanied by a few other similarly attired gents, some with beards. This being well before the advent of hipster/MTV tattoos and Williamsburg facial hair, their vibe is totally and authentically "biker." In fact, the Ear Inn leads a double life. A home for wayward musical weirdness, it is also—with its proximity to the piers and the West Side Highway—a hard-drinking longshoreman's bar frequented by dockworkers, teamsters, truckers, and bikers. It's clear that this particular group of the latter have been imbibing. The one next to Joel takes the lead: "Hey, what is that shit?"

"It's just music."

"That ain't music."

What I'm thinking, channeling my old postal mentor: *This IS music, motherfucker, and do you know why? Cuz I'm playing it.*

I'd been through this movie many times, in many venues. On this particular evening, the dialogue bounces back and forth for a few more rounds but doesn't go much beyond the basic hostilities. When it threatens to advance further, Joel stands up, mustering his full height. The critic sinks back onto his stool.

I excuse myself to begin the second set.

Over the course of this set, most of the diners finish and leave and the front tables are occupied by a dozen or so dedicated listeners. There's some positive response, very heartening, as well as continued heckling and catcalls from my biker fans at the bar. The second set is longer and I start with the fretless, move back to the electric and then, to bookend the evening, return to the soprano sax. During this number, my dedicated critic, three sheets to the wind, stumbles up to where I'm performing and grabs my bass clarinet from its perch atop the upright piano. I stop playing and grab the tail end of the horn. The instrument is a cheap Bundy that sounds decent considering it's just one step up from PVC plumbing, but it's the only bass clarinet I have. Unwilling to let it be snatched or smashed, I'm acting without really thinking where this might go. He pulls. I pull. I'm staring him straight in the eyes and, adrenalized, finally jerk the horn out of his hands. Joel is now working his way over from the bar. The critic's buddies are watching the show with glazed eyes, apathetic or too soused to care. The guy's eyes are bulging and his nostrils flaring like a cartoon bull's. Finally he shouts, "I do not feel safe with the likes of you walking around loose!" He turns around, grabs his friends and leaves.

A mention of Bachelors, Even in a fanzine in 1981 intrigued me with its Duchamp reference and the use of records as source material, something most definitely in the air at that moment as Grandmaster Flash was blowing minds with his turntable gymnastics on the Wheels of Steel. I was a fan of John Cage's use of phonographs and records in *Imaginary Landscape No. 1* and *Credo in US*. Invited to a dinner at the apartment of Martha Swetzoff, I soon learned that her housemate, Christian Marclay, was one half of Bachelors, Even. Christian brought me into his workroom, where I was struck first by records on the wall pieced together from varied discs, then by the piles of LPs: exotica, easy listening, avant-garde. Christian talked a bit about his work and played me some samples of his vinyl cut-ups. I was in the midst of assembling the first *State of the Union* compilation of one-minute pieces and immediately invited Christian to contribute a piece. The resulting opus very clearly deserved the opening spot on Side 1.

We found ourselves crossing paths at the various obscure dumps where improvised music was presented, and played our first duo in 1982 at the notorious Pyramid Club in the East Village. That set established the basis of much of what followed between us, with gestures shifting between timbral counterpoint, imitation and transformation, pure noise, and oblique puns, always accomplished without any prepared structure or prior discussion. In August of 1983, we performed at the Ski Loft, an underground venue in a construction site on Avenue A. Christian brought his "turntable guitar," a record-player worn like a guitar and used to manipulate guitar music through effects pedals and an amp. It was a clear and powerful manifestation of Christian's use of elements transplanted from one medium to another—a way of recontextualizing both—and a perfect match for my defretted Stratocaster, a sound source more than a guitar, which I attacked with extended techniques and mechanical preparations and processed with distortion. The harsh reality of life in the crime-sodden East Village of the early '80s intruded post-concert: hailing a cab, Christian briefly put his turntable guitar down on the sidewalk and in a flash it was gone, never to be seen again.

A mutual friend suggested that I audition as bassist for *Village Voice* columnist Michael Musto's Motown tribute band, The Must, a forum for him to channel his inner Diana Ross. I brought Mark Miller to the audition; he was awarded the drum chair and we became the rhythm section. The backup singers included underground film star Donna Death; Brant Newborn, an editor at *Rolling Stone*; and a girl named Mary, an editor at *Us* magazine. The women singers wore shiny evening gowns with foot-high beehive wigs and pointy augmented bras, while we men wore pink jackets with black velvet trim. The tenor saxophonist, a statuesque blonde, wasn't the greatest musician but more than compensated with her visual presence, which featured six-inch platform shoes and a skimpy leopard-skin outfit. There were two guitarists of decidedly unconventional abilities, Vinnie and Ruben, both adding some special sauce to the stew. We had a huge book of tunes and for a bassist it was a dream gig. The Motown songs were mini-concertos for the talents of legendary bassist James Jamerson, a musician of astounding invention and touch. I worked hard to do justice to the parts he'd created.

Musically speaking, The Must had a fairly ragged superstructure built on the rock-solid groove laid down by Miller and me, but that wasn't the point—it was a show, and an entertaining one at that. Michael was a genial host who seasoned his welcoming patter with just the right amount of sarcasm. The group was extremely popular and we played some of the biggest rooms in town circa '80 to '81: Bonds, The Ritz, the original

Peppermint Lounge in Times Square. The Must attracted a glitzy show-biz crowd, making for a fun hang both during and after. Michael decided that The Must would sponsor a Diana Ross look-alike contest, with the winner to make a guest appearance singing with us. This ultimately generated some problems, as the winner thought she'd be commencing a high-powered entertainment career. When the more prosaic reality hit—a gig on a rainy Tuesday night at The Vault in Mount Vernon—her thug of a boyfriend showed up at a show of ours at S.N.A.F.U., a cabaret in Chelsea, and threatened to make trouble for Michael and everyone else. It was after this show that Miller and I went to the Binibon on Second Avenue for a bite.

The Binibon was a nexus for artists, musicians, neighborhood characters, and bohemians true and faux. From 1979 to '81 I spent many an hour there drinking bottomless cups of terrible coffee, reading, meeting people, hatching projects, observing, listening. Typical guests at the Binibon might include sundry No Wavers and Lounge Lizards; bebopper Jimmy Lovelace and free-jazz gypsy Don Cherry; artists Keith Haring and Jean-Michel Basquiat; writers William Burroughs, Quentin Crisp, and Allen Ginsberg; Kid Creole, Coati Mundi, and various Coconuts; Johnny Thunders; members of Liquid Liquid; and legions of avant-garde filmmakers, actors, and directors famous and non-. I was friendly with the all of the staff at Binibon and the events that unfolded affected me greatly.

Jack Henry Abbott was a talented writer and imprisoned killer. He'd become the protégé of author Norman Mailer, who had helped sponsor his release into a halfway house around the corner on 3rd Street. He was now well known in the neighborhood and, if notoriety was currency, had become a very rich man thanks to the NYC press. Miller and I were leaving the Binibon around 3 a.m. just as Abbott was entering with his entourage. I found out about the murder of night manager Richard Adan a few hours later. This tragic event came at a time of transformation in the neighborhood—its culture, its daily life, its real estate, and its future identity. Soon after, I began thinking about how I might tell the story, not just of this event, but of the environment in which it occurred. It was nearly 25 years before I was able to finally manifest this work as the opera *Binibon*.

Contact with Mark Kamins at Island continued and though he didn't want to sign Human Error, he was interested in producing a record of some of my more accessible music. With the four-track deck at Andrew's studio, I was now layering guitars, bass, horns, even vocals over grooves composed with a drum machine. Knowing that the state of my personal economy was usually just a few small steps from collapse, Kamins unofficially hired me as an "assistant A&R" at Island Records. It was a position without title or salary but the job description was clear. Listening to demo tapes was not one of Mark's favorite activities, so he would install me in his office at 6 p.m., as most of the employees were leaving, and for $25 and pizza I would slog through the huge cardboard boxes filled with cassettes. The standard technique was to pop the cassette in, hit "play" and, if nothing brilliant was evident after five to ten seconds, toss it in the "reject" box. I was amazed at the poor quality, both sonic and aesthetic, of 99 percent of the submitted material. I don't want to demean anyone's sincere efforts, but what I was hearing was not diamonds in the rough, just incompetent renditions of banal clichés. (Perhaps too many people were taking H.L. Mencken's famous, and usually misquoted, dictum to heart: "No one…has ever lost money underestimating the intelligence of the great masses of the plain people.") Submissions that included a self-addressed, stamped envelope would be returned to sender but any high-quality cassettes without the means of return would be donated to my own research and development. A high point of my time at Island was when the visionary Jamaican producer Lee Perry, one of my sonic heroes, showed up with a large and noisy entourage, smoking and snorting and spray-painting the walls of the offices with graffiti.

Mark DJ'd at Danceteria and would invite me up to the booth to listen and see how different grooves might affect the mood and movements of the crowd. Dancing in front of him most nights, or hanging out in the booth, was a blonde who went by the name of Madonna. He was producing her first record and I was somewhat shocked to hear she was being offered a huge deal with a major label. I was less surprised when Mark told me later that as soon as she inked the deal, she promptly told him to get lost.

For our project, Mark was finally able to get a very modest budget from Island's edgier subsidiary label Antilles, allowing us to book a studio and record. I would call the band Moving Info and for personnel, we agreed on drummer Phillip Wilson, bassist Bill Laswell, percussionist Mark E. Miller, and trombonist Art Baron. The session was held at Greene

Street Recording. Mark was the producer, Roddy Hui the engineer, and the overall atmosphere was one of overheated and hilarious chaos. This was my first "real" recording session and I was incredibly nervous. I was hoping to make my "grand musical statement" but Mark wanted at least one track that could be played at prime time in the dance clubs. This, obviously, would be titled "Obvious." It took full advantage of Laswell's and Wilson's menacing groove, with a double-tracked Art Baron solo channeling both Bubber Miley and Tricky Sam Nanton. Taking heed of Charles Mingus' admonition to white musicians trying to play jazz—"Let the white man develop the polka"—led to another composition: "Happy Chappie Polka." This was a blast of hyperspeed punk rock with Miller drumming and a solo as I imagined Albert Ayler would do it, a mix of honky-tonk, wide-vibrato melody and blow-your-brains-out squealing. The musicians all remained focused and played at the highest level, though in quite an elevated state—brilliantly creative and consummate professionals. We recorded slamming rhythm tracks and a few overdubs and by the time I left the studio at 8 a.m. with a rough mix on cassette, I too was quite elevated from all that had gone down.

A few months later we did overdubs and mixing with engineer Doug Epstein at Mediasound on 57th Street, an industry favorite housed in an old church. I was anxious for the music to see the light of vinyl, hoping it would allow me to perform my own work rather than continue with piecemeal gigging. Antilles, alas, did not share my enthusiasm; the label head, Herb Korshack, found the material a bit too weird and abrasive, hence uncommercial. A week later, a complimentary article about some gig of mine in the *Village Voice* or *Soho Weekly News* might prod Korshack toward putting the record out; a week after that, back to thumbs-down. This seesaw continued for months.

In the meantime, I succumbed to harsh economic reality and in September of 1980 took a job as a bar cleaner at The Library, the disco in the basement of the Barbizon Plaza Hotel on West 56th. Miller, Wayne Horvitz, and Joe Casalini were already working there and introduced me to the protocols. It was a great job in many ways, though it meant punching in by 8 a.m., often just an hour or two after I'd gotten to bed. As it was a union gig, we were paid for seven hours though the job could be completed to perfection in three. The manager was an ex-Playboy Bunny "kept" by a hotel bigwig and installed in this position. She could be incredibly nasty and was nicknamed "The Witch" by the janitorial staff. She resented all of us grunt workers and, counter to union rules, would try to find ways to augment our strictly defined tasks. A showdown finally happened in May of 1981 and I was forced to walk off. An attempt to collect unemployment compensation was shot down at the hearing: with The Witch wearing a low-cut blouse and flirting with the crusty old adjudicator, I didn't stand a chance.

I was still hoping Island would release the Kamins tracks and to nudge that along, Mark helped me book shows at Mudd Club and Hurrah for Moving Info with a crew including Wilson, Miller, Baron, and either Laswell or Brand X bassist Percy Jones, a virtuoso and innovator known for his work with Brian Eno and Jon Hassell. In the meantime I continued to compose, getting closer to what was knocking around the Inner Ear. Exploring a timbral and textural approach far removed from that of the funky Greene Street session, these pieces used grooves inspired by Burundi drumming, Jajouka music from Morocco, Javanese gamelan, and industrial sounds. On top were fragmented melodies, their contours mostly dictated by the natural overtone series. There would be thick chunks of greasy noise from prepared and fretless guitars, odd electronics, and Miller's unorthodox drumming. I took the money I'd saved and booked time at Martin Bisi's OAO Studios in Brooklyn and recorded the tracks that would become the zOaR release *ism* with a crew of Miller, Laswell, Art Baron, Charles K. Noyes, and cornetist Olu Dara, with Diana Meckley providing electronic processing of the percussion on two tracks. The album was released on zOaR in the fall of 1981 and met with an excellent response, leading to a licensing offer from Glass Records in London. The ensuing English album, *Nots*, combined the *ism* tracks with the pieces produced by Kamins.

Things began to heat up. November of 1981 saw the premiere of my first opera, *Innosense*, at Harvestworks/Studio PASS, then operating out of a tiny office in Chelsea. Through simultaneous involvements with Mark Dagley's Hi Sheriffs Of Blue and original no-wavers Mofungo, I was given Tuesdays at a tiny hardcore punk joint, A7 Club, on Avenue A and 7th Street to use as a laboratory in the form of a concert series. It began that November and followed a simple formula: I would invite musicians I knew from the realms of rock, jazz, hardcore punk, improv, and avant to play music together without songs or any sort of chordal structure. The music was sonic- and groove-oriented and used simple frameworks as starting points, usually timbral/rhythmic cells. The owner of the club would direct bands from the more radical end of the spectrum over to me and they might also perform on these nights. Inside A7, outside reality was suspended as the club had no windows and no clocks. There was a loud but low-quality PA as well as a house drum set and amps fixed onstage for the musicians' use.

A7 Club would open around 1 a.m. and the last set might finish at 9, with the musicians emerging into the daylight, pale and blinking, while the workaday world revved up around them. It was a bizarre and entertaining hang with an audience of international thrill-seekers and local artists sometimes performing deviant antics much wilder than anything happening on the cramped stage. Besides my Tuesday night series, I might guest with various bands or jam with HR and Earl from Bad Brains or hang at the bar with an ever-changing cast including Wayne Kramer, Alfonia Tims, Von LMO, the nonverbal guitarist we christened "The Heavy Metal Kid" and his frequently naked girlfriend, or Jan, a street-singer from Warsaw never without his silver-sprayed guitar and a sign bearing the message "SONGS FORBIDDEN IN POLAND." Jan could also be found singing on Astor Place or hanging out at the bar at the Baltyk, a 24-hour Polish restaurant on East 1st Street. When the *New York Times* wrote articles about American reactions to the Solidarność movement in Gdansk and quoted "sources in the Polish community," they were usually referring to the barflies at the Baltyk.

For the long-running A7 gig, I played the fretless Strat, soprano sax, bass clarinet, and a cheapo import copy of a Fender Jazz Bass. The series ran until April 1982 and with the help of the contacts it afforded, I put together a band, I/S/M, to help realize the buzzing in my Inner Ear. On bass was Michael Brown, whose style of two-hand tapping on an authentic Jazz Bass perfectly interlocked with my own. Percussion was played by Al Diaz, longtime partner with Jean-Michel Basquiat in their graffiti duo SAMO as well as a member of Liquid Liquid. On drum kit was either Bobby Previte or David Linton, sometimes both. I/S/M would on occasion gig outside our normal home base, making hits at the Mudd Club, CBGB, Darinka, or Plugg, Giorgio Gomelsky's 24th Street loft. To open one of the shows at Danceteria, our full squadron unleashed its percussive attack on the Surfaris' hit "Wipe Out," which segued seamlessly into one of our own twisted originals. We also performed at the *New York/New Wave* show at PS1 Contemporary Art Center, where I encountered Alanna Heiss, visionary director of the center. She became an important mentor for me.

Butch Morris and I first met on January 25, 1982 at the "Benefit for Nothing," an event at Symphony Space on the Upper West Side of Manhattan organized by Peter Cherches (editor of *ZONE* Magazine) and me. Butch's five-minute set was a marvel. Slowly circling the expanse of stage at Symphony Space, he was a brooding presence, blowing and vocalizing into the bell of his horn and producing a panoply of captivating sounds that I'd never before heard emerge from a cornet. Backstage after the set, I was just as taken with his warmth and good humor, qualities that prevailed in his approach to life. A later revelation came from witnessing the David Murray Big Band under Butch's Conduction at the Groningen Jazz Festival in 1988, where a slightly disorganized group of virtuosi was transformed into a tight and roaring sonic force. It's never enough to say that Butch Morris was a brilliant musical thinker who created Conduction, a system for spontaneous musical composition. One must add that using Conduction, Butch composed beautiful, visceral, and expansive music in real time. To hear or perform Butch's music was a transformative experience—the ears and heart were opened.

Conduction began as a thought process about music-making but then became the music. Butch didn't just theorize and analyze but acted firmly in the belief that his ideas could positively affect our lives through sound. Conduction is a set of tools that will be recognized as a milestone in the history of systems for organizing improvisations into a coherent architecture in real time. Over the years, there have been numerous attempts to develop methods for conducted improvisation. What sets Butch and his system apart is not only the detailed codifying of the techniques but his own refined use of them, a function of his unique ears and intelligence. In a piece like *Skyscraper*, for example, his prepared written parts gave the music a sonic identity present in every performance, no matter how much the internal arc and actions varied. Butch would set up situations where the composed elements would bear improvisatory fruit that he could harvest and serve in myriad ways, each course providing the nucleus of the next. His memory cues seemed to be modeled on the "memory locations" found in many electronic keyboards, a clear and convenient way of conveying this technique to the players. As a conductor, Butch was extremely disciplined and expected the players to take the Conduction as seriously as he did. "Watch me!" was both an imperative and a mantra, oft repeated.

Planning for the UK release of *Nots,* David Barker of Glass booked a mastering session for February 1982 with John Dent at Island Studios, as well as a concert at the legendary Band on the Wall in Manchester where I would collaborate with Danielle Dax of the Lemon Kittens and The Mothmen. The venue was a large and ancient pub that derived its name from the caged bandstand about twelve feet up and behind the lengthy bar, a construction designed to keep the musicians safe from the usual floor-level mayhem. With modern times and a more civilized ambience, the musicians now performed on a ground-level stage. A call to drummer Paul Burwell (whom I had hosted and performed with in NYC) led to a booking at the London Musicians Collective for my solo plus a trio with Paul and Terry Day on a bill with the duo of George Lewis and Lindsay Cooper.

I now had to get a passport and find a cheap way to get to London. The first was easily accomplished and for the second, I followed the path of least resistance to the lowest price, booking a package deal of a round-trip flight on Laker plus three nights at a hotel for a total of $199. My first intercontinental flight was smooth and uneventful, most of the plane filled with members of the Mormon Tabernacle Choir, no doubt scheming polygamy to add to their polyphony. My defretted Fender Stratocaster in its Fender-labeled case accompanied me and I was stopped by a customs officer who very brightly chirped, "Ooh, a Fender—I might know someone who would be interested in buying it. Please let me see it." Having been hipped to the entrapment policies of English immigration officers but speaking the truth in any case, I told him I had made it fretless solely for my own needs and that it was of no commercial value, it was unique, and I was not interested in selling it. Cleared, I headed out to Arrivals and the bus to my hotel where I happily crashed out. Coming down to the lobby a few hours later to meet Barker, I was greeted by newspaper headlines shouting that Laker Airlines had folded—I was on the last flight from New York and there would be none to follow in either direction. I was thrown for a loop but, at the moment, had other fish to fry. After some incredibly bad coffee, all too typical of London in those days, we headed over to Island Studios.

As a geek, I was fascinated by the enormous multi-channel console and racks of high-end outboard gear, much of which appeared to have been custom-built. Dent, patient and jovial, explained some of the more esoteric equalizers and limiters and gave me a primer on the process of mastering. My concerts were enjoyable, and attending our LMC show and hanging out after was a most gracious Keith Rowe of AMM, improvising guitarist extraordinaire and inventor of the "guitars on the table" approach. With British Airways generously honoring my Laker ticket back to NYC, I successfully completed this first foray into international touring.

In September of 1982 I produced and released *Peripheral Vision: Bands of Loisaida* on zOaR. The bands of the East Village ("Loisaida" in the Spanglish pronunciation of "Lower East Side") were a diverse group whose output ranged from the tightly arranged near-orchestral forces of The Ordinaires to the reductionist blasts of The State, Mofungo's wry cultural commentary in a no-wave matrix, and V-Effect's Leftist art rock. The compilation also included art-punk auteurs Crazy Hearts (led by Victoria Vesna), Mark Dagley's Hi Sheriffs Of Blue, no-wave veterans Chris Nelson, Phil Dray, and Susie Timmons in The Scene Is Now, and my seven-minute collage of the history of I/S/M titled *Sample/Hold,* created by editing together on reel-to-reel numerous tape fragments ranging in length from 5 to 30 seconds, transferred from cassette recordings of every gig to date. This use of the jump-cut technique was inspired by films of Meliès and Vertov as well as Godard's *Breathless.* I continued with this approach in the compilation *State of the Union,* a December 1982 release and collaboration with Peter Cherches to which 34 artists each contributed one-minute tracks. These were edited together to provide a seamless flow thanks to hours spent with razor blade and Editall on Wayne Horvitz' Revox. *State of the Union* included in its roster of artists Tuli Kupferberg, Squat Theater, John Lurie, Spalding Gray, Peter Blegvad, Fred Frith, and Pulsallama. Peter Cherches and I recorded Tuli at his Sixth Avenue apartment, a special thrill as I had been a longtime fan of The Fugs. Spalding was recorded at the Performance Garage and Pulsallama at a scuzzy rehearsal room on 1st Street. The zOaR catalog was now up to eight LPs and two seven-inch EP's and all of a sudden began receiving positive press attention, college radio airplay, and repeat orders from record distributors.

A typical trajectory in the indie release world played out for me: Mr. X at Distributor Y would order 200 records and a month later order another 200, after which I would ask for payment, which would be promised. More records were ordered, payment requested again, followed by notice of said Distributor Y declaring Chapter 11 bankruptcy, making its debts uncollectable. The same Mr. X, now working for Distributor Z, contacts me to order 200 records... And so on. We would get paid occasionally by the few honest distributors, but payments rarely squared with the number of records consigned. Though I loved the entire process of making records, this mode of operation was financially suicidal. By 1984, as more requests for licensing came in, zOaR became a production company only, thereby avoiding the expensive headaches of manufacturing and distribution and after-the-fact collection of payment. For a one-time payment, a master would be licensed for a set period: a simple arrangement without unrealistic expectations.

The year 1982 also saw the Bowery Project emerge: a series of concerts at the loft of dance trio Kinematix riding the underground wave and tapping into the incredible cross-disciplinary energy of the scene. I was part of the organizing group and we booked an eclectic array of performers, including one of Sonic Youth's first shows; the duo Dog Boys, consisting of Steve Buscemi and Mark Boone, Jr.; the band Interference, including Michael Brown, Joe Dizney, David Linton, and multi-instrumentalist Ann DeMarinis; and my own premiere of the "active bows," an invented instrument consisting of piano wire stretched on a metal frame to create multiple string lengths and amplified with a piezo pickup. It was played with two metal rods on which bass strings were stretched and tuned, each with a piezo pickup on its bridge. The three outputs went to three separate amplifiers, creating a massive low-frequency rhythmic din.

All of this activity did shine some light on my compositional ideas and offers for higher-profile concerts began to appear. When Ann DeMarinis became music director of The Kitchen in the summer of 1982, she immediately commissioned a large piece from me to be premiered in October. This was *Crowds and Power*, inspired by Elias Canetti's seminal volume discussing the nature of group dynamics, from hunter/gatherers to fascist governments. His chapter "The Orchestra Conductor" compared the symphony to a hierarchical and authoritarian society and inspired Fellini's short slapstick film *The Orchestra Rehearsal*. For *Crowds and Power*, I/S/M was augmented to a 21-piece ensemble with the addition of strings, horns, more guitars, and more drummers (Miller and Noyes). I'd used Fibonacci numbers in my 1981 opera *Innosense* and decided to use them again in *Crowds and Power* to organize the proportions of the macro-structure as well as in counted rhythmic sequences. The Fibonacci series is created by summing a number and its predecessor, beginning with (0,1). This equals 1 and the next in the series then equals 2 (1,1). The numbers that follow are 3, 5, 8, 13, 21, 34, 55, 89, and so on. The average of the ratios of adjacent numbers in the series forms the proportion known historically as the Golden Section, φ (1.61803...). φ has long been employed as an organizing principle in architecture and art and reveals itself in nature as the logarithm representing the spiral, found in such places as galactic form and construction, the cochlea of the ear, the shape of the DNA molecule, and the growth patterns of flower petals, seed cones, and the shell of the chambered nautilus. While some have attributed mystical properties to anything constructed using φ, I never counted myself among them; I did, however, greatly appreciate the formal beauty of the pattern and its remarkable currency in both nature and culture.

Within certain sections of *Crowds and Power*, improvisation occurred. Particular players might have carte blanche in their allocated segments; for others, improvisation might be guided by keywords or simple instruction sets. Sections would be cued by sudden changes in the lights—alternating from pitch-blackness to extreme brightness—with each section manifesting different permutations of players from within the ensemble. There might be quiet duos, full massed forces, or any quantity in between. Presented by Ann with this opportunity to do exactly what I wanted, I felt that the various elements of IrRational Music were now coming into balance. The philosophy behind the sonic organization was echoed by the mix of freedom and discipline required of the players. *Crowds and Power* had some delicate moments but given the instrumental forces at hand, it made both my Inner Ear and the outer ring for days after the shows.

It was now time to record I/S/M and a session was booked at Plaza Sound, a spacious recording studio in one of the upper floors of Radio City Music Hall. Riding the freight elevators, one might encounter stagehands hauling scenery, Rockettes in full regalia, even (on one occasion) a horse. The rates were low given the size of the room, the wonderful Neve console, and a collection of vintage microphones, limiters, and EQ's. The Ramones and Blondie had all recorded here and it had become a favorite for many of the experimental downtown bands. Because of budget considerations, we tracked and mixed in one eight-hour day. Though we played songs with well-defined structures, the music remained open-ended, with a fair amount of improvisation. In recording it, therefore, I took the approach one might take with a jazz group. We set up in a circle in the room and played without headphones, the amps and drums achieving some sonic separation thanks to judiciously placed gobos.

The music was stark and vicious and Joe Dizney, guitarist with The Ordinaires, created a suitably brutal album cover. The record release was slated for our February 1982 gig at the legendary Folk City in the West Village, a club with a grand tradition across many scenes. The series we were taking part in included such groups as The Minutemen, The Ordinaires, Hüsker Dü, Yo La Tengo, V-Effect, Fred Frith's Skeleton Crew, The Scene Is Now, and Sonic Youth. We hired poet Barbara Barg and her van to transport us to the show. The pressing plant had given us 100 advance copies of the LP in two boxes of 50, one of which we brought in with us at our soundcheck while the other was left in a hidden storage area underneath the van's floor. After our performance the LPs sold out quickly, so Barb ran out to retrieve the other box, only to find her van ransacked and the box of records stolen. I can only imagine the look on the thieves' faces when they took stock of their loot and realized its sales potential.

A lesson learned around the time of my concert at The Kitchen was that in New York City, there were no unimportant gigs. A solo show in an ill-conceived Sunday matinee series at Folk City didn't even net me enough money to take a taxi with my gear back to my hovel, but it got me a guitar student and an offer to perform in the Tone Gegentone Festival in Vienna, Austria from a curator who happened to be at the show.

Thanks to Daniel Waldner at Recommended Records Switzerland, the Viennese festival offer was expanded into a one-month European van tour together with V-Effect. From a base in Zurich, we made a number of journeys ranging from two to ten days around Middle Europe with concerts booked in theaters, clubs, galleries, youth centers, and squats. Our first concert in Germany, arranged by the triumvirate of Bernd Leukert with Heiner Goebbels and Christoph Anders, both of the band Cassiber, was at the Batschkapp in Frankfurt, on a bill with David Thomas of Pere Ubu accompanied by Chris Cutler and Lindsay Cooper. Doing his best Jackie Gleason impersonation, David fired Chris three times during the course of their set. I marveled at David's personal rider specifying the exact measurements and orientation of the ham, cheese, and bread in the backstage catering. We spoke of Cleveland.

Our itinerary included 24 concerts in Zurich, Basel, Berlin, Lichtenstein, Erding, Brno, Prague, and other towns in Germany, Switzerland, and Austria. The Berlin shows were part of a festival curated by that city's one-woman force for alternative music, Monika Döring, at her venue, The Loft, in the Metropol building on Nollendorfplatz. We had four days in Berlin with two concerts and I loved the feeling of this island floating on an East German sea. Edgy music and art were integral parts of the lifeblood of the city, and its general air of physical decrepitude was quite reminiscent of the East Village. I felt very much at home.

Our much-anticipated shows in Czechoslovakia were next, and after a day off in Regensburg, we headed east, the van subjected to painstaking inspection by the Communist guards at the border. The guards were quite friendly to us but with great hostility addressed Daniel Waldner only as *Schweitzer*. They focused special attention on our books, magazines, newspapers and tour posters. A gift of one of the posters bought some good will and eased our entry into the country.

The Brno concert was organized by singer/violinist Iva Bittová and percussionist Pavel Fajt. The sound engineer, Peter Werner, had built his mixing desk from scratch using components obtained on the black market or smuggled out of the factory where he worked. While portable cassette recorders were a common sight at Stateside gigs, in Brno a number of audience members were lugging huge reel-to-reel decks and ancient-looking microphones to record the show. Knowing of the difficulties in presenting this music added an intensity to our sets. While in Brno, we learned that our concert in Prague scheduled for the next evening was cancelled because of a government "anti-new wave" campaign. We decided to go anyway.

Our host in Prague was Dona Nemcova, grand matriarch of the Prague underground scene. Her daughter was married to Milan Hlavsa, founder of the band Plastic People of the Universe, and her son David Nemec was a member of Group 309. The Plastics and everyone around them were often carted away to prison solely because of the perceived subversiveness of their music. The Charter 77 of Human Rights written by Vaclav Havel in 1977 was focused on the government's persecution of the Plastics. Their songs, sung both in English and in Czech, were inspired by Frank Zappa, the Velvet Underground, The Fugs, and William Blake and the music was dark, heavy, angry, and molten. Through David, I met a number of musicians all creating work in the interstices between hard rock and more experimental sounds, with a favorite of mine being the MCH band of Mikoláš Chadima. Sitting in David's kitchen at 2 a.m., we discussed releasing underground Czech music on zOaR. Dona, asleep in the next room, heard and hurried out to chasten us, gesturing to the air: if we must discuss such matters, it should be done someplace like the park where the conversation would be less likely to be monitored by the secret police.

Through a sort of *samizdat*, a concert was arranged for us in the large back room of a pub for the next day and word given to all who might be interested. The sound system had already been set up when we arrived and the house was packed and expectant. My solo began the evening but after a few minutes, the angry pub owner stormed into the room announcing that he would never allow such music and if we didn't clear out in five minutes, he would call the police—not an idle threat in Prague at that time. With no other choice, we quickly packed up and repaired to someone's house to drink the excellent local beer and discuss the situation.

The next day started out very touristically with a visit to the Altneuschul and Old Jewish Cemetery where Rabbi Loew, protagonist of the Golem legend, was buried. Around noon we received word that another attempt to have a concert would be made, this time in the backyard of a house on the outskirts of town, facing a railroad yard. The audience was not allowed to applaud, only to wave their hands together without touching to indicate their approval—a surreal scene worthy of Prague's own Franz Kafka. The story continued when, post-concert, our entourage went to the only open restaurant, a most elegant Russian nightclub situated in a downtown basement. The waiters were impeccably tuxedoed and the ambience was dark and deeply crimson. The place was filled with Arab and Russian businessmen, accompanied by the only hookers we saw in the city. Serenading the assembled guests were a keyboardist playing a huge clunky synthesizer that sounded like an accordion, a drummer whose somewhat martial beats were clearly derived from hours spent listening to cheesy electronic Rhythm Aces, and a small round man with wrap-around shades who doubled on electric guitar and clarinet. They played a mix of polkas, businessmen's bounce, and light surf instrumentals. We had a final day free in Prague and David brought us up to the old church in Loretánská, maintained but not open to the public. A friend of his worked as a watchman and he let us in to breathe its ancient air in appropriate darkness. Poking around in the eaves, I found the power switch for the pipe organ and improvised on it for some minutes, the sound in that room making chills run up and down my spine. We also rang the church bells, causing a stir in the town below.

The tour continued to Vienna and the Tone Gegentone festival, an international conclave featuring New York City artists but also including groups from Hungary, Germany, and Austria. Our concerts here were as packed with enthusiastic listeners as the other events on our tour. The hang between artists, promoters, friendly audience members, and stray journalists was extremely convivial and often extended to late-night post-concert dinners at the Beograd, a Yugoslavian restaurant with an interior encrusted with tchotchkes and a soundtrack provided by a pair of seedy yet elegant musicians playing *cimbalom* and violin. At one of these dinners I had a long and inspiring conversation with Achim Roedelius, elder statesman of electronic music and Krautrock.

After Vienna, there were a few more concerts, with a finale in Zurich together with percussionist Z'ev at a converted porn theater. V-Effect returned to NYC and I headed down to Italy to meet up with Steve Piccolo, now expat and living in Florence. We performed there, in Turin, and in Milan and I returned to Zurich for one more show at a gallery before heading home to New York, my head spinning from the journey, another American artist energized by the European experience of knowledgeable audiences loving to be challenged by hearing something heretofore unheard.

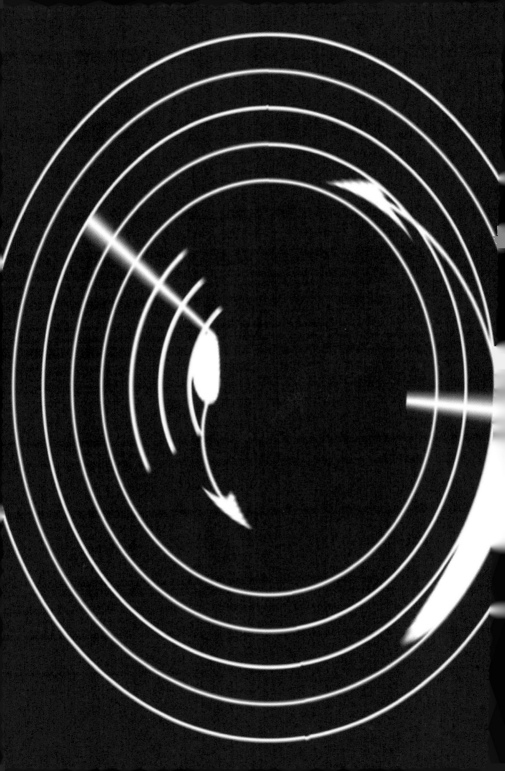

VIII.

A Brief
Carbonic History

In January of 2009 I found myself once again composing new short pieces for my usually loud and spiky band Carbon, to be released as an album titled *Void Coordinates*. Thanks to the efforts of Patrik Landolt of Intakt Records in Zurich, Carbon would again record and tour. This was indeed a welcome return plunge into the Void: I was thrilled at the prospect of reconvening the Carbon quintet of 1991 to '96, the band that had manifested the music on *Tocsin, Truthtable, Amusia, Interference,* and *Autoboot.* I'd suspended work with this constellation to focus on larger ensemble projects using more conceptual approaches and formal systems, as well as more integration of acoustic instruments and real-time computer processing. Carbon, rather than disappearing, had metamorphosed into Orchestra Carbon, with performances and recordings of the long-form compositions *Rheo~Umbra, SyndaKit,* and *Radiolaria.* Even though I was jacked into a nice jolt of electricity with Tectonics and Terraplane, I missed the extreme dynamics and suppleness of this self-contained band of powerful musicians.

Carbon was first conceived in April 1983, shortly before my first full-on European tour, by cross-breeding the language of my solo music with the heavy grooves of I/S/M. Carbon debuted at the Speed Trials festival at White Columns Gallery in Soho in May 1983 alongside performances by Lydia Lunch, The Fall, Swans, Sonic Youth, Beastie Boys, and Toy Killers. The name appeared earlier as a song title on my 1981 disc *ism* and seemed perfect for the band concept of a sound that would be both earthy and ethereal, groove-oriented but never aiming for the lowest-common-denominator beat, and powered by cracked math and punk mania. The band's first phase included either Jonathan Kane or David Linton on drums, with sundry guests from various scenes including abstract *schrei* vocalist Marie Pilar (whom I'd met at Giorgio Gomelsky's) and steel drummer/mallet bassist Rick Brown. In addition to a Frankensteinian double-neck guitar/bass that I'd rebuilt from an ancient flea-market Höfner, I used soprano sax and bass clarinet as well as my invented string/percussion instruments: slabs, pantars, and violinoid. By theory and design, no digital effects were used in this first iteration of the band; all sounds were generated using extended techniques, amplifier distortion, and high volume with vibrating strings, membranes, or columns of air.

Returning from that first European tour, I was struck by the stark contrast between the sort of artistic existence one could lead in Europe and the one I led in New York, where my work felt marginalized and my economic survival precarious. The increasing gentrification of the East Village and Tribeca led to the closing of many venues, with nothing opening to take up the slack. There were intermittent guitar students but I was forced to take temp warehouse jobs and sell any equipment not in frequent use. Situational depression was the immediate result but soon a deeper gloom settled in.

In October of 1983, Carbon had another short tour of Europe, beginning in Zurich. Just after soundcheck, without any thought, just pure panic, I ran to the roof of the venue, the Volkshaus, and found myself staring down at the ground below—but also deeper, into an abyss. Timeless, frozen, I sat there as the sky darkened. The source of my distress was distributed between exhaustion, chemical imbalance, and a painfully microscopic examination of my own work and activities in the larger context of my art and life. I was most definitely not suicidal, yet this act could have been fatal. Pulling back from the edge—back from my immediate horror—I tried to take stock, to see things with as much perspective as I could muster. The concert we played later that night felt like a cleansing purgative, an outburst of pure noise and fire.

The next day we went to Frankfurt for an event at the Batschkapp organized by Karl Bruckmaier, our first meeting. Carbon's set was brief and intense, a blast. Now on to Berlin for a festival at The Loft, on a bill with Sonic Youth. Our hotel was a nightmare so we ended up crashing at promoter Monika Döring's apartment, where we found Blixa Bargeld of Einstürzende Neubauten asleep under the dining room table. As Berlin gigs often do, this one felt like home, comfortable in its noisy extremity. Then Munich: a gig organized by a Communist squat, cold and unheated with a huge poster of Karl Marx and a bathtub in the main room. They put us all in one room with no beds, mattresses, or even blankets. Our set was interrupted midway by a bevy of city police in green uniforms. The concert was over.

The evening was split with the Serbian gypsy-fusion band Beograd. We both had contracts specifying a certain amount of money, more than the squat was willing to pay. Beograd wanted it all; I was willing to split it 50-50. There was a standoff. In retrospect, it's amazing that the evening didn't turn violent but remained simply a test of wills. I held my ground and eventually at 3:30 a.m. the money was split fairly, with an equal amount for each person performing. By that time, there was no reason not to go straight to the station, where we took the first train back to Zurich.

There were two days off before the next spate of shows. I was exhausted, drained, fed up. I asked Marie Pilar and David Linton to return to NYC while I played the remaining shows solo. I needed to reflect, and didn't want to be responsible to or for anyone else.

I had brought a copy of *Gravity's Rainbow* with me. Rereading it for the fourth time, I felt a kinship with Tyrone Slothrop as I bounced from city to city in a suspended and dissociative state, not happy to be touring but not looking forward to finishing either. The concerts were a blur of sound and surreality, the moments onstage lost in the music my only respite. Playing a gallery in Trier, the birthplace of Karl Marx, I was approached by an African-American gentleman with a big smile and an expensive-looking leather outfit. "Yo New York, what's happenin'? You travel around a lot—do you want a gig? I work for the Company and we need people." "The Company?" I half asked, half smirked. "Which company is that?" "You know, business, import-export, business." To this day I don't know if he was trying to recruit me as a drug mule or as a spy.

Returning to New York, I had come to a crux point. After four years of intense involvement in the scene, I felt that I needed a major change in direction, a hiatus from music and Downtown life. During this period I completely cut myself off from almost everyone I knew. I have no memory of even touching an instrument. I'd finally lost all patience with the sacred totems of postmodernism and their ascendance as the defining paradigm of our little world: appropriation, deconstruction, irony. These techniques had many historical antecedents but first became prominent in NYC visual arts early in the 1960s, with some parallels in Frank Zappa's music. By the time they hit Downtown in the 80s they were devoid of transformative power, mainly present for their entertainment value. Postmodernism gave the audience license to smirk, to cultivate a smug sense that they, and only they, were in on the joke. It felt trivial. So voracious was the referential irony that moments just past were already placed in quotation marks. This general relativity of affect dissipated true feelings or cloaked them in theory to the point of emptiness.

There was no resonance in this for me. I studied Spanish and mathematics texts in an effort to fight my overwhelming feeling of dread, the sense that my artistic work had hit a dead end.

In November of 1983, I traveled for a month in Mexico with Marie Pilar, riding across deserts and mountains from Mexico City to Puebla to Oaxaca to Puerto Escondido in old yellow school buses reeking of fuel exhaust and animals, in *cooperativo* combis, in the backs of open trucks. Passing through a village as we walked down from the archaeological site on the summit of Monte Albán, I heard some of the strangest music I'd ever heard. Following our ears, we came upon a dark and tiny tavern, open to the gravel road, with three musicians—trumpet, electric guitar, snare drum—playing a primeval song, pure melody scraped to the bone. It was like the rawest blues and haunted me, entering heavy rotation in my brain over the next two weeks while I tried to formulate a plan for my immediate future—whether to contnue as a composer/performer or to set off on a completely different tangent...but if so, what and where?

We returned to NYC, the backdrop an increasingly paranoid nation that seemed to have little place for me or what I wanted to do with music. It was cold, 7th Street was a wreck, there were no gigs in sight, and I took temporary work at a book depository.

In February of 1984, through Felipe Orrego, I met and began to collaborate with the Bolivian multi-instrumentalist and instrument maker Hilario Soto, a virtuoso on q*uena* and *siku*. He was interested in cross-cultural fusions and in our sessions we would improvise using both Bolivian melodic gestures and more abstract sonics, often built on drones or repetitive rhythms. I concentrated on electric bass and Korg MS-20 analog synthesizer. Hilario would be returning to Bolivia in May and suggested that I come to La Paz, where there would be many opportunities to perform together. It was a tempting idea and it remained in my consideration.

March 4, 1984: a blisteringly cold night outside and pretty chilly inside my 7th Street pad as well. After a supper of psylocybin mushrooms, I set out to explore the sonics of the Fibonacci numbers and their application to guitar. Having found that certain ratios of adjacent Fibonacci numbers coincided with ratios of just-intoned intervals, I translated these ratios to a guitar tuning with 1/1 = C and restricted myself to playing only the open strings and overtones, using various picking and tapping techniques. The intervals, from low to high: C (1/1); A♭ (8/5, a just-intoned minor 6th); C (2/1, an octave); G (3/2, a just-intoned perfect 5th); A (5/3, a just-intoned major 6th); and C (3/1, two octaves up). By the time I was ready to hear my thoughts in sound it was after midnight, so I hunkered down next to the amplifier with a blanket over it and myself so as not to disturb the neighbors. That tube amp also generated a nice amount of heat, very welcome. The amp's pilot light glowed red and I found myself in a cave, womb-like.

As I began to excite the strings with plectra, fingers, and EBow, I was astounded at what I was hearing: liquid harmonic melodies of a nature both exotic and familiar poured out of the speaker. I wasn't playing it. It was playing me, a powerful inevitability in the waves of overtones as defined by the physics of a vibrating string. Under that blanket, there was no amplifier, no apartment, no guitar, no self, even—just the sound.

It was nearly sunrise when I finished. Time had stopped in those hours hunched next to the amp, one with the sound, much as it had in my marathon sessions with the shortwave radio as a teen. I emerged, changed.

There was no choice now but to dig in deeper and I devised a number of strategies for utilizing the Fibonacci series. Besides the primary approach of harmonic tuning of guitars, this included mapping the ratios to rhythms and to the overarching structure of the pieces. In addition, the techniques derived from these ratios were applied to various other instruments, including bowed strings and saxophones. Trombones also received the treatment because I liked that instrument's essential simplicity and inherent purity of tone, its relation to the didgeridoo and the Tibetan *rag dung*, its extended downward range using pedal tones, its ability to produce an array of overtones, and, finally, its incredible potential in the wrong hands to produce an astounding array of onomatopoeic sounds.

Over the course of the next two months, I composed the core elements for six pieces that would fuse extended techniques and radical sounds with the Old Math, the natural overtone series, sounds and approaches from many of the non-Western musics that I loved and learned from, and the grooves of urban life. The music would be played by a band that would include Linton, Miller, and Charles K. Noyes on a variety of drums and percussion instruments, plus Lesli Dalaba on trumpet. My main instrument was the Höfner double-neck, augmented by soprano sax, bass clarinet, sopranino clarinet, trombone, and my own voice using variations of *kargyraa* and *khoomei* throat-singing techniques that I'd continued to practice. We premiered the music at Giorgio Gomelsky's loft that June and I decided that we should record it in July, after which I planned to head down to La Paz.

Sometimes plans change. At a Linton Kwesi Johnson concert on May 4 I ran into Hope Martin, an artist and budding Alexander Technique teacher whom I'd met soon after arriving in NYC but hadn't seen since. At that first meeting she'd told me with a grin, "My paintings are black." Now we began an exciting and promising relationship, a wrench in the works of my departure.

More disruption on July 1, 1984: the publication of William Gibson's seminal cyberpunk novel, *Neuromancer*. Sitting in Hope's loft, I blasted through the book. I'd abandoned sci-fi years ago but this volume pulled me back in with the force of a singularity, stoking my dystopian fantasies while stimulating a notion of myriad possibilities in the realm of the digital. John Brunner's *Shockwave Rider* preceded *Neuromancer* in positing a cybernetic alternate reality, but Gibson captured the zeitgeist and the growing submission of all life to the powers of the corporate plutocrats. He saw the shiny future as well as its gritty and terrifying underside and how we might inhabit and operate in this reality, a virtual one separated from the weight and wisdom of flesh and blood. I began to seek out like-minded authors: Lucius Shepard, K.W. Jeter, Bruce Sterling, Pat Cadigan, Lewis Shiner, Jonathan Lethem. This opening to the cyber world hinted at the infinite: a Void of our own making but with rules yet to be written, realms to be discovered. How to map it to the music? The Inner Ear was buzzing and beeping, demanding attention.

In the meantime, Carbon. I couldn't say that the music was cyberpunk, but I couldn't argue that it wasn't. I was shooting for something at once archaic and futuristic; despite my new infatuation with the Web, I used no digital processing on the recording. It was all vibrating strings, columns of air, membranes, objects of metal. We recorded the basic tracks in one live session in July at Martin Bisi's BC Studio, with overdubs and mixing happening over the course of a few days. That first Carbon record was released simultaneously, in September of 1984, by my own zOaR label and the Atonal label in Berlin. For all my confidence in this music, I was nonetheless quite surprised at the positive response it received in the NYC press as well as in Europe and Japan. Invitations for European concerts and festivals began to appear and between the reception of the music and the positive state of my personal life, it seemed that I was falling back into the full-time routine of a New York-based musician. Instead of a new life in the Andes, the next year was spent in planes, trains, and vans and in concert halls, theaters, rock clubs, jazz clubs, galleries, lofts, basements, and squats in the US, Europe, and Japan.

Flush from touring, I had a custom double-neck guitar/bass built to my specs by Ken Heer to replace the rustic Höfner barely held together with duct tape and mismatched hardware. This new instrument included a hexaphonic pickup feeding a MIDI converter to trigger samples that I would prepare on an Ensoniq Mirage, one of the first affordable samplers, only 8-bit resolution but sounding very juicy. By sampling sounds, processes, and phrases produced on the various homemade instruments as well as on guitars and horns played with the extended techniques that were to form the sonic cores of my compositions, an additional reflexive and recursive element could be layered into the mix. The triggering of samples also greatly extended my timbral range. Editing samples in the Mirage was accomplished by manipulating numeric buttons and monitoring the results on a two-digit hexadecimal readout. Now I had the explicit cyberpunk connection, the Inner Ear interfacing with one version of a virtual reality. Immersing myself in the hexadecimal universe created a synesthetic reality shift—one could *feel* the samples, their shapes and textures, and thereby know their sounds. You pull the edge of a sample and it gets longer. You massage a crossfade and you can feel the sound change. With time-stretching using repeated downward transposition, the transient of a sound might be expanded from a few milliseconds to over 30 seconds, revealing surprising melodic contours and alien harmonies that could then be transcribed and orchestrated or used as the basis for layering. Using individual chains of processing on each neck played by tapping and triggering the samples, I could generate a truly orchestral range of sound.

Touring continuously between 1984 and '87 with a shifting cast of musicians, the band clarified into a pool of players who had learned not just the riffs, the vocabulary and syntax of the pieces but also the reasons behind the construction. Carbon might range from a duo with Linton, or a trio with Bobby Previte and Pere Ubu bassist Tony Maimone, to larger groups adding some of my invented instruments to the mix of brass, reeds, and percussion required to perform *Marco Polo's Argali*. During two tours in Japan in 1985 and one in 1986, I lectured on my compositional strategies and performed solo as well as with many Japanese artists: musicians Yūji Takahashi, Toshinori Kondo, Chiko Hige, Sabu Toyazumi, and Reck; the Butoh dancers of Byakko-Sha; video artist Keisuke Oki; plus sets of Carbon music in duo with percussionist Katie O'Looney. I also met controversial art provocateur John Duncan on that first trip, marking the beginning of a long friendship and varied collaborations.

Saxophonist Ned Rothenberg was booked for a concert at the Cooper Hewitt Museum in April of 1985 and asked percussionist Samm Bennett and me to join him. I had known Samm in Massachusetts and dug his explicitly African approach, with a hybrid drum kit comprising various cowbells, drums, and timbales. Ned and I shared certain technical and aesthetic approaches on our instruments that dovetailed nicely: polyrhythmic interlock, multiphonics, open tonality. Ned was also an accomplished shakuhachi player with a beautiful sense of abstract narrative. We established some simple structures on which to improvise and hit. That set felt great and we decided to form a band, which I named Semantics. Dubbed "the first Downtown supergroup" by members of the press, we were able to exploit the hype and book a number of concerts and tours in Europe and on the West Coast. We returned to Plaza Sound and recorded an album of works both composed and improvised for the German label No Man's Land.

Also in 1985, I became aware of the fractal geometry of Benoit Mandelbrot through an article in *Scientific American*. This was as life-changing as *Neuromancer*. I felt a strong resonance with Mandelbrot's mapping of mathematical functions to such forms and phenomena of nature as turbulence, chaos, and seeming randomness. A surprise National Endowment Fellowship award that spring gave me the funds to put up pristine sheet-rock walls and a ceiling in my apartment as well as acquire an Atari ST computer. A fractal generator was one of my first software purchases. Falling into the infinite regress of an iterated Julia Set, I sensed that I was looking at a picture of time rather than space—

not linear but jagged, reticulated and looping. Guitar or horn in hand, I would use the fractal images as my score, the perfect substrate for sonic explorations into the Void. Using graphic editing software, I also created a primitive notation "construction set" to facilitate the creation of my scores, a vast improvement for any of the musicians who had previously attempted to decipher my illegible scrawl.

Back to Europe in October 1985 for a long tour both with Carbon and solo. I spent a few days running around Budapest with Tibor Szemső and Arnold Dreyblatt, hitting their favorite cafes, flea markets, and forgotten squares where the bullet-pocked buildings screamed history. Judit Kiss brought me to a gypsy club at 3 a.m. It was closed to the public but open to those who knew somebody who knew somebody. Gypsy musicians from all over the city would congregate there when their gigs in tourist-trap restaurants ended. The music never stopped, nor did the little glass cups of espresso coffee thickened with brandy, even at 7 in the morning when most people were heading to work. Permutations and multiples of violins, cimbaloms, contrabasses, singers male and female: keening and wailing in a dark and passionate stew that left my head spinning as I made my way back to the hotel.

Carbon toured Europe again in the spring of 1986 and during a four-day break I stayed with a friend in Karlsruhe. There was a beautiful grand piano and while she was at work I found myself drawn to it like a moth to flame. I'd had a deep antipathy toward the piano since my childhood battles but now it was time to make amends. I tried some stride and blues, plunked out some Monk, then began transferring my two-hand tapping from guitar to the monster, focusing on the lowest keys. With the sustain pedal down, and alternating my fingers from left to right on a single key, I could emulate the sounds produced with analogous techniques on the bass strings of the double-neck. Restricting myself to the same ratios of 1/1, 2/1, 5/3, 8/5, I had a pitch set based on Fibonacci numbers. Varied combinations of notes and rhythms produced luminous arrays of harmonics floating above the rippling drone. These experiments yielded the score to *Mapping*, my first solo piano piece. After returning to NYC from the tour, I recorded it at The Kitchen with John Erskine capturing the sounds using a pair of Schoeps microphones placed in close proximity to the soundboard, contrary to "classical" piano recording technique, and thereby revealing a detailed attack and dancing overtones.

Inspired directly by *Neuromancer*, I began work on *Virtual Stance*, a performance project using the Atari computer as a platform for real-time improvisation. The software M was an open and flexible programming environment that could be used to create and mutate loops and grooves as well as perform radical orchestrational shifts using MIDI gear. With M, I could control samplers, drum machines, and processors, and trigger them all with the MIDI signal converted from guitar, soprano saxophone, or bass clarinet. When all was flowing in the *Virtual Stance*, I operated inside the circuits: Inner Ear, breath, fingers, and processing controllers inseparable from the emerging sounds. It was absolutely essential to have the sounds of vibrating strings, reeds, and columns of air as well as digital samples. The result was close to the electronic dance music found in some of the clubs I frequented, except that *Virtual Stance* required dancers of uncommon flexibility.

When my guitar or horn were interfaced to the computer, I could set up complex chains of triggering conditions that would be so confusing, the only way to play them was to not think about what was happening and just listen, be in the moment. This worked beautifully, at least until the computer crashed. It was a question of when, not if, the small buffer of the Atari ST would choke on the large amounts of data passing through. The ST was a brilliant machine with a low price and built-in MIDI interface aimed directly at musicians. Genius design, but not too robust. The DRAM chips would get dislodged out of their supposedly secure sockets by transport or less: a small vibration on the table might sink the machine. Sometimes the only cure was to lift the computer about six inches and drop it, reseating the chips in their sockets. I kept a looping delay on the output of the system so that when the inevitable crash occured, I could hold and repeat whatever was in the buffer until everything rebooted.

With the album *Fractal*, recorded in the autumn of 1986, I set out to capture various aspects of fractal geometry as translated to the Inner Ear. I wasn't interested in generating tables of fractals to construct musical material, feeling that this approach was too mechanistic. Instead, I was attempting to sonify such notions as self-similarity and the echo between micro-structure and macro-structure, translating them into musical terms. Each piece balanced elements of fixed structure and guided improvisation, layers of interlocked order and chaos. I looked to the math for catalysis, inspiration, and allusion. Methodology included creating small sonic fragments whose contour would then be expanded proportionally to form riffs and structures of various magnitudes. These fragments might be conceived on a guitar or horn or might start life as a bit of notation or instructions for manifesting a specific technique. This approach echoed the methods used to create the string quartet *Tessalation Row*. For example, "Singularity," from the the *Fractal* album, used layers of guitars, basses, and drums played in nested proportional rhythms: microscopic to macroscopic. The guitars and basses used a variety of tunings that ranged from near unisons to larger intervals, all in reflective proportions.

In 2002, chemist and Nobel laureate Roald Hoffmann invited me to perform in his series Entertaining Science at the Cornelia Street Café on a program together with Benoit Mandelbrot, who would present his work on fractals. I performed a fractally inspired improvisation on electroacoustic guitar, after which we all dined together. Benoit Mandelbrot was a large man and a grand presence. Convivial and erudite, Mandelbrot possessed talents extending well beyond mathematics and computers. He was not humble. He would wax eloquent on painting, music, wines, and the proper way to make *bouillabaisse*, or detail how the need to present his thoughts on fractals led him to invent word-processing software and computer graphics. It was beyond inspiring to meet him and I was fortunate to have another dinner with him some months later. I was deeply saddened at his passing in 2010.

In May of 1987, I was walking up Avenue B after taking care of various errands prior to leaving that evening for JFK and a long tour of Europe with Carbon. There was Marion Brown! I hadn't seen Marion since moving to the City. We exchanged jazz-hugs and he told me that he, too, was leaving for Europe that night. After a few more words, we parted with Marion shouting "See you in Germany!"

Mid-tour there was a short break, after which we were to rendezvous with our driver at the Frankfurt train station. Before leaving for the five-hour drive to Düsseldorf, I had a flash and ran back into the station to pick up food for our journey. Coming out of the kiosk, there's Marion! Laughs and jazz-hugs and time for a quick catch-up before Marion's parting "See you soon!"

The last two weeks of the tour were pretty wild, especially the 48 hours without sleep in Berlin with concerts on two nights and running around in the free moments to various clubs with our friends from the NYC band Bite Like A Kitty. After Berlin we performed our final concert in a festival in Hanover, with the plan that our driver would bring me to the Frankfurt Airport in the Land Rover on his way home to Würzburg. The Rover was pretty erratic in its operation and had a maximum speed of about 80 km an hour, so it was imperative that we leave Hanover no later than 5 a.m. to get me to the airport in time for my flight. We returned to the hotel at 3 and I decided to just stay up the last two hours before we departed. When touring, one always devises alternative plans, so I perused the train schedule posted in the lobby. In the worst-case scenario there was a train at 6 that would just barely get me to the airport in time. Exhaustion was looming. I sat down with a pot of coffee and a book and the next thing I knew I was popping up awake to the sight of 0530 on the clock.

In a panic I ran to the driver's room and began banging on his door. It was nearly impossible to rouse him but he finally emerged and I explained that we had to get to the train station—I had to make that 0600 train! We went down to the Rover. It wouldn't start. Drawing on reserves of panic adrenalin, I push-started the heavy beast myself. We're heading to the station as the clock is ticking away. Arriving, I'm out of the Rover and dashing up the stairs as best I can while carrying the huge roadcase containing my double-neck and bass clarinet in one hand, a bulky electronics rack in the other, a soprano saxophone in a case strapped around my neck, plus my backpack. Up the stairs to the track just as the train is slowly rolling out, the doors still open. With a last surge I throw my gear on and jump in after. Made it! Sweat is streaming down my face. I lurch into the first compartment in the dark and throw in my case.

There's Marion!

The next manifestation of Carbon took the form of a large ensemble with thirteen members: Orchestra Carbon. On November 13 and 14, 1987, this ensemble premiered my *Larynx*, a commission of the Brooklyn Academy of Music's Next Wave Festival. For *Larynx*, the group included the Soldier String Quartet (Dave Soldier, Laura Seaton, Ron Lawrence, Mary Wooten), four drummers (Previte, Linton, Noyes, Bennett), and four more musicians (Jim Staley, Lesli Dalaba, David Fulton, Ken Heer) doubling on brass instruments and my slabs and pantars—invented instruments that took on increased importance in this work.

Some of my sound-producing creations were designed and constructed by intent; others emerged from a chance look at a piece of detritus found in my junk box or on the street. Partch's *Genesis of a Music* always had a place of honor on my bookshelf and, catalyzed by it, I began constructing crude acoustic instruments to obtain "other" sounds in 1969, while still a high-school student. Plucked chordophones made from plastic coolers and storage boxes, with necks carved from scrap wood, were a good match for my primitive instrumental technique and perfect for use in our jug band. Later, my approach evolved as I studied electric-guitar design and construction and my technical abilities on guitar grew. I had defretted a $9 garage-sale Norma electric guitar in 1973, opening up a universe of non-tempered sounds and uncategorizable noises. The violinoid, built in 1978 from a scrapped violin, features multiple bridges, with magnetic pickups on either side. It produces only a raw semblance of traditional violin sounds, though it can be bowed conventionally as well as plucked, struck, prepared, and attacked with objects of various materials.

Pantars followed in 1983, fashioned from the stamped steel tops of large storage cans used for such substances as monosodium glutamate or sweeping compound, easy to find while walking through Chinatown. A domed cymbal serves as both bridge and resonator and amplification is by contact microphone. The pantar is held like a guitar and may be picked, bowed with an E-bow, or hammered. Variations include the triple-course bass pantar and the hammerpan, purely percussive and played with mallets. In its essential sound, the pantar can be described as a cross between a tamboura and a dumpster. The slabs are horizontal basses with movable bridges and two pickups with separate outputs to generate a stereo field. They can be played with a variety of techniques: with metal mallets or slides, muted with cloth or the palm or side of the hand, plucked with fingers or picks, strummed open, bowed with E-bow or cello bow. Open to a range of tunings, the sound of the slab runs the gamut from deep *mbira*-like clangs and polyrhythmic bass webs to warped tympani and Tibetan *khoomei* singing. Sampling allows these large and unwieldy constructions to be used virtually in many contexts, notably in the composition and performance of *Larynx*.

"Larynx" is analogy: the orchestra as throat. It follows as corollary to the throat as orchestra: the throat singing of the Arctic Inuit, the *khoomei* singing of Siberia and Mongolia, as well as related jaw-harp techniques found throughout the world. The natural overtone series is the melodic core of much of these musics and of much of *Larynx*. The Fibonacci series was again used to generate tunings, rhythms, melodic/harmonic material, and structural proportions, while my studies in fractal geometry provided a conceptual framework on which to hang the sounds and interactions, expanding the techniques used in the *Fractal* album. I wanted the music to dance on the always changing boundary between a Cartesian geometry derived from the Fibonacci series and a fractal geometry of turbulence, chaos, and disorder. The explicitly ordered materials are embedded in a dense flux of multiple processes: layers of micro-melodies and micro-rhythms, active crosstalk between the players. In the five interludes between the six major sections, new landscapes and new processes emerge. The opening and closing use all four drummers while the remaining sections each feature one, with the others playing slabs or samples. Each drummer has developed a unique sound and vocabulary; I enjoy the contrast between them as well as their singular understanding of my strategies. This applies to all of the musicians in Carbon, who are given instructions of varying degrees of specificity in the different sections, ranging from exact rhythms, notes, or playing techniques to more general notions of density and texture.

The same processing algorithms are mapped into each section, cross-referencing them while yielding radically different sonic results. One is transported, via the interludes, into each section; the terrain is different yet the functional identity of process is the same. (An analogy from topology applies: a torus is a torus is a torus.) The interludes form a cycle of their own while connecting the cycle of main sections. All string instruments are tuned to the just ratios of 1/1, 3/2, 8/5, and 5/3. Throughout the piece, string instruments are predominantly played using only open strings or their overtones, while brass instruments use open pedal tones of these notes and their overtones. There are, however, a number of places in *Larynx* where the players are called upon to use the variety of their own idiosyncratic extended sound-production techniques, well outside any system.

I was apprehensive about the premiere of *Larynx*, but felt the band was well prepared and the sound nearly optimal. On the first night, I counted off the opening and heard… very little. The sound engineer had not brought the master faders up. As I tried to fathom what I was or wasn't hearing, the levels quickly rose and we were on our way, recovering the momentum lost in those first few seconds. The second night went perfectly, the music following the path of inevitability.

In Cleveland, 1954

Performing with St. Elmo's Fire, Sunshine Festival, Cornell University, Ithaca, NY, May 1970

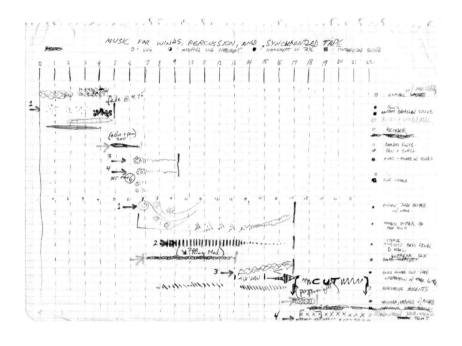

Excerpt of graphic score *Yugen*, 1973

With Buffy, Williamsburg, MA, 1978

With active bows, Bowery Project, NYC, 1982

With triple-course bass pantar, Studio zOaR, NYC, 1991

Drinking Turkish coffee with Hubert Sumlin, East Village, NYC, 1994

Trying the sumsumiya with Muhammad Abu Ajaj, Sinai, 2000

With Janene backstage at Hi-Teca Festival, Porto, Portugal, 2004

Conducting *Quarks Swim Free,* Issue Project Room, Brooklyn, 2006

With Godin electroacoustic guitar, Klangbiennale, Frankfurt, 2007

Performing with Michiyo Yagi and Tomoyo Honda at Shinjuku Pit Inn, Tokyo, 2012

Studio portrait with Lila, Kai, Janene, Brooklyn, 2012

With Koll eight-string guitarbass, Shapeshifter Lab, Brooklyn, 2013

With Bachir Attar and Mustapha Attar of the Master Musicians of Jajouka, LPR, Manhattan, 2014

With Cecil Taylor at benefit for Brooklyn Music School, Brooklyn, 2014

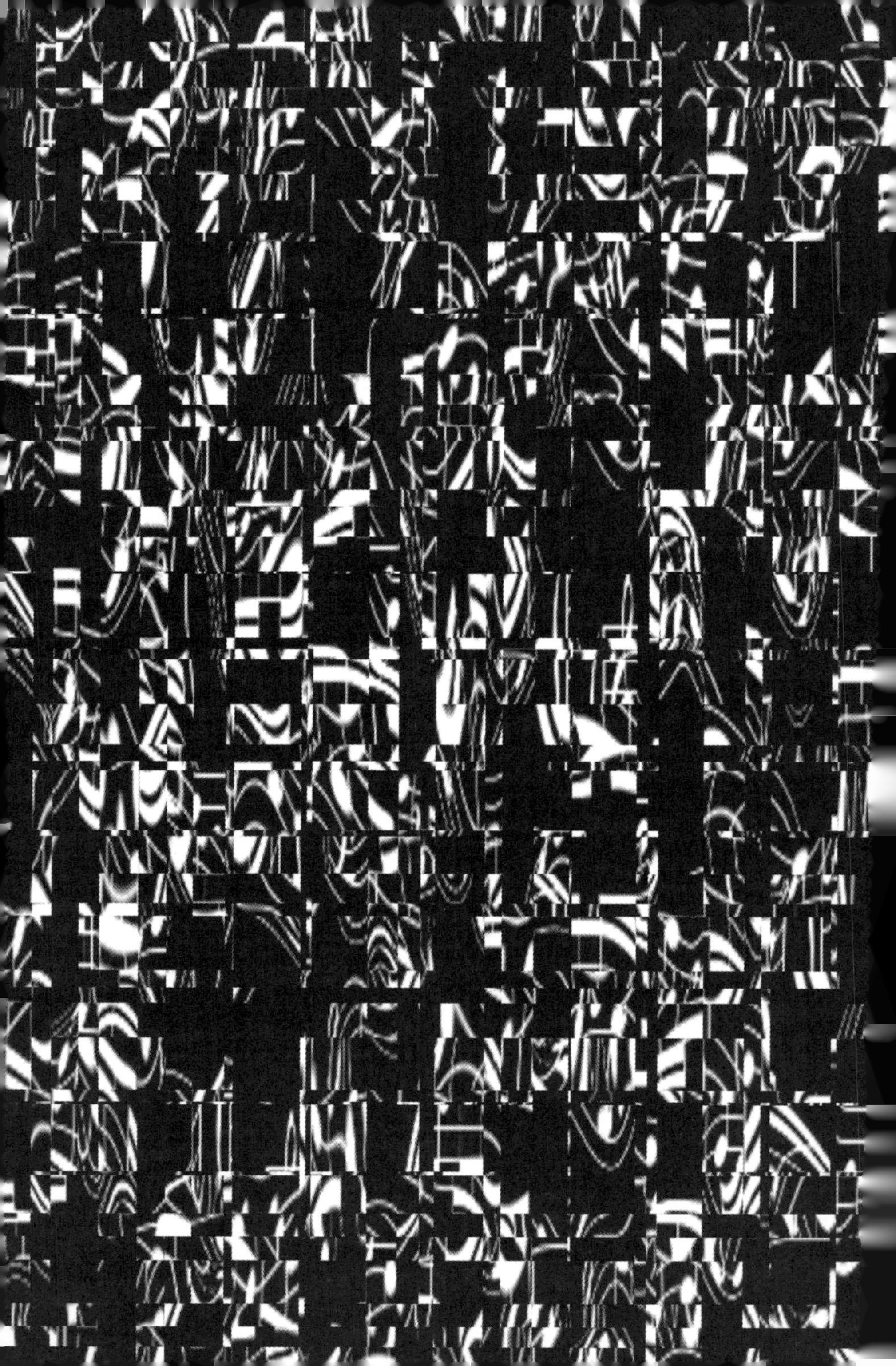

IX.

Self-Organizing Systems from Cyber to Punk (With a Side of Blues)

In the months following the premiere of *Larynx*, there were a number of short European tours and festival engagements, an enjoyable diversion from the Carbon work. Finland's Pori Festival, taking place in early July, was a venerable institution for mostly mainstream jazz and fusion. Wanting to bring in a more "avant" element, curator Matti Laipio created the Ultra Music Meeting within the larger Pori organization. For the 1988 UMM I was among the invitees, as were Andrew Cyrille, Joseph Jarman, Bobby Previte, Sonny Sharrock, Edward Vesala, Wayne Horvitz, Vinny Golia, Tomasz Stańko, James Newton, and Connie Bauer. We would perform in impromptu combinations as well as present our compositions in varied settings.

After we'd all arrived in Helsinki from our various points of embarkment, we were brought by bus to the town of Pori, a two-hour drive. Matti was there to greet us at the hotel, along with his assistants. One, a striking girl with synthetic "Euro-Red" hair, promptly informed me, "In Finland, we drink all summer because it's light all the time and we drink all winter because it's dark all the time." Indeed, there was a distinct alcoholic haze surrounding almost everyone we met. I did a 10 a.m. lecture on improvising with the Atari 1040ST computer, and even at this sober event there was an open bar. By the time the crew found an elusive but necessary cable, the audience was completely snockered.

That evening, the trio of Sharrock, Previte and me rocked in high intensity from start to finish. (We reprised the experience the following year at a concert in Vienna, in a large and longstanding squat on the outskirts of the city.) The entire group of UMM players took part in performing my composition *Self-Squared Dragon* in front of the full festival audience of 10,000, all baking in the blazing sun. It began to cloud up, and just as we completed our set the skies opened, drenching those not lucky enough to be under the tarpaulin covering the festival stage.

Virtual Stance was performed in clubs in NYC and in Europe as well as at the New Music America festival in 1989. Along with Sonic Youth, Fred Frith, and Henry Kaiser, I'd been signed by SST Records, the influential post-punk label started by Black Flag's Greg Ginn. Booked by the label on concert extravaganzas, I would sometimes present *Virtual Stance* in addition to a set by my more rocking band Bootstrappers, with Mike Watt and George Hurley of the Minutemen and Firehose. A huge fan of the Minutemen's compact blasts of smart and incisive punk, I'd been devastated by the death of guitarist D. Boon. Minutemen sets were completely composed in advance, including segments that sounded like high-velocity improvisation. Watt and Hurley were not at all experienced in improvising, especially in performance, but after some initial coaxing took to it readily, honing their chops onstage. The SST audiences, ever loyal and supportive, cheered Bootstrappers on but seemed thoroughly confused by *Virtual Stance*. Music that was loud, atonal, discordant, and grating was all fine as long as it was produced by guitars, bass, and drums—no computers, please.

Bootstrappers performed up and down the West Coast on the SST circuit, splitting bills with Firehose and Screaming Trees and once even opening for metal guitar god Joe Satriani at The Palomino in North Hollywood. Satriani was riding high at the moment, buoyed by a chart-topping record and appearances with Mick Jagger. Bootstrappers had been playing a series of shows in the LA area and we had garnered our own share of highly vocal fans who were in attendance. While our set thundered to a climax, there was a mini-riot as the opposing forces confronted each other, with the Bootstrappers fans yelling "Go! Go! Go!" and the Satriani dudes, mulleted and shagged, yelling "Stop! Stop! Stop!" The vocal protests escalated to widespread throwing of plastic cups filled with ice cubes or beer. As Hurley grooved, Watt began to play his bass by banging it on his head while I fed back and triggered samples of machine guns and metal springs dropped three octaves.

We were having great fun playing the role of "power trio," but there was much more to it than that. I do love the physical act of playing the guitar to its limit but at a certain point, lots of fast screaming notes and scalar runs just sound like nothing much—tires spinning or a phone off the hook. No information. Using samplers as well as radical sound worlds created with extended techniques, I found a need to expound sonically on a world plunging into a technological and psychological sea-change. Sometimes it takes a blast of noise to clear the buffer, jam the usual patterns of perception and open the way to others. Cyberpunk caused us to look around and realize that we had other realms to explore, untapped resources, but also new traps and dangers. The old musical models (especially when they're wearing spandex and playing wheedly-wheedly on guitars) seemed pretty tired and empty. I thought of the model for improvising in the Bootstrappers style as a self-organizing system in the form of a cyberpunk-rock band with the samples taking the place of the lead vocalist, whether the sounds were of a smarmy radio announcer, a melody derived from digital aliasing errors on a sax sample, or a blast of noise from a pantar, transposed down and stretched way out.

Back in New York, I wanted to return to a small band-format for Carbon and assembled Samm Bennett on drums, percussion, and sampler; Linton on drums and tapes; and electric harpist Zeena Parkins doubling on slab and keyboard. All were players with a wide timbral range—anyone in the group could deal the woofers or the tweeters, beats or melodies or pure noise. This group had been performing the long-form *Jumpcut* but I decided to focus instead on composing short pieces, which we recorded and released on Enemy Records in 1989 as *Datacide*.

Taking a brief sabbatical from Carbon, I continued touring as a soloist and in various collaborations. The gigs were necessary for economic survival but I enjoyed them all. More important, each situation fed all of the others musically while also feeding the resource library of the Inner Ear, surprising the synapses and building new connections. Stopping in San Francisco on my way to Tokyo to perform a concert with Korean *komungo* player Jin Hi Kim, I accompanied her on a visit to the late composer David Wessel, who very generously gave a full explanation and demonstration of Thunder, the latest invention from Don Buchla. Thunder was a controller of unprecedented power and flexibility, with each of its numerous keys location-, touch-, and pressure-sensitive. Each could function as a keyboard to trigger sounds, as a sequencer, or as a set of continuous controllers, and each could send MIDI data on multiple channels simultaneously. It was ergonomically designed and the experience of using it fell somewhere between playing tablas and giving a massage. The Ear was joyously dumbfounded by its potential and a good chunk of my touring income went towards the purchase of one. I could now manipulate samples in real time with the intuitive ease and transparency of playing the guitar. Also in real time, I could use the prodigious controller abilities of Thunder to manipulate vast amounts of sound using my hardware reverbs and pitch-shifters.

For the next record, *Tocsin*, Joseph Trump replaced Epstein on drums. More explicit song structures emerged with Trump, a veteran of such groups as Brian Brain and Pigface, bringing a deep groove and double-kick speed and intensity. For this phase, I didn't want Carbon to hew to any one formal agenda, but instead to be the carrier of many mutant strains. Continuing from earlier records was the use of extended timbres to orchestrate a melodic or harmonic idea or to create the full sound design for the piece. Samples were played from my MIDI'd double-neck or from Weinstein's keyboard, allowing sounds developed in the lab to take their place on stage. Some of these sounds were the result of time-stretching extremely short impulses sampled from my various instruments to reveal melodic contours and hidden voices. These were all integrated into the Carbon sound, soundscape as pop instrumental.

To today's ears, a short and pungent sound can function just as a catchy hook or lyric refrain once did. We heard this in the early days of hip-hop when a DJ would present the identifying sonic icon for a track. It might be a fragment of an instrument from another record; it might be something off of a sound effects album; it might be a melodic fragment teased out of a longer phrase. Whatever it was, it made the song. A car might pass you on the street, that certain sound blasting from an open window, and in a few brief seconds you knew the song. It was timbre that first tuned my ears into the panorama of sounds, timbre that first hooked me on guitar. Whether punch press or overdriven fuzz, Balinese gamelan or Mongolian *khoomei*, it wasn't the song or the structure but that quick hit of sonics. Timbre and texture remained my guiding lights.

In parallel with Carbon's evolution, I translated the *Virtual Stance* project to an Apple laptop and it molted into a new identity, Tectonics. During 1991 I had been a rabid fan of the UK's jungle scene, with its high-speed asymetric dance rhythms and saturated synth timbres, work that resonated with techniques I was developing in *Virtual Stance*. The "psychedelic jungle techno" of Tectonics melded extended guitar with warped grooves in a real-time processing environment using the software Cubase. I was performing it mostly at Soundlab, a party in a loft on Canal Street that had previously been shared as a rehearsal space by Marc Ribot, David Linton, and myself. At Soundlab I met composer and programmer Frank Rothkamm. He whipped up some drum loops and from them grew the song "Krkd," the opening track on the first Tectonics album, *Field & Stream*. The album met with an excellent response and received widespread radio play. Soundlab interfaced closely with NYC's small jungle scene and I quickly met its local pioneer and evangelist, Carlos Slinger (a.k.a. DJ Soul Slinger), a turntablist and proprietor of the Jungle Sky label. We began to perform in duo together and, one wild evening, in trio with Christian Marclay.

The personnel of the *Tocsin* band continued to work together despite everyone's involvement in many other projects, and over the next five years we toured extensively in Europe, Japan, even the United States. This latter tour took place in 1995, using a rented van. We played 29 concerts in 35 days, ranging down to Texas, through Arizona and California, and up to Seattle in a sleep-deprivation experiment of continental proportions. Returning to our NYC base, we added *Truthtable, Amusia, Interference,* and *Autoboot* to the discography. My strategy for the songs varied: sometimes very detailed structures, sometimes simple riffs or just conceptual sketches consisting of a few words, an image, an abbreviated narrative, a sample or a guitar blast. Lyrics were written and sung by KJ Grant, DD Dorvillier, even myself. Sample programming and sound design for each song would follow. The band would rehearse a bit and knock out very live-sounding versions in one or two takes, after which I would use ProTools to edit and process the tracks and in some cases create new songs from fragments, using a few bars of drum grooves and odd sounds from everyone else: sampled, sequenced, and twisted. Finally, everything would be remixed and edited until master tracks emerged.

During the time of the mixing of *Amusia*, a chance sidewalk meeting with Denardo Coleman led to an invitation to visit the Harmolodics studio on 125th Street. Ornette's music had long been a pleasure and influence for me and his expositions of Harmolodics, an enigmatic collection of sometimes contradictory notions on music, retained a poetic power to inspire, perhaps because of an ambiguity that allowed a wide range of interpretations. Ultimately, Ornette's instrumental voice, uniquely inventive and affecting, transcended any verbiage. A beautiful surprise on his seminal 1977 album *Dancing in Your Head* was the musical meeting with the Master Musicians of Jajouka.

I arrived at the building on the appointed day and time. I'd been warned about the elevator operator in Ornette's building, and indeed, ascending to the studio was akin to being an astronaut in a low-tech launch. No sign of Denardo. The recording engineer brought me into a control room dominated by a massive Harrison console, where I was privileged to witness Ornette overdubbing alto sax solos on a track for the *Tone Dialing* album. Each solo was a masterpiece of invention and articulated melody, virtuosity not for its own sake but for the song. I heard over a dozen solos, any one of which I would proudly call a "keeper" but none perfect enough for Ornette. I was agog at this overdose of riches. We had met briefly on a number of occasions and when Ornette emerged from the iso booth, he greeted me warmly and graciously invited me to tea, showing no interest in auditioning his overdubbing marathon. We chatted about the recording, the studio, Denardo (as yet unarrived), and electronic music. No deep words of wisdom were transmitted from Ornette to me, but I felt that just being in his charismatic presence (especially after hearing his series of brilliant solos) was a lesson in centering. Ornette returned to the booth to play more overdubs, and I, downtown.

Before heading back out on tour, I convened Dave Hofstra on bass and Joe Trump on drums to record a set of classic blues and two originals that would be released under the name *Terraplane*. After the disintegration of a three-year relationship, it was deep balm to play instrumental versions of tunes by Otis Rush, Robert Johnson, Howlin' Wolf, Muddy Waters, Albert King and more. I'd spent decades working on channeling the sound of my blues heroes through my fingers. While it's good to be able to execute anything that you're hearing, ultimately mechanics are not that important: anyone can learn licks. The asymptotic returns: I'd rather hear and play the search than crank out a flashy lick, a worn cliché. I'd long felt that attempting the impossible is a lot more exciting than waltzing through gestures that are nearly automatic.

With our recording, I felt we'd done a little justice to the music and I hoped to perform it live, perhaps add a vocalist or horns. Over the next two decades, Terraplane did indeed expand to encompass a wide range of soulful and talented artists, among them Eric Mingus, Tracie Morris, Lance Carter, Sam Furnace, Curtis Fowlkes, Alex Harding, Tony Lewis, Dean Bowman, Terry L. Greene II, Mollie King, and our most esteemed special guest, guitarist Hubert Sumlin. I'll never tire of listening or playing classic and country blues: the poetic and expressive lyrics delivered by voices rich and rough, embodying pain, anger, and joy; the African-derived rhythms; the vocalized guitar; the wisdom and humor. Sometimes my synesthesia takes the form of taste. I like cooking and eating good food and when playing blues, hitting certain notes brings forth tastes: salty, sweet, sour, bitter. Tastes like life.

Flash to September 2011: the master himself, Hubert Sumlin, enters producer Joe Mardin's studio for an overdub session for the new Terraplane album *Sky Road Songs*. He's carrying his oxygen tank like a guitar case. "Like an astronaut," he says, chuckling slyly.

It's two years since I've seen Hubert and I'm surprised by his frailty, but reassured by his strong hug and joyful demeanor. Soon we're all laughing over a story about his early days with James Cotton. He downs an espresso and fingers my white Strat while we play the basic track "This House Is For Sale," on which he'll overdub. Magic in that right hand—not to mention the left. Over the years I've spent many an hour watching like a hawk, trying to figure out just how that magic is conjured. A relaxed brushing of the strings with those *lo-o-ong* digits: totally casual, but the sounds that emerge are anything but. No matter what kind of guitar he's using (and I've seen him play them all), it always sounds like Hubert.

I first met Hubert in 1983 in a Chicago dive, where he was alternating sets with guitar trickster Lefty Dizz. The regulars were none too happy that the pool table had to be moved to accommodate the music. Hubert played salty and sweet, fire and ice. We spoke a bit about guitars but I didn't want to bug him on his break. I was happy just to hear him play and, in fact, thrilled to actually exchange a few words with this man whose sound had moved me for so many years. Like so many other suburban white kids, I came to the blues through Paul Butterfield, the Yardbirds, the Stones. But once I heard the source, the real thing, I was hooked and had to dig in deeper. Howlin' Wolf's music always grabbed me: the feral gravel of that voice and the perfect foil, Hubert's acerbic guitar. On first hearing "Goin' Down Slow," I was floored by the strange and vocal quality of the guitar leads, the aggressive angularity and brilliance of the lines. There were no credits on the albums and it took me till 1970 to find out this guitarist's name. "Shake for Me," "Killing Floor," "300 Pounds of Joy," "Wang Dang Doodle" are all prime examples of Hubert's genius: he gave each song a clear identity through a few terse licks filled with emotion, wit, and a Cubist take on melody.

Through vocalist Queen Esther, Terraplane was booked to back up Hubert at NYC's Knitting Factory in 1994. I was nervous: could I ever have imagined standing on stage trading licks with one of my all-time heroes? In the dressing room, Hubert was all smiles, calling us "my guys." We played some blues chestnuts and a couple of Hubert's songs; the gig was a gas for all and led to my producing some sessions of Hubert's, both live and in the studio.

Before a solo gig of his in a West Village club in 1996, I interviewed him at a nearby pizzeria and we spoke about many things. After the show we had an encounter with the club's owner, so typical of the music business. We had planned to record both nights of Hubert's run using the house DAT deck. The deal was that I would take the DAT tapes and give the owner identical, 1:1 digital copies for his archives. The first night found Hubert in great form, playing some beautifully lyrical and insanely wild guitar and singing both his songs and the classics. I took the tape and ran off the 1:1 copy in my studio before returning to the club for the next evening's show. After Hubert's set, I brought the club owner the copy of Day 1 and asked for the new DAT to copy. "No!" he shot back. "This one is for me." I called over Hubert's manager, Red, and explained the situation. Soon Red and the owner were shouting at each other while Hubert and I stood back, exchanging grins and eye-rolls. Finally Red pulled out his trump card: "I'm Jewish, too, so God will punish you if you fuck with me." End of fight and the owner hands me the tape.

Later in 1994, Red asked me to produce an all-instrumental session. At Seltzer Sound in Chinatown, we recorded some duo tracks of Hubert with pianist Dave Maxwell, as well as some trios with bassist Fuzz Jones and drummer S.P. Leary, the hard-swinging rhythm section of Muddy Waters' 1970s bands. I asked Hubert to throw in some electric solos for possible future overdubbing; he obliged with a vicious boogie and a pungent version of the eternal "Rollin' and Tumblin'." When, in 1996, my Studio zOaR moved to a shared recording suite on West 30th Street in what I called the Spinal Tap Building and I convened the members of Terraplane to work on the double-CD *Blues for Next*, we finished both those skeletal songs. Though I'd have much preferred for Hubert to join us in the flesh, his busy schedule and recent change of management made it impossible. Sim Cain on drums and Dave Hofstra on bass overdubbed first, laying down a solid foundation congruent with Hubert's quirky phrasing, after which saxophonist Sam Furnace and I put down our tracks.

After that release and its positive reception, Terraplane performed extensively in Europe. American gigs were harder to come by, as we were too weird and angular for the very conservative blues clubs but not arch and ironic enough for the "Downtown scene." On the Continent, though, we played to huge and ecstatic crowds at clubs, theaters, and festivals. Whenever possible, our tours featured Hubert as a guest and he was a gracious and loving presence, never failing to astound guitarists in the audience—and those onstage.

A memorable two-week tour in the UK in 2003 began with the Belfast Jazz Festival. Empty, with fluorescent illumination and a sticky floor, the venue—the Guinness Spot, on the campus of Queen's University—didn't present an appealing first impression. But with the stage illuminated, the house lights down, and a packed audience of 500 (the show was sold-out three weeks in advance), it became a funky roadhouse with a glitzy sheen. The acoustics, dauntingly reflective at soundcheck, were likewise transformed by the the presence of the audience. Starting our first set with horns, no guitars, we soon brought up Eric Mingus and finally Hubert. With Hubert, we begin with the classic "Sittin' on Top of the World" and move on to other Howlin' Wolf songs. Having had a cancerous lung removed the previous year, Hubert lacks his full singing strength, so Eric sings most of the Wolf songs. Hubert takes over on "Howlin' for My Darling" and burns up the solo on our set closer, "Stop That Thing."

The second set follows the first in structure but the heat is turned up a few notches, fueled perhaps by fresh Guinness for both audience and band. After fiery versions of "Oil Blues" and "Please Don't," Hubert returns to sing and play "Little Red Rooster," always a rush for me. It's a little strange to be playing back to Hubert the licks I learned from his records with Wolf; the irony is certainly not lost on him as he flashes me a smile when I hit him with one of his classic lines, lines etched deeply into my ears and fingers. The band really begins to meld in this set, taking chances and just missing trainwrecks with gnarly shifts of direction— not least on "Back Door Man," where we enter *Bitches Brew* territory and inhabit it. Hubert finishes the set with us, tossing in an uptempo "Lost Soul." Huge acclaim brings us back for a long pulsing encore somewhere between *Rollin' and Tumblin'* and psychedelic trance.

Back at Heathrow we meet our driver, Patrick, and have our first ride in the posh and comfortable bus that will be our home for the next week: upper and lower lounges, sleeping berths, refrigerators, coffee-maker, microwave, DVD decks.

The next night in Birmingham, Hubert amazes with his biting tone, spontaneous invention, and incredible exuberance. Driving all night, we arrive in Scotland at dawn. Haggis and single malts are prime topics of conversation as we approach Aberdeen. Our show at the Lemon Tree builds and builds, but since the club is licensed to operate only until midnight, we must cut the show off precisely at that point. We're surrounded by autograph seekers and Hubert, pleasurably besieged, is happy to sign anything: CDs, LPs, magazines, hands, a woman's thigh.

Next night we're in Newcastle, reputed to be a rough town. Walking to the club after dinner at a nearby Chinese restaurant, we encounter a small gang of young white toughs who throw rocks and yell "nigger" from across the road. Tony would like to "discuss" matters with them but the majority would rather just go and play our music. The club operates in a disused opera house, a long thin room with a small stage. The layout is awkward but the sound is quite good and our set seethes with anger, spicing our joy in playing. In contrast, the next night we perform at the Opera House of the Royal Northern College of Music in Manchester. Typically for university facilities, this 600-seat hall has a spacious, well-equipped stage and a big sound for the instruments even with little amplification. Hubert plays some unbelievable chords and licks in "They Say We Is"—jagged, visceral, and sonic. Can these notes even be transcribed into Western notation? Lots of students come up after to ask questions and get autographs.

Returning to London, we're booked to perform a short set from the Foyer of the Queen Elizabeth Hall "live" on BBC3 for the opening of the London Jazz Festival. It's potentially a logistical nightmare and, in fact, soundcheck takes much longer than it should. We have the first check and last set of this concert. The BBC crew is predictably competent and the sound is quite good considering that we're in a vast open room with huge glass windows. When the time comes for our 20-minute set, we play a compact and tight "Work or Leave," then bring up Hubert and Eric Mingus for blistering versions of "Wang Dang Doodle" and "Lost Souls." Expecting an indifferent response from a snobbish jazz audience, we're blown away by the applause and cheers.

The next morning, Hubert and I are guests on Paul Jones' show "Jazz Me Blues" on a small London jazz radio station. Paul is a huge fan of Hubert has done his homework on me as well. We play three improvised blues live in the studio; Hubert plugs into a small Peavey amp, while I play direct into the desk and monitor with headphones. Tuning is a bit out on the first number but we tighten it up for the rest of the set and have some fun, a conversation in the language of the blues but with liberal doses of alien argot.

After the radio set, we cruise through the afternoon rush-hour traffic in the Mall and are amused at the plethora of American flags erected to welcome W, due in London in a few days. For welcome balance, there's an ample set of anti-Bush signs and information tables. We soon arrive at the club in East London, which hosts a trendy restaurant and two live rooms. Our show is in the larger one upstairs, with a capacity of about 300 and a tight stage in the middle. Looming over us is the balcony/backstage area, making us feel as if we're in a low-ceilinged basement. The sound is warm and resonant, though, and we play two sets to a packed and rowdy house with many friends in attendance, the perfect finale for this tour. After the second set's *Wang Dang Doodle*, Hubert's manager, Toni Mamary, brings out a blue Stratocaster-shaped cake in honor of Hubert's 72nd birthday. The entire crowd joins in singing and we bring it on home.

But I digress. Back to 1996: I'm taking stock of my activities and how best to perform them. Touring with the double-neck guitar/bass and its associated electronics had begun to wreak a physical toll. Back strain from using the weighty instrument onstage was one factor, but perhaps even worse was carrying it around in its sturdy road case, with another case of similar weight keeping the racked electronics safe. I began imagining a single-necked instrument that could cover the full range of bass and guitar. After sketching out some ideas I commissioned Carlo Greco, a master luthier who'd designed instruments for Guild Guitars for many years, to make a neck for me that would be wide enough for two bass strings and six guitar strings. I then asked Doug Henderson, a sculptor and guitarist, to fashion the body and tie it all together with appropriate hardware. I chose three Bartolini Jazz Bass pickups because of their clarity and full frequency response. Doug's design paid homage to the classic Gibson "Flying V" favored by Albert King, Lonnie Mack, and Jimi Hendrix but in a compact and futuristic variation. Using stereo sound processers and linked guitar and bass amps, I could now cover the full tessitura of the double-neck in a lightweight instrument that could easily be carried on any plane without argument from security or flight attendants. The final element was a track pad velcroed to the body with which samples could be scratched using the software LiSa, which I'd worked with during a brief residency at STEIM in Amsterdam in 1996. Instead of emerging from 40 pounds of metal, the samples would now be output from my laptop. This eight-string made its debut on the second Tectonics album, *Errata*.

Reviewing in 1998 my studies in self-organizing systems, algorithms, genetics, chaos theory, flocking behavior, hunting packs, street gangs, and African drum choirs led to the next phase, the composition *SyndaKit*. My first impulses leading to the construction of *SyndaKit* were purely musical but reflecting upon the work, it's clear to me now that there are simultaneous channels being translated between world, mind, and Inner Ear. Carried on these channels are notions I've held close for decades: this would not be hierarchical music but anarchical in an ideal sense, a utopian vision of musical natural selection, invisible rules derived from biological interaction, a socio-acoustic paradise shaped by pheromonal handshaking and killer grooves. Rather than a fixed score on a timeline, this was to be a construction set to allow the musicians to generate the work in real time, creating an ever shifting rhythmic and timbral matrix, unified in identity but different in each performance. Improvisatory and algorithmic but not improvisation, SyndaKit's essence is a generative organism consisting of 144 composed cores on twelve pages divided among the twelve players, with a set of simple rules for their use through processes of imitation, addition, recombination, transposition, and mutation. Paradoxically, the organism's prime objectives are to form rhythmic unisons and grooves while continuously evolving and transforming. I felt that with this piece, the notion of IrRational Music was hitting its stride: pure process to create a music without fixed form or content, yet inevitably itself.

Cores are looped by the musicians or may be used as "objects" to be injected into the sonic flux. The four pitches C, G, A♭, A act as nodes of attraction in *SyndaKit* and draw all sonic activities towards them: four possible dronalities. Cores are composed of these pitches or nonpitched materials. Pitched Cores may be transposed to any octave. When imitating pitched Cores, players may transpose to any interval. Players may add one of their Cores to any other one that is looping, thus forming a new loop, but they may not add together their own Cores unless they happen to be attached to another Core already in use by another player. Players may "pop out" with short improvised statements at any time and then return to the flux. These "pop-outs" may be used by players as source material for looping thereby adding fresh "genetic" material. Players may enter or leave the flux at will. Theoretically, an entire set of *SyndaKit* could be performed without players ever consulting the sheets of Cores, only operating from "pop-outs." There is no "right" or "wrong" version of *SyndaKit*. Valid performances of *SyndaKit* could be unison quarter notes for the entire duration of the set or a single held tone.

SyndaKit received its premiere at the NYC club Tonic in November 1998, performed by Orchestra Carbon. The group included Zeena Parkins on piano, David Weinstein on sampler, Marc Sloan on bass, Joseph Trump, Rea Mochiach, and Elliot Humberto Kavee on percussion, Judith Insell on viola, David Soldier on violin, Tim Smith and Evan Spritzer on bass clarinet, Ted Reichman on accordion, and myself on electroacoustic guitar. A Godin Duet Multiac was modified with an extra metal tailpiece, which allowed behind-the-bridge clanks and plinks plus koto-like bends and added resonance. The combination of piezo pickup and internal condenser microphones made for a detailed and hyperreal sound. A long rehearsal in the afternoon at Tonic was followed by two intense and strenuous sets with Cores appearing then evaporating, only to reappear with changed aspect. The inventiveness and creative abandon of the players matched their discipline, and global listening allowed them to hew to the composed Cores while recombining them in oblique extrapolations of great intensity.

For a January '99 concert in Berlin, Reinhold Friedl invited me to bring the *SyndaKit* score for a performance by his ensemble Zeitkratzer. One of my favorite Berlin sights from the air is the Fernsehturm, the "space needle" TV tower in the Alexanderplatz that was once a symbol of Communist East Germany's vision for the future. As we came in for our landing, the silvery globe of the tower floated above a low and thick layer of clouds, the sky glowing red from sunrise, the ground below still dark with greys and blacks. *SyndaKit* with Zeitkratzer had a very different feel than the sets with Orchestra Carbon. At the risk of stereotyping, I'd say the Berliners were a little cautious in their transformations, but also more willing to let the ensemble sound gel into the monolithic unisons that are an essential part of the piece—something those individualistic New Yorkers seem to avoid like the plague. In the years to follow, *SyndaKit* was performed throughout Europe and Asia by both ad hoc ensembles and such groups as NY's Tilt Brass and Prague's Agon Orchestra. Though the international mobility of many musicians may have diluted the national character of these performances, having *guqin* and *guzheng* players in the Beijing New Music Ensemble gave its 2006 realizations of *SyndaKit* a distinct local flavor. I found that ensembles comprising only one type of instrument made for very successful performances; versions of *SyndaKit* with twelve brass, twelve electric guitars, or twelve acoustic string players were especially resonant.

A most welcome commission by Meet The Composer led to the next composition for Orchestra Carbon, *Radiolaria*. With operations modeled on biological metaphors for growth and reproduction, the title was a tribute to the hugely influential biologist and artist Ernst Haeckel, perhaps Charles Darwin's most important acolyte. The commission had an extra wrinkle in that the premiere would be performed at the 42nd Street branch of the Whitney Museum in Manhattan. Formerly the atrium of a bank, the huge space had floor-to-ceiling glass windows, making for incredibly reflective acoustics. As fighting the sound of the room made no sense, the composition of the piece would try to make the quirky acoustics a virtue. Full drum kit and intricate melodies were most definitely contraindicated. The orchestration included pairs of alto saxophones, trumpets, bass clarinets, and trombones, as well as a pair of keyboardists playing samples made from my own soprano sax, radically transformed through editing, time-stretching, and pitch-shifting. Percussionist Jim Pugliese played timpani, bongos, and a small selection of unpitched metallophones, while I performed on soprano sax and laptop.

Again, a simple algorithm formed the underlying strategy of each section within the piece: to transform horizontal gestures of rhythm or melody into stratified, vertical layers of sound. This would be enhanced by live computer processing of the sound from the ensemble. Extracted overtones and subharmonics would be fed back into the mix, conjuring "ghost instruments" from the resulting difference tones. To this end, a patch in the application Max/MSP was sketched out and then programmed by artist, educator, and Max-*meister* Luke Dubois. Based on the object ~*fiddle*, a plug-in "external" that analyzes audio and allows the results to be used in various ways, the patch contained a filter that would divide the sound spectrum into 24 bands with great selectivity. The material in each band could be freely transposed up or down in pitch, then reintroduced into the sound mix.

Each section in *Radiolaria* uses composed cores, with the musicians following sets of simple instructions to manipulate their core materials. For example, the opening section uses proportionally-spaced unison hits over an eighth-note pulse. Each musician adds a different length of rest (in increments of sixteenth notes) at the end of their cycle to throw the unison out of phase. In addition, the musicians increase the duration of one of their notes, the target pitch, to transform the hocketed pulse into a multi-layered drone with intermittent rhythmic crosstalk. For the penultimate section, a simple set of rules allows the players to construct complex chains from provided Cores (as in *SyndaKit*) recombined with the material imitated from the output of the other players. In the finale, each musician begins by oscillating between a home pitch and a target pitch, gradually increasing the speed of oscillation. As this section proceeds, the ensemble's intervallic range and the range of the target pitches increases, adding to the density of the totality until the soundfield is nearly a solid mass, but one fibrillating with ricocheting microsounds. Many of these same strategies were put to use in another piece for Zeitkratzer, *Coriolis Effect*, which was re-orchestrated for the New Juilliard Ensemble led by Joel Sachs for performances in Paris and New York.

Radiolaria was performed a number of times in New York over the next year and after recording and releasing a CD of it on zOaR, I turned to other projects. Besides curating the upcoming exhibition and overview of sound art, *Volume: Bed of Sound*, for PS1 in NYC, there was seemingly non-stop international touring as a soloist with Tectonics and my blues band Terraplane, as well as more collaborations with Zeitkratzer; DJ Soul Slinger; guitarists David Torn and Vernon Reid in our trio GTR OBLQ; the group of oudist Muhammad Abu Ajaj; kotoist Michiyo Yagi; and vocalist Saadet Türköz. In May 2001, Saadet and I went to Istanbul for performances and on a free day visited Butch Morris at the university to attend the class he was teaching. That evening, I was saddened to hear him lament that most of the students did not wish to draw on the deep heritage of Turkish music and instead wanted to play a "jazz" closer in spirit to the Yellowjackets or Kenny G than to the AACM, Ornette, or Butch's own Conductions. Butch loved Istanbul and it was fantastic to hang out on the deck of his apartment overlooking the Bosphorus, or go over to the night market for *mezze*. Walking around Istanbul day or night, we'd find that every taxi driver in town knew Butch and greeted him warmly.

One of my favorite Orchestra Carbon shows was a concert in the bandshell of NYC's Central Park for the Downtown Festival in July of 2001. We performed *SyndaKit* for a large audience of festival-goers, dedicated followers of my work, curious onlookers, and those who might normally be found hanging out in the park on a hot summer day. In general, I much prefer an audience that is not too "well trained," too predictable in its response to the music. The free outdoor festival is perhaps the most open format of all and the experience may vary greatly. On this occasion, we garnered some very enthusiastic applause, some sustained booing, and the spontaneous appearance of a self-appointed "conductor" in the guise of a young woman who had obviously been indulging freely in an uncertain mix of alcohol and illicit substances. She staggered and stomped around in front of us, waving her arms and shouting imprecations in an unsucceful attempt to get the musicians to stop playing. Distracting, to be sure, yet somehow inspiring.

From 2003 to 2005, Orchestra Carbon performed only sporadically, presenting *SyndaKit* and a new piece, *Quarks Swim Free.* For *Quarks,* Butch Morris guested as conductor on a number of occasions with the group. Butch would hone in on specific passages of the written material or hear things in my improvisations that might have been tossed off as asides or parentheses. Finding the value in them, he would elevate these items to iconic status or transform them into structural points of great weight. The material was always expanded. Indeed, I keep returning to "expansion" as a catchall phrase for so much of the magic in Butch's approach to life and music. His hand signal for "expansion"—open hands moving apart and together, like wide-range slow-motion clapping—took on an important role in my own Conductions, a simple sign that so completely captures the adventure of going beyond limits combined with the discipline of staying within the operating parameters that define a particular musical gesture.

After this hiatus from Carbon performances, I was primed to put the 1991 quintet back in operation, even if only briefly. *Void Coordinates* has multiple meanings: the exact location of The Void (a contradiction in terms); the process of eliminating exact location; a cutting loose of all previous references. The titles for the individual pieces serve (as most of my titles do) as pointers, references, and keywords to various strains in music, mathematics, natural history, philosophy. I'd long wished that my album covers were loaded with hypertext links so that while listening to a track, one could check out definitions, etymologies, and usages related to current events. The track list here included "Eskatones," "Eukaryonic," "Hypercubus," "Fermion," "Holoscenic," "Index of Minerals," and "The Younger Dryas." Recorded "live" with a minimum of edits and overdubs, the album is an accurate representation of what Carbon sounds like in performance: operating in the service of groove and psychoacoustic chemical change, IrRational Music rendered loud.

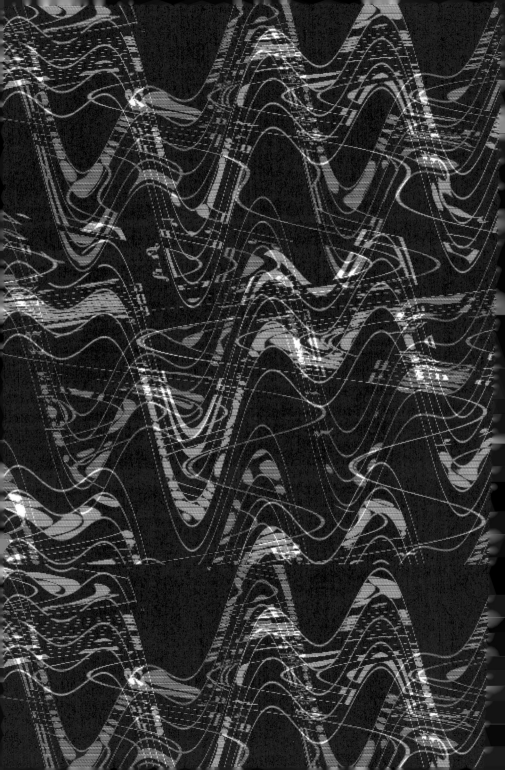

X.

Out in the Worlds

Nusrat! Hearing *qawwali* singer Nusrat Fateh Ali Khan's album *En concert à Paris* on the Ocora label in the late 1970s was an earthshaking experience. Since then, I'd seen two of his performances in NYC, set apart from any other concerts I'd witnessed by the powerful and frenzied devotional nature of both music and audience. Nusrat's fans, transported by the ecstatic sounds, would jump on stage and plaster bank notes—$20s, $50s, $100s—to his sweat-drenched forehead or toss them on the stage while the music continued, inexorable. There was the same intensity in his music that I found in Hendrix, Coltrane, Xenakis.

My solo concert in Montreal in 1990 led to meeting and playing with Nusrat, something I could hardly have imagined. The McGill University radio station, CKUT, that organized my concert had, on the previous evening, produced Nusrat's, which I unfortunately missed because of my travel schedule. The station's program directors, Brian Zuraw and Julia Loktev, floated to each of us separately the idea of a live session at the studio the next day. We were in mutual agreement and it was on.

We set up in a small room, perhaps 100 square feet. The staff rolled out a canvas tarpaulin over the grey industrial carpet and placed microphones, after which Nusrat and Party (as they were called) quickly set up on the floor. Besides Nusrat, his band consisted of Nusrat's brother singing and playing harmonium, a tabla player, and two clappers who also sang on the choruses. I had the double-neck guitar/bass running through a delay pedal into a small amplifier and the bass clarinet played acoustically.

I was extremely grateful for Nusrat's openness to this experiment. Welcomed as a guest in *qawwali* music, I couldn't participate with abandon. The amazing melismatic extrapolations of Nusrat's voice are the result of years of discipline and practice. While I certainly had my own longstanding praxis, I wasn't sure if it would enhance or even fit at all with Nusrat's. In the close quarters of that tiny studio, the sound of his singing was overwhelmingly gorgeous, and frankly I would have been quite happy just to listen. His brother's voice was equally virtuosic, if lacking a bit of the high-tenor intensity so prominent in Nusrat's sound.

In a very informal and personal way, I had studied Hindustani and Carnatic music enough to know just how little I knew. Still, I could recognize the ragas used in the various songs and where they intersected with Western modes and scales, and thereby find a way to contribute to the mix. With guitar, I mostly used the EBow to generate sounds that fortified the drones of the songs. Likewise, I approached the bass clarinet as if it was a chromatic didgeridoo enhancing the bottom layer. I did play some melodic runs and add other sounds to the crosstalk, but ultimately I tried to stay out of the way.

Even within a well-defined scene, improvised collaborations can be tricky. At their best, they're conversations full of unpredictable interplay, with participants fluidly shifting between foreground and background, engaging, enhancing, even contradicting and arguing. But when players from radically different cultural traditions are improvising together, common ground must be found. Needed is the creation of a mythical locus equidistant to all participants, one where all are at ease in a suspended space. This space should be comfortable enough to let the music flow as if from "home," but enough outside of one's own realm to enable a semi-formal channel: a clear table, a village square, a blank space. There is always the danger in cross-cultural interfaces of what, at its worst, I would call "cultural imperialism," a type of condescension where the exotic sounds of the foreigner are brought in only to add spice or a touch of mystery to a musical gesture controlled by the Westerner's rational sense of structure. Such an imbalance of power can produce results similar to the *chinoiserie* of the 18th century, a decorative style that (as Edward Said showed in his landmark work *Orientalism*) projected

European fantasies and stereotypes. Yet when one is confronted with a vast body of musical knowledge of great beauty and historical depth, how can one not attempt to learn from it, to channel techniques, forms, and gestures? To approach the music of the other with openness, humility, and an analytical ear has always seemed to me a good mechanism for meeting in the middle.

My favorite collaborations with non-Western musicians have all attained that quality of a shared space "out of place." They've felt effortless and energizing, drawing new musical gestures from all participants. Especially cherished meetings have been with Jajouka master Bachir Attar, Japanese kotoist Michiyo Yagi, the Bedouin musicians Einad and Mhamad Synk, and a young Palestinian oudist, Hisham Abu Muatiqud.

Michiyo Yagi and I first met when she performed in an ensemble playing my composition *Spring & Neap* at the Tokyo Music Merge Festival in 1996. I was astounded at her inventiveness, power, and virtuosity. Her playing is technically advanced and in addition to her encyclopedic knowledge of Japanese music, her vocabulary includes "traditional" techniques from the Western avant-garde such as preparations and the use of electronics, as well as using objects as exciters and alternative bows that bring the koto into the realm of pure noise. She's a seasoned improviser who enters into any musical interaction with both humility and presence. After our initial introduction, we went on to perform frequently and record in duo as well as with other Japanese musicians.

A trip to Israel in May of 2000 to perform a concert with poet Ronny Someck in Tel Aviv led to the meeting with Muhammad Abu Ajaj, Mhamad and Einad Synk, and Muatiqud. Ze'ev Schlick of ZuTa Music had the idea of bringing me down to the Negev to collaborate with some Bedouin and Israeli musicians. The morning after my arrival, we picked up an acoustic guitar from a used-instrument shop—a Canadian-made Horabe that sounded and played surprisingly well—then headed down to the desert near the Egyptian border. The ostensible leader of the musicians was Abu Ajaj, an oud player and leading teacher of Arab classical music (Simon Shaheen is one of his more renowned students).

We rendezvoused with Amir, an Israeli lawyer who'd been involved for many years as an advocate for the Bedouin near the kibbutz on which he was raised. The Bedouin leader of the Azazme tribe, Suleiman, considered Amir "a son" and allowed him to erect his own tent, where he lived part-time. Around 2 p.m., a few of the Bedouin arrived: Muhammed and the two *sumsumiya* players, Einad and Mhamad. They were from the Abu-Kaf tribe and lived in Embatin, a Bedouin village in the Negev.

The *sumsumiya* is a six-string zither or lyre made from whatever materials are at hand. I'd seen pictures of a full spectrum of "box zithers" in use across a wide swath of geography, from Sub-Saharan Africa and the Middle East to Indonesia. Among the Bedouin, the body may be plastic, metal recycled from tins or oil cans, or specially crafted by a luthier from wood. For strings, either communications wire from the army found in the desert or bicycle cable may be used. The sumsumiya is played with a soft plastic plectrum cut from water jugs. The name comes from "sesame": ancient versions of the instrument used strings made from sesame fibers. The strings can be tuned to different *maqamat*, scales associated with the various songs. The technique is based on a very fast, steady, and rhythmic right-hand strumming; the left hand stops and unstops the strings at various nodal points. The result is a combination of groove, drone, melody, and chordal movement. The effect is hypnotic; revealed in the sound is the wide horizon of the desert, its space and light, drama and shadow, with neither beginning nor end.

The Bedouin all seemed to have cell phones, indispensable in the desert (especially as smuggling over the somewhat porous border between Egypt and Israel was a major source of income), but at that time far from ubiquitous in NYC. The first to arrive called the others, and within two hours there were about twelve musicians in the tent, playing continuously: five sumsumiyas, two oudists, a rebab player, a few drummers, and one musician playing the *azzam*, or "inviter," a large mortar and pestle used to grind coffee beans, with a steady syncopated rhythm that accompanied the drone of the sumsumiyas. The rhythm of the azzam is the signifier for a party and what better way to enhance partying then with little cups of strong Arabic coffee, served with lots of sugar.

Songs build, or rather get deeper, as they progress. One may last for fifteen or twenty minutes. They often have unison chanted lyrics over simple chordal patterns, which are woven into intricate tapestries by the sumsumiyas. The oud commonly doubles the main melody and provides additional ornamentation. I try my hand at playing the sumsumiya, with limited success. With the guitar I'm able to find various ways to join in on the Bedouin songs, providing drones, doubling melodies, or playing obligati, even chord progressions. My straight soprano sax also works well, its nasal sound emulating the rebab. Throughout the day we hear the muffled roars and booms of the munitions of the Israeli army on maneuvers a few miles away. Stepping out of the tent at one point, I'm shocked to see Israeli paratroopers jumping from low-flying transport planes perhaps half a kilometer away. A camel browses peacefully nearby.

Later, another oudist arrives, Hisham Abu Muatiqud. Perhaps seventeen, he lives in Jordan and is in the camp visiting family. He's an incredibly inventive virtuoso. At one point we engage in an extended duet, getting hotter and wilder by the minute. Muatiqud makes full use of a variety of extended techniques I'd never before heard on the oud; we play storms of tremolos, clouds, lightning-fast atonal flurries, and dense granulations. We exchange addresses, as I would very much like to release a recording of his. Later, there's a dinner break to eat hummus, chopped vegetable salads, grilled chicken, and the delicious pita bread handmade by the wife of Suleiman. Then back to the music. Around 10:30 p.m. the Bedouin suddenly all leave, quickly and with little ceremony.

I had also met and rehearsed with two young Israeli percussionists and though they spoke English perfectly, there was little in the way of fruitful communication. Our improvising together seemed without center, without meeting place. I suggested some approaches for our playing but whether out of contrarianism or lack of interest, they consistently did the opposite and little progress was made. Though we met the next day in a recording studio in Tel Aviv, those sessions yielded nothing of worth, only a few hours of frustration.

The day after this minor debacle I returned to the studio, this time with Einad and Mhamad and their sumsumiyas. They had never been in a recording studio before but were immediately comfortable with the use of monitoring and concepts of microphone placement. We dug right in, recording about 75 minutes of material in a variety of flavors. No evaluation distance was necessary; I was immediately and incredibly excited by what we'd recorded. Hearing the detail of the sumsumiya recorded with good microphones was astounding, as the richness of the overtone fields enhanced the feeling of timelessness I'd first experienced on hearing them. I took the recordings back to New York to mix at Studio zOaR for release by ZuTa.

Back in time to 1990: I was in preparation for upcoming European tours with Carbon. The personnel went into flux and the new touring band included Zeena Parkins, bassist Marc Sloan, David Weinstein on keyboard and sampler, and Blind Idiot God drummer Ted Epstein. For these tours we would be joined by Bachir Attar, the leader of the Master

Musicians of Jajouka. Attracted by its aura of psychedelic exoticism, I had picked up a copy of *Brian Jones Presents the Pipes of Pan at Jajouka* on its release in 1971. Instantly enthralled by its intensity and otherworldly ambience, I incorporated this village music of the Moroccan Atlas Mountains into the soundtrack of my college years at Cornell and Bard. This record led me to further explorations of Moroccan music, including the Paul Bowles collections on Folkways and recordings on the Lyrichord and UNESCO labels.

In the early 1980s, my friend Charity Martin, a San Franciscan, budding ethnomusicologist, and clarinetist—and identical-twin sister of Hope—told me tales of her travels to Jajouka and encounters with Bachir Attar, the young leader of the musicians, a multi-instrumentalist who revered Brian Jones and Jimi Hendrix. In 1988, I again heard talk of Bachir from another friend, New York photographer Cherie Nutting. She'd met Bachir in Tangier through Bowles, and now told me he would soon be visiting NYC. (They later married.) When he arrived, we first met at Cherie's for dinner, a relaxed occasion with lots of wine and laughter. Slim, sporting a trim mustache and 'fro, Bachir was not tall but had a large aura. He was an excellent cook and made most of what we ate that evening: fish, couscous, aubergines. Next he visited my studio just to drink coffee and listen to music: North African records, Ornette (whom Bachir played with in Jajouka), Korean *samul nori*, country blues. I played him some of what I was doing with Carbon and we began to play together, finding our way to that "outside" place—sessions that led to gigs as an informal duo at CBGB and the Knitting Factory.

Bachir taught me some of the Jajouka rhythms, which I translated to programs on a Roland TR707 drum machine—a gadget he loved because it could relentlessly repeat a pattern without the variations spontaneously invented by human drummers, which he found a distraction. Philosophically speaking, I was diametrically opposed to this view, as I thrived on the continual elaboration of rhythm as produced by my many favorite drummers. But I was keen to find my way in to the music of Jajouka. I wanted to hear and make the music as Bachir might and if this meant deferring to Bachir's judgment, so be it.

In 1989, the aptly named Enemy Records asked us to make a record, which we did very quickly under low-budget conditions. We experimented with sounds and textures in our attempt to create a fictional locus halfway between NYC and Jajouka. I made extensive use of the EBow on guitar to create sustained textures, over which Bachir would improvise, in the *maqam* section of each piece—a free-time intro where material for later exploration is introduced. The EBow was also used to generate a massive, dark, and salty-sweet sound for solos, reminiscent of both a bowed string and the *rhaita*, the double-reed horn. With the slab, I could create sounds reminiscent of both a bass and a *bendir*, the Moroccan frame drum. Jane Tomkiewicz added some actual *bendir* as well. Bachir played *rhaita*, *lira* (a type of wooden flute), and the *guimbri*, a lute with a goatskin soundboard. With this project he had his first taste of overdubbing and got it immediately, building up multiple tracks of rhaita to recreate the sound of the larger ensemble of the village. The record, titled *In New York*, has now been reissued as *Jajouka New York*.

Bachir joined Carbon for our European tours in October and November of 1990 and again in January of 1991. Repeatedly, the band would build up a seething intensity under Bachir's magnificent and relentless rhaita solos. At the end of our fall '91 tour, we were scheduled to fly back to NYC on Pan Am from Frankfurt just before Thanksgiving. Things were heating up in the Middle East prior to the first Gulf War; security was tense and paranoia the rule at airports. Arriving at the Frankfurt Flüghafen, we entered the security lines at check-in, where we were separated and asked the ritual questions. I had to supply Bachir's interrogator with our tour itineraries, posters, newspaper previews and reviews, hotel and travel receipts, and all other related documents. As he carefully perused our materials, we waited for nearly 30 minutes with no results. Our group was taking up all four of the security stations and behind us an impatient crowd was rumbling; the flight would be departing in less than one hour and everyone was determined to be on it.

Frustrated at the inaction and getting anxious, I beckoned over two stern-looking security officers who seemed to be supervisors and asked what the problem was. After a moment's consultation, they told me that since Bachir was an Arab he couldn't be cleared for the flight, and therefore none of us could fly. I pointed out that he was not Arab but Maghrebi and had a passport from Morocco, a "friendly" nation. No go. I then added that Bachir was a USA resident with a Green Card, married to an American citizen whom I had known for years. No go. Dumbfounded, I asked if we were all expected to spend the rest of our lives in the Frankfurt airport. Shrug. I then stated that Bachir was an internationally renowned musician who had played with the Rolling Stones, and... Before I could finish, the security guards looked at each other and said, "The Rolling Stones?....Okay, you can fly!"

XI.

Lines, Planes, Jews

Why should artificial divisions between the various disciplines of musical theory and practice be enforced or even exist? Music is one translation of the Inner Ear; at the core of the creative impulse, Mind. Mind is flexible, porous, quicksilver, open. Whether improvising or creating through-composed works, I always hope that they can be heard without the framing effects of preconceptions regarding ensemble, setting, even dress on stage. How do we listen or compose with the spontaneity and unpredictability that might be present in an improvisation? When improvising, can the music display the inevitability and arc of a well-structured composition? Will listeners treat music heard in a rock club with the same attention and gravity they might bestow in a concert hall? Can they feel the music in their guts when sitting in one of those red plush seats beloved of Morty?

As the Inner Ear gathers its abilities, these questions may become moot. Sonic strategies become well-worn pathways, deeply ingrained and even unconscious. Work in any realm will inform and feed back to the others without restriction or limitation. The essence of composing for me is to take the creative impulse within the Inner Ear and translate the output into the truest form of that impulse in whatever medium. Inextricably linked to this process is the notion of the synesthetic: the output may smear across the full frequency spectrum of sensations and perceptions. Hearing the sound generates the score that triggers the taste that catalyzes the music. Or the reverse. Mind doesn't make walls or insist on rigid tactics. Translating Inner to Outer might mean picking up an instrument and improvising; it might mean meticulously placing every element in a fully notated score for orchestra. It might not even lead to the making of music at all. As I developed strategies, my aesthetic sense coalesced around certain gestures with which I found deep resonance. I tried to resist defining my work so completely that it would be recognizable as a style. A danger to be avoided: the fine line between personal style and self-parody.

As much as I considered myself a composer, after my time in Buffalo I adamantly refused to write for other musicians. Instead, I held to the idea that music should be created to be performed only by its composer. I must thank flutist Barbara Held for changing my mind. In the fall of 1983, she requested a solo piece from me and when I expressed my thoughts on being a composer (or not!), she explained that a composer hears the production of sound in her own unique way and that interpreters may be the best, perhaps even the only ones who can properly bring those sounds to life. In response, I composed *VX* for her using only simple sixteenth-note rhythms, plus the overtone series of the lowest C and D on the instrument. The score also required that a contact microphone be affixed to the body of the flute, with the signal amplified by a guitar amplifier in front of which is placed a snare drum with the snare unmuted. By this means, the physical action of playing the flute transforms the flutist into a percussionist producing a duet of upper-partial sweeps and a web of polyrhythmic noise.

Around the time of the recording of the Carbon album *Fractal* in 1985, David Soldier told me of his decision to start a string quartet and asked if I would write a piece for the group. By happy coincidence, Paul Dunkel, then associate conductor of the American Composers Orchestra, contacted me in January 1986 about a commissioned piece for the orchestra. I had been contemplating the application of my Fibonacci-series work to an ensemble of strings, essentially re-orchestrating ideas evolved on the guitar. The two pieces would be closely related and I began work first on *Tessalation Row* for the Soldier String Quartet, then on *Re/Iterations* for the ACO. Both pieces use the Fibonacci series to generate tunings, rhythms, and forms. All pitches are played on open strings (tuned to 1/1, 3/2, 5/3, 8/5 with C = 1/1), a mix of open strings and overtones, or only overtones. I created a tablature to transmit the instructions to the players, with the modules in the score giving exact rhythms, timing, and the fundamental pitch. At times the players must loop overtone melodies, their actions moderated by a number indicating loop length. I felt that to maintain the essence of the piece, the score should not use standard notation. My main concern was to create a clear sonic identity: in every performance, the composition would be the same length and have exactly the same structure, though the sonic flux and internal detail could vary greatly.

Having seen a Carbon performance, Dunkel requested that I compose a work in which I would also perform, preferably with the drummers I was currently working with. In its original conception, *Re/Iterations* would be a concerto of sorts for three soloists—percussionists Bobby Previte and Charles K. Noyes, and myself on double-neck guitar/bass—and string orchestra (fourteen violins, four violas, four cellos, two contrabasses). The sole performance, at Merkin Hall, NYC in June of 1986, revealed both potential and problems. The orchestra was not overly receptive to any composition that required *scordatura,* let alone a recalibration of score-reading skills. Even though the new tunings for the strings were well within the range of accepted practice, the players refused to consider them for their own instruments, instead insisting that cheap substitute instruments be rented for them. Perhaps the greatest issue with the full-orchestra version of *Re/Iterations* was amplification, or the lack thereof. Though not at all keen on the idea of competing in volume with an electric guitarist and not just one, but two drummers, the players seemed to find the obvious solution—amplifying their own instruments—equally abhorrent.

As to my score, Dunkel was sympathetic but made it very clear that the orchestra would not even consider learning my tablature. Instead, he took it upon himself to create a version of the score in standard notation. This was an admirable gesture and made the performance possible, though I felt that it did not completely capture the intended sonics of the piece. The budget allowed only one dress rehearsal for the concert and to my amused dismay, the entire orchestra showed up with large wads of cotton overflowing from their ears. Since the density and transients produced by drums and electric guitar (even a just-intoned one) would likely mask the delicate "ghost instruments" produced by the difference-tone effects of the orchestra, the drummers and I limited our dynamic range so as never to overpower the strings. This translated to *pianissimo!* Ironically,

Re/Iterations was the quietest piece on the program and our restraint in the service of transparency of sound resulted in what I would consider to be a bloodless simulacrum of the work as intended. The audience response was still extremely positive, but after the applause abated the first violinist remarked in a stage whisper, "Why didn't he just ask us to stomp on our instruments?"—a rather tempting gesture to include in the event that I'm ever commissioned again by the ACO.

The premiere of *Tessalation Row* by the Soldier String Quartet took place later that month at Columbia University's Miller Theater and was much more felicitous. Here the acoustics favored the unamplified quartet and this realization of the piece felt completely successful. The quartet also performed a piece by legendary producer Teo Macero and I was thrilled to meet him. In the fall of 1986, I brought the Quartet (augmented by bassist Ratzo Harris) to OAO Studio to record, with Previte and Noyes joining us on the second day. Two takes of *Tessalation Row* were committed to tape, with excellent results. The instruments were recorded acoustically as well as with contact mikes processed through Tube Screamers, distortion devices beloved of guitarists that enhance the production of even harmonics. To record *Re/Iterations*, the quartet overdubbed themselves twice over the master take; the bass did the same. Thanks to the slight delay in attack times and to variations in the strings, the multiple tracks of acoustically miked and direct electronic sounds combine to give the effect of a much larger ensemble. The next day, the drummers and I overdubbed over the rough mix of the orchestra. Unfortunately, even in the controlled situation of the recording studio, I felt that the subtle acoustic phenomena produced by the strings were masked by the transients produced by guitar and drums. The original conception, it seemed, was simply not viable, and the final master take of *Re/Iterations* consisted of strings alone.

Also recorded at this session were *Digital*, *Diurnal*, and *Ringtoss*. *Digital* is an orchestration of music that was conceived and first performed by myself on prepared guitar. The instruments were prepared with flat strips of spring steel woven through the strings near the bridge, with piezo contact microphones mounted on the bridges. Six unison rhythms serve as connection points; the players improvise between them, always tapping on the strings with the fingers of both hands. The only strict requirement is that the ensemble must groove. The combined effect of the preparation, tapping, and amplification creates the sound of a mega-*mbira*. In my opinion, the best performances of the piece have been by the Soldier Quartet, though quite a credible version was performed by the

Smith Quartet at the London Musicians Collective Experimental Music Festival in May 1993. *Digital* was also recorded by the Kronos Quartet, though their interpretation diverged widely from the intent of the piece. In a surprising variation, Kazue Sawai's all-koto ensemble Koto Vortex performed *Digital* in 1992, preparing the instruments with wooden rods.

The simple scoring construction set I'd made on my Atari 1040ST and used to create the score of *Larynx* was used as well for *Hammer Anvil Stirrup*, an algorithmic piece commissioned by the 1988 Ultra Music Meeting in Pori, Finland for the Avanti String Quartet. This work is based on a single core rhythm used as an ostinato, as well as on sets of pitches that may be used by the players explicitly as foreground, as background for a variety of operations, and as source material for improvising. Each section has a simple iconic instruction such as "drone," "groove," or "canon," sometimes layered with improvised "pop-outs." In certain sections the ostinato can be transformed by adding notes to create phasing effects. The instruction "shuffle" appears in one section, not for playing the blues but to allow players to bring in any and all previous elements of the score. I illustrated each of the operations with a graphic depiction.

The next scored pieces were written during January 1991, as the Gulf War unfolded. Though there was no conscious link to the horror show revealed on televisions everywhere, one cannot discount the subliminal effect. *Shapeshifters* could easily serve as soundtrack to a vampire or were-creature film; not coincidentally, I felt that the pretenses used to rush to war could very well have been the work of were-humans, their brains and hearts replaced by alien lizard organs designed to suck the lifeblood from humanity. Mostly through-composed, the piece is defined principally by hocketing and by a melody that creates a spiny thicket of verticality when the players, using a simple set of instructions, throw the unison theme out of unison and into a varying phase relationship. Improvisation appears briefly in the form of "pop-outs" over certain sections of the written material. *Twistmap*, also mostly through-composed, is a score designed to guide the quartet overland through rough terrain. Hocketing, overtone grooving, and explicit melodies appear and evaporate. In both of these works, the overall approach is again that of a clear overriding identity with the internal detail varying from one performance to the next, the Inner Ear dictating instruction sets rather than black dots.

By the end of 1991, relentless gigging gave me the funds to finally upgrade to an Apple computer and I began using SoundTools software on a Mac IIx, a huge and heavy machine operating with a massive 16MB of RAM and a processor running at the blinding speed of 16MHz. I purchased an external hard drive as well, a weighty metal chest with a 640MB capacity, enough to hold an entire audio CD! Working with SoundTools (later upgraded to Pro Tools) made for a vast improvement in my work flow. This was a self-contained and efficient system—a far cry from my first attempts at computer music, using the Music 4 programming language, in studies with John Myhill in the back in Buffalo. At that point in its development, Music 4 allowed one to create instruments, a relatively simple but tedious process. After writing out the code specifying every parameter of an instrument, one would punch the code into cards line by line on a hippo-sized terminal. The completed box of cards would be transported across town to the mainframe residing in the computer center on the new Amherst campus. After a number of hours, or more likely the next day, one might receive a digital tape—or, more commonly, a "bug report" listing all of the places where the code was faulty. Once the code was debugged and a digital tape was in hand, it would be brought to the chemistry department on the main campus in North Buffalo to be run through one of the two digital-to-analog converters then residing in New York State, and finally transferred to an analog tape that could then be brought back to the music department for auditioning. Frequently, if one was successful, the results were a few seconds of hum or a simple tone or click. That this process could create sound at all was remarkable, but it seemed to me there was quite a distance yet, both sonically and temporally, to the sounds I was hoping to produce. It was all there in my imagination but not in the grubby reality. These were the pioneering days of computer music and incredibly exciting in the abstract, but because of my own impatience I couldn't muster the enthusiasm necessary to stay the course. "Just give me a guitar and a fuzzbox!" was my battle cry then—I would check in a few years later and see how things were going.

With my new setup, already obsolete in 1991 but still a great leap beyond my Atari, I could hear the fruits of my labors relatively quickly if not immediately. With the processor speeds of my setup, rendering a pitch shift to a 60-second soundfile might take twenty minutes with the computer's little brain doggedly gnashing code, chunk by 8-bit chunk. As these rendering breaks usually meant running to the stove and putting up a pot of espresso, a major project would find me even more caffeinated than usual.

The first composition to be realized in this work mode was *Cryptid Fragments*. A menu of sonic gestures was created and the wonderfully talented twins, cellist Margaret Parkins and violinist Sara Parkins, were recorded to DAT tape performing multiple iterations of them. These gestures included some pitched material but also made extensive use of preparations and bowing with metal springs and thin wooden dowels. The results were then dumped into the computer and subjected to a series of processing strategies by which the raw string sounds would be transformed—expanded or compressed in time, transposed (sometimes by multiple octaves), reversed, chopped, merged, radically equalized. Samples could then be sent back out to hardware processors for further twisting using distortion, delay lines, reverberation, or modulation and then returned to the computer for more of the same. My work model was derived from the noble techniques of *musique concrète,* which involved much cutting of tape—a process I greatly enjoyed delving into in the 1970s and early '80s. Sequences of processed samples could thus be rendered into cells that might themselves be further processed. Cells (and cells-of-cells (and cells-of-cells-of cells...)) would be nested and sequenced in a fractal process that eventually crystallized into its ultimate form—approximately 100 hours of work yielding the seventeen minutes of the finished piece.

In other ways, too, 1991 was an extremely important year. At the farewell concert for the band The Ordinaires on May 6, I ran into Rosalie Sendelbach, the publicist for Enemy Records. As the set was winding down, she dragged me off to a party. Walking in the door of the loft, I was introduced to a radiant woman: Rosalie's roommate, Janene Higgins. Her eyes were alive and filled with intelligence and humor. I was thunderstruck by a powerful recognition: she could very well be the person with whom I was meant to share my life. She joined Rosalie and me for drinks later that evening. The next day, I left for a three-week tour in Europe and she remained in my thoughts. On my return, Rosalie—in an obvious but welcome ploy—mentioned that Janene was a graphic designer and perhaps I could hire her for my next album. We began to meet to discuss the artwork for *Twistmap.* The meetings became more frequent and, most happily, veered from the specific task at hand and toward our future together.

Fast forward: when, in 2007, Janene and I decided to get married, we discussed how to have a ritual event for our families without bringing in religious components that were spurious to our existence. It was a short leap from the first thought of how a ceremony could be conducted to inviting the Master of Conduction, Butch Morris, to be the presiding entity. To our delight Butch readily agreed, and Janene worked on a text with him. In his inimitable manner, he treated the rehearsal with both extreme seriousness and great levity. The wedding itself was perhaps the only time I ever saw Butch the least bit nervous before a performance. He officiated with great love, and we cherish that day.

Rosalie would often hold gatherings at her apartment for Enemy artists and a loose constellation of friends and colleagues. In addition to her wide circle of associates from both upper and lower echelons of New York society, the musicians in attendance would often include Kelvyn Bell, Jean-Paul Bourelly, Melvin Gibbs, Gary Lucas, Peter Scherer, Arto Lindsay, Yuka Honda, Chris Haskett, Dougie Bowne, and Sonny Sharrock. Sonny was quite the joker and a bottomless fount of surreal stories, especially of his Harlem gigging days in the late '60s. (If Chicken In A Basket is ever revived, do not patronize it if you value your life!) When the hilarity reached critical mass, we might pile into a taxi and head over to where one or the other of our bands was performing: venues such as the Cat Club, the Gas Station/Space 2B, Sybarite, Tramps, Wetlands, CBGB, or S.O.B.'s. We were absolutely floored and saddened at Sonny's sudden death in 1994. The funeral in Ossining was a convocation of friends and musicians there to see Sonny off. Unfortunately, none of Sonny's music was played; instead, the minister led a "light jazz" combo. It was an open-casket funeral and Sonny, lying prone and cradling his wine-red Les Paul Custom, looked so good that everyone half expected him to sit up and yell "Gotcha!"

The concept of "radical Jewish culture" was introduced to me in 1990 by the Jewish Austrian musicians and organizers Edek Bartz and Albert Misek. Partners in the neo-klezmer duo Geduldig und Thimann, they shared the notion of a contemporary Jewish music that looked both backward and forward and wanted to present a number of artists in a compilation that would examine this idea. For *A Haymish Groove*, we were invited to compose or arrange modern music inspired by klezmer. Included in the roster were Shelley Hirsch, Don Byron, Arnold Dreyblatt, Ruth Rubin, Guy Klucevsek, and Mark Feldman. For my piece, "Stetl Metl," based on a nigun of uncertain origin, I overdubbed multiple tracks of guitar and bass clarinet, together with intense Afro-metal drumming by Ted Epstein, then added soprano sax and an improvised solo.

I'd long felt that Jewish culture was, for the most part, inherently radical. Over the centuries, no matter how much they contributed to or were integrated into the societies in which they lived, Jews still faced severe limitations and prejudice, often expanding into pogroms and worse. Besides escape, the primary response was discussion, argument, and visionary art, philosophy, and science. So many Jews have been associated with revolutionary concepts—Baruch Spinoza, El Lissitzky, Walter Benjamin, Leon Trotsky, Frida Kahlo, Albert Einstein, to name just a few—that one might consider it a characteristic of the group. Was it necessary to wave a new radical flag? Weren't memory and current practice enough?

Late in 1991, an invitation from John Zorn to take part in a Festival of Radical Jewish Culture—a concert at New York's Knitting Factory, as well as some programs in Munich as part of a larger festival called The Art Projekt—resulted in my composition *Intifada*. Though quite opposed to John's idea of an ethnically identified cultural manifestation of this sort—and concerned that it was primarily about marketing—I nonetheless hoped that the events would reflect a wide range of thought and viewpoints and that my voice could be constructively added to the mix. I found it difficult to connect a self-consciously defined "radical Jewish culture" with such precursors—with which I actively and wholeheartedly sympathized—as the American civil-rights movement and the many ethnic liberation movements stemming from anti-colonialist battles in Africa and Central America. After the horrors of the Second World War and the Holocaust, Jewish economic and political power was greatly magnified in the United States and Europe and, needless to say, in the nuclear-armed state of Israel. The final and most salient factor for me was the reactionary specter of Zionism, radical only in the way that other nationalist and right-wing movements had been. What had begun supposedly as a utopian philosophy and inclusive blueprint for a greater socialistic Palestine quickly transformed into a viciously nationalistic and self-serving philosophy, replete with early definitions of ethnic cleansing implied by the quest for a Jewish state as presented in the writings of Weizmann and Herzl.

Haunted by my mother's experience of the Holocaust, my parents were determined that I should be fully immersed in the Jewish religion. Up through my high-school years I was forced to attend Hebrew school, where the prevailing narrative about Israel was swallowed without question by myself and my friends. Yet I considered myself an atheist well before my bar mitzvah, with much thanks due to a rabbi who presented his version of the philosophy of Baruch Spinoza as part of a discussion of the heretics who would destroy Judaism. My early interest in physics and math helped me to resonate with Spinoza's thoughts about the tight feedback loop between microscopic and macroscopic in the universe, the infinite in everything. Though rapidly on my way to eliminating organized religion from my life, I was still held hostage, twice a week, by those long afternoons studying the Hebrew language and arguing the fine points of a religion that I disbelieved.

In the media and in family discussions, Israel was always presented as a heroic victim suffering the ever-present threat of annihilation from its Arab neighbors. Though the threat was not unreal, there was more to the story, as I was to learn. During the 1967 war, Israeli victories were cheered in our public school class and I joined in. Yet an editorial by Edward Said, likening Israel's presence in the Middle East to that of the West in Vietnam, entered my thoughts and shook my beliefs. My doubts were amplified during the 1973 Arab-Israeli War and its aftereffects, the illegal Israeli annexation of the West Bank and subsequent suppression of the Palestinian people. I certainly couldn't deny the threat to Israel, but began to see Israeli policies in defiance of supposed global standards of human rights as hypocritical, to say the least, and as continually and cynically exacerbating the problem. Another factor of great importance was Israel's aiding and abetting of the apartheid regime of South Africa. Finally, there was the matter of the unholy alliance between the Israel Defense Forces, American military contractors, and AIPAC.

At the first Radical Jewish Culture Festival at the Knitting Factory, the alliance with Zionism was made all too clear in much of the music and peripheral discussion. *Intifada* was written to be performed by the Soldier String Quartet augmented by my fretless guitar and B♭ clarinet. In this modular piece mixing full notation with instruction sets, each clearly defined section presents a sonic vignette with a different flavor and point of view. The work is not programmatic and has no text; it takes no sides and presents no argument but is more of an angry lament. At the premiere, I prefaced the performance with this statement: "As the son of a Holocaust survivor, I am appalled at the suffering inflicted on the Palestinian population by Israel's illegal and immoral occupation of the West Bank. Judaism, whether cultural, historical, or religious, is not Zionism." I finished these words to stony silence, except for one booming male voice hollering "What is it then? A bowl of fruit?" At the end of the performance, the audience response was split between cheers and jeers, strong applause competing with loud boos and indecipherable shouts. A number of people accosted me after the performance to express their deep disapproval of my words, though some added that they liked the music in spite of my politics. In the days that followed, a number of anonymous and thinly veiled threats of violence appeared on my answering machine and my picture was posted on extremist Zionist websites with a caption stating that I was a "self-hating Jew" who denied the Holocaust.

At the concert in Munich's Philharmonic Hall, *Intifada* was performed along with *Tessalation Row*. Here there was no tumultuous aftermath; the response was overwhelmingly positive, and thoughtful discussions of the Middle East situation and the relationship between art and politics filled the air and appeared in the press.

Dave Soldier approached me early in 1994 about composing a new piece for the Soldier String Quartet to be premiered at Ars Electronica Linz in October. This would be *X-Topia*. Once again, I judged that the proper strategy would be to create an open-ended composition based on a set of resources including simple instruction sets and four melodic sequences, all designed to provide a bubbling lattice of pitched sounds— fertile ground for real-time processing to be controlled using my Buchla Thunder. I couldn't separate my compositional ideas from the technical innovations of Thunder: it made a music possible that I could not realize in any other way. In four sections, the musicians would repeat a sequence while applying operations of elongation or transposition to selected target notes. These sections were separated by extended-time drones with pitches derived from the target pitches. Patches in the TSR-24 were created mixing multiple delays with filters, flanging, and multi-voice pitch-shifting, with the option of adding varying degrees of feedback. The system worked perfectly, except for one intermittent and unpredictably fatal glitch in the Buchla hardware. Thunder might run for weeks operating flawlessly but then it might suddenly crash, erasing everything loaded into its internal memory. I'd learned to program Thunder quickly but would never be fast enough to do it in the midst of a performance. My fallback was to load all of the Thunder patches as System Exclusive data in a sequencer running on my PowerBook 100, an early laptop. These data could then be loaded back into the controller, an approach that was slightly clumsy and too slow to be workable in the middle of a performance. As an alternative, I began running performances of the patch in the studio while recording all of the MIDI output into a software sequencer. With this backup in place, I could take comfort in having multiple levels of fail-safe for each performance. If Thunder failed, I could run a simulation of real-time manipulation by triggering strings of MIDI controller data using the QWERTY keyboard of the PowerBook.

By the late '90s I was doing most of my processing on the laptop using Max/MSP or SuperCollider and, for performance, various plug-ins within a sequencer, either Cubase or, later, Ableton Live. The GRM Tools were a favorite because of their range, power, and ability to make confoundingly beautiful sounds. I continued to use Thunder in the studio, but since I was already carrying a laptop and audio interface on tour, it made sense to leave Thunder and the rest of the hardware safely behind. In fact, the idea of touring only as a composer and not as a performer came into focus as a very appealing notion, especially as I was feeling the effects of years of dragging cases filled with equipment denser than osmium in and out of vans and cars, through airports and train stations, up and down stairs, and on and off stages of all sizes and shapes. I needed to shift into a mode where I would be seen primarily as a composer, and I couldn't do it without help.

XII.

Black Dots, Caves, and the Frozen Zone

Over the years, Bernd Leukert and I had remained in touch and early in 1996, in his capacity as director of *Ernste Musik* at the Hessischer Rundfunk, he contacted me about the possibility of a future Ensemble Modern concert in which they would perform *Tessalation Row*. I sent a copy of the original tablature score, to which Bernd responded with the suggestion that I rewrite it in traditional notation; the Ensemble would certainly prefer that and it would make rehearsals much more efficient. In making the new score, I was faced with the same problem I'd confronted with the American Composers Orchestra: how to maintain the sonic essence of the original compositional impulse without using my own specialized notation. As I began translating the score from my tablature, I began to breathe easier with the realization that neither the sound of the work, nor how the players or even the composer regarded it, would be in any way compromised by the notation and its inherent qualities. I had to laugh at my silliness—it was as if I'd thought a typewriter could limit what you could write with it.

The Tokyo Music-Merge festival in November of '96 provided the catalyst for my return to graphic notation. Asked to compose a piece for an ad hoc ensemble with thirteen players of varying music-reading abilities, I determined that a combination of conducting and a graphic score would be the best solution. To compose *Spring & Neap*, I scanned a curve from a graph of the tidal energy over a twelve-hour period in Tokyo Bay, and assigned parameters including relative pitch, density of activity, dynamics, even the shape of the players' featured solos: all would follow this curve. The group assembled to perform *Spring & Neap* featured some especially dynamic soloists, among them Zeena Parkins on Celtic harp, Michiyo Yagi on koto, Yumiko Tanaka and Yoshiki Fujio on shamisens, and Makoto Nomura on piano. All the players displayed a high level of attention, commitment, and skill.

Just before leaving for Tokyo, I'd received another call from Bernd informing me of a modest commission from the Hessicher Rundfunk for an orchestra piece to be performed by the Radio-Sinfonie-Orchester Frankfurt in 1998. This would be *Racing Hearts*, a piece that began life as an algorithmic score for a Bang On A Can Spit Orchestra concert at The Kitchen in December of 1994. Each section defined the transformation from a "horizontal" sound field of short cycles of hocketed rhythms into a "vertical" one based on extended durations of target pitches, harmonic saturation, and textural density. Each performance would provide a unique manifestation of the internal detail while retaining the overall identity, one of my longstanding strategies.

Over the course of 1997, between tours, studio work, and other composing projects, I was able to complete the score, a task rendered possible but also somewhat frustrating by the notation program Overture—an extremely useful tool for projects with smaller ensembles but one that lacked the flexibility and quality of output needed for an orchestral work. In this sixteen-minute version, I retained the overall architecture of the original with a series of modules, each presenting a process of hocketed pitches interlocking to form a horizontal melodic pattern that would lengthen and then blend to build into stacks of shimmering, harmonically ambiguous chords animated with difference tones. The score was sent to conductor Peter Rundel well in advance, and we were able to clarify some ambiguities and tweak a few problems by means of fax, phone, and even one face-to-face meeting at Frankfurt Airport, with both of us in transit to different destinations. *Racing Hearts* was programmed together with works by Heiner Goebbels, Michael Mantler, and Frank Zappa for this November 1998 concert. The score endured my last-minute adjustments at the dress rehearsal but the premiere in the Sendesaal crackled with energy, the excellent acoustics of the hall enhancing the music.

My meeting with Rundel at FRA occurred as I was changing planes en route from NYC to Ljubljana, Slovenia for participation in a new film project by American director Michael Benson. His documentary *Predictions Of Fire*, about the Neue Slowenische Kunst movement centered on the band Laibach, had met with very positive critical response and illuminated many of the factors that would lead to the dismantling of Yugoslavia and the attendant ethnic wars. This new film, *More Places Forever*, would be less a narrative than an open-access discourse about a number of overlapping topics, form and function linked. Prime focus would be on the intersection of art, science, and commodification, but running through the film was a discourse on dislocation, whether physical or abstract, and how it may both positively and negatively affect perception of self and the world. That first evening in Ljubljana, Michael filled me in on the details over dinner, explaining how he wanted to shoot me playing in the Postojna caves on the border with Italy, about an hour's drive.

The next day, we arrive around 5 p.m. and descend for about fifteen minutes into the cave, the crew carrying my equipment down wooden ramps laid on the stony pathways. We have to snake our way around the thick power cables running from the generators up top. The caves are absolutely spectacular, rendered more so by the lighting that has been installed for the shoot. Occupying a rather conspicuous place in the main cave is a huge state-of-the-art remote-control boom on which is mounted a broadcast quality video camera owned by TV Slovenia, one of the sponsors of the film. A Fender Twin Reverb amp has also been brought down and is nestled between a pair of stocky stalagmites. We set up my pedals on a wooden board placed on some layered carpets, on which I also stand. I have the new solid-body eight-string and my straight soprano sax. I'll be playing over Tectonics rhythm tracks so there are speakers for monitoring. I've prepared a variety of grooves as well as the drums to the tune "Krkd," built on drum loops created by Frank Rothkamm. All will be played back from my laptop running a Max patch that, in addition to playing back the multiple layers of grooves, allows me to scratch samples using the trackpad velcroed to the body of the guitar. We spend most of this first night tweaking the sounds as well as hunting out and killing hum from ground loops. It's damp and 50 degrees F. in the cave, so we have to go above ground every hour or so to warm up at the canteen, where we are refreshed by the warm night air and espresso fortified with locally made grappa, potent stuff. Around 5 a.m. we begin to film some takes.

Ironically, this very moist environment features a very dry sound. Though "cavernous," the complex interior structure dampens most reverberations, so I have to rely on the spring reverb in the amp to give the guitar sound some life. Once we're running, time flies. By sunrise at 6:30, it's quitting time and we drive back into town. My hotel room has thick purple drapes and I feel like Nosferatu as I draw them closed against the sun and go to bed. I rise around 2 in the afternoon for breakfast or dinner, whatever it can be called: numerous cups of espresso and the hotel's specialty of thick buckwheat blini with salmon caviar. At 5 p.m. we return to Postojna. We work all night for the next two nights and get a number of useable takes, playing with the grooves as well as performing some free improvisations. When we wrap, we're happily loopy from our work of these nights (not to mention the canteen's refreshments). My last night in Ljubljana is spent giving a solo Tectonics concert at the K4 cultural center and I return to New York the next morning.

Sidetracked by many intervening events, in April of 1999 the Ensemble Modern would finally perform *Tessalation Row*. After all of my trepidation at rewriting the piece in traditional notation, hearing the Ensemble tear into it at the first rehearsal was exciting and liberating. With an early landing at Frankfurt after a red-eye from JFK, I was met at the airport by Clair Lüdenbach, radio journalist, old friend, and partner of Bernd. She whisked me to their flat for *Frühstück,* after which Bernd and I, score and parts in hand, headed to the Sendesaal of the HR.

The beauty of standard notation is that it's almost universally understood and practiced. The long-running issue for me has been how to bend it to do the things that will get the musicians to make the music I want to hear. It's like hacking a synthesizer with an antediluvian operating system: if you can tweak the code well enough and put the black dots in the correct place, the device will do what is required. In this case, it meant adding icons for the operations of open-string, overtones, and mixed fingering, as well as bowing location and direction and looping numbers.

Unlike the ACO, the string players from the Ensemble had absolutely no objections to my proposed *scordatura.* Nor did they object to amplification; in fact, they welcomed it. The Ensemble had preferred that *Tessalation Row* be conducted and Kasper de Roo was engaged. Over the arc of the rehearsal, we adjusted some performance parameters and then added the element of sound modification, with the tonmeister of the group mixing their lavalier microphones through a subtle distortion patch in his processing rack that would add even harmonics and two milliseconds of delay, both contributing to a rich and animated sound. The piece sounded fine acoustically but the processing added just the perfect touch of hyperreality.

The performance went exceedingly well, as did another (sans conductor) at Lincoln Center later that year where I met pianist Jenny Lin, a virtuosic and forward-thinking player and soon to become a frequent collaborator. She requested a piece from me, which I finally composed in 2004 during a brief teaching residency at Dartmouth University. This was *Oligosono*, twenty minutes of permutations of short fragments inspired by genetic processes. The title means "a few sounds" and indeed, the piece recombines sonic cells in a number of sequences, using a variety of extended techniques. It's an extremely demanding piece requiring great velocity and endurance, perfectly suited to Jenny's talents.

I will always feel deep gratitude to Bernd for believing in me as a composer and for putting the resources of the Hessischer Rundfunk to work on my behalf. Both *Tessalation Row* and *Racing Hearts* had been recorded for broadcast by the HR and Bernd had the idea of making a trilogy, with a new piece for the Radio-Sinfonie-Orchester Frankfurt to be conducted by Peter Rundel at the legendary Internationale Ferienkurse für Neue Musik at Darmstadt in 2002. The three pieces would then be released together on the HR's label, hrMedia. This news was both inspiring and daunting. In the music departments at Bard and Buffalo, Darmstadt was spoken of by all composers in hushed tones, as if it were the most sacred of pilgrimage sites. The deadline for the score would be January of 2002, plenty of time to listen deeply inside and hear what it might be.

This wonderful news came at a time of hectic touring, thanks to a number of interrelated projects and the constructive actions of a new booking agent. Throughout 2000 to 2001, it seemed as if I was commuting to Europe nearly every week, to say nothing of concert tours in Japan, Turkey, and Israel. There was no chance of falling into a rut, as every week brought something different—Tectonics solo, Terraplane, GTR OBLQ; the cooperative jazz group Oblique Ah Blue with Billy Hart, Arthur Blythe, Oliver Lake, and Santi Debriano; a panoramic array of duo concerts and recording sessions with such wonderful musicians as cellist Frances-Marie Uitti, guitarists Nels Cline and Marc Ribot, violinist Mari Kimura, cellist Diedre Murray, komungo player Jin Hi Kim, harpist Zeena Parkins, and

Carlos Soul Slinger. To top it off, I began composing and recording the score for Dael Orlandersmith's wrenchingly powerful Pulitzer Prize-nominated play, *Yellowman*. Rather than fragmenting and dissipating my creative energies, I found that I was further energized by these radical shifts in compositional perspective. Each new project was informed and enhanced by the others, another type of feedback loop.

Carlos was organizing Ecosystem 1.0, a marathon rave in Manaus in the Brazilian Amazon, as a benefit for Greenpeace and he invited me to take part. My solo Tectonics set took place on a stage set up on a tiny island in a lake with the audience mostly on the shore. The international cast of artists featured many DJs, but also musicians representing each of the regions of Brazil, with their unique grooves and sonic flavor. Carlos and I did a long jungle set on another stage for thousands of dancing revelers. There was no sleep during the 30 hours I was in Manaus—just about the same amount of time I spent flying there and back. The festival was filled with incredible music and company, great food, and nonstop espresso and guarana, a local herbal stimulant usually mixed with fruit juice. Returning to NYC after Manaus afforded me time to complete some studio projects and then head to Warsaw with Carlos to perform a club concert. We returned to New York on Sunday, 9/9, flying just past the World Trade Center towers as we made our approach into Newark Airport.

On the evening of the 10th I received a call from Patrik Landolt, freshly landed from Zurich: we would meet for breakfast the next morning at an East Village cafe. Janene headed to midtown early for work and I started the day with some coffee, planning to take care of correspondence before meeting Patrik. Unable to get online around 8:45, I called the telephone company and was told that some of the lines were down; the representative had heard that "a plane had hit a building" and it might have affected service. Hearing and seeing our landlord talking animatedly with some people on the sidewalk, I joined them and found out what had happened—and that another plane had just hit the second WTC tower. I ran over to the cafe, occasionally looking back over my shoulder in disbelief at the massive roiling cloud filling the air, my mind filling with dark thoughts of a potentially huge loss of life.

After breakfast watching the cafe's television, Patrik and I returned to the apartment, spending the day in front of the tube, drinking never-ending pots of coffee, trying to glean useful bits of info from the noise, discussing theories. I was able to reach Christian Marclay around 11; he and Lydia lived quite near to the towers but they were fine, she uptown at work and he preparing to go to safer quarters. Over and over we watched the shocking footage of the planes hitting the towers, the images burning indelibly in the brain. Bits of news about the Pentagon hit and Pennsylvania crash would work their way in to the mix. Panix, my ISP, was down as their dialups were in a building quite near the WTC site, but I was able to log on to AOL for email and get news direct from the AP feed, as well as take in network and CNN blather. Janene finally made it back home in the late afternoon, easing that worry. The area of lower Manhattan below Canal Street was to be evacuated and the area between Canal and 14th Street, where we live, was closed to all but residents. This was dubbed the Frozen Zone by the news and police checkpoints were set up to screen people trying to enter.

As day turned to evening, the brain was numbed and twisted. "President Bush" (I'd always had a difficult time writing or even saying it without air quotes or gagging) spoke at 8:30 p.m. in a typically inarticulate and uninformative manner, often invoking "God" and "prayer." My thoughts swirled around the notion of blame, of punishment, around the use of fear to control and crush the creative spirits of people everywhere. Self-interest, greed, and lust for power are served by state and individual terror, with innocent civilians manipulated and victimized. The self-righteousness of the West continues to amaze me. As a Jew and the son of Holocaust survivors, I must protest. But how? To whom? It continues to bring up deep questions of our role as artists, as humans.

Wednesday, September 12: too much television, too much web, too much coffee. Walking around the Frozen Zone, I'm struck by the eerie tranquility, a slightly subdued party atmosphere. When encountering friends, there are inevitably deep hugs—we're happy to see each other alive, to be together somehow in this place and time. The cafes are all full, with long queues for seats. People eating, drinking, laughing, kids playing. The air is filled with a slight haze: not so visible, but it stings the eyes, smells of burnt electrical apparatus, wood, paint, we don't want to think what else.

I return to the studio late that morning with the idea of working, but tempted by paralysis. I open up the score template that I'd prepared for the Hessischer Rundfunk commission. A field of empty staves greets me, daring me to take part in something so trivial as composing music when the world around me is crumbling and burning. Somehow, though, nothing makes more sense right now than despoiling that whiteness with some black dots… then more and more. The sound begins to form, perhaps an alarm, an interruption. A title appears: *Calling*. I collect thoughts and references: A transmission, an infection, an inheritance. The Old English battle herald, *hildecalla*. The Old Church Slavonic *glasu*, voice. A challenge, a censure. The characteristic note or cry of an animal. A demand for an investigation. Testify. Radio waves or over a wire. Signals across synaptic contacts are essentially pheromonal. To predict. Convocation. To charge, to act, to announce.

While the lure of the internet keeps pulling me out to the consensus reality, the new work sustains me. So many emotional states run through me as I sit staring at the screen, mostly centering on fury and grief. Dare I hope that this music might engender something positive? I work on into the evening, alternating composing with small doses of news. Patrik was supposed to return to Switzerland today but is now stranded in Manhattan until commercial flights resume. Janene and I meet him for dinner; we must go to the "border" with our credentials to escort him into our own little soft internment center.

When the adrenaline, fear, anger, and disbelief of those first days wore off, the sadness hit. Now, a time for coolness, objectivity, analysis—which yielded a fresh anger. Gazing out the window of my studio, I could hear and see the F16s patrolling the City, enforcing the protection of the Great Leader, here to inspect the Front, here to act in pious pretension, beating his chest and proclaiming that he will banish "evil" from the world. Astonishingly, Bush uses the word "crusade," which only a boor could employ without any understanding of its historical resonance. Bush's presence truly signifies that New York, our city, our place of life and work, has been conquered; it is now Occupied Territory, captured by America. The occupation began over a decade ago and was, at first, relatively peaceful: mouse ears on Time Square, mall-ing and McDonaldization. But the stage was set: New York City, hated by Americans for its culture, its diversity, its soul, its brains, was transformed into a sacrificial lamb, an excuse for vengeance against the "enemy." Where does the blame lie? Who is the real enemy? Deep Throat's putative words seem relevant: *Follow the money*. So do those of Malcolm X: *Chickens coming home to roost*.

Over the next few weeks, there seemed to be a return to a state of near-normalcy in everyday life. The travel restrictions had mostly been eased and items other than the 9/11 attacks appeared on the news shows. The Bozzini Quartet plus guitarist Tim Brady were booked to perform at The Kitchen on September 21; denied entry to the USA at the Montreal airport, they rented a car and drove without a hitch across the border, arriving just in time for the show. The Bozzini played *Tessalation* Row with incredible fire. On September 22, Joel Sachs brought the New Juilliard Ensemble to Juilliard Hall for a set of orchestral works devoid of political commentary. *Racing Hearts,* receiving its US premiere, was played with a transparency and brilliance in the difficult hocketed sections that allowed the processes at work to be clearly defined, yet without reducing the mystery of their unfolding. It was a distinct pleasure to host both Janene's and my parents for the concert and to talk about nothing but the performance. The following July saw *Calling* premiered at Darmstadt on a program with premieres by Wolfgang Rihm and Sebastian Claren. Claren's piece was a cello concerto, *To the People of New York City,* combining seething sound masses with whimsical moments. Rihm's piece, dedicated to Luigi Nono, included a second piano situated at the side of the hall. The sound world ranged from transparent delicacy to heavy explosions, with timbres and passages transformed across the orchestra, both instrumentally and spatially.

I was surprised that there would be only one three-hour rehearsal for a piece as complex as *Calling.* I knew, though, that I could trust the instincts and skills of conductor Peter Rundel, and before the rehearsal we combed over the score to find areas of potential trouble. The recording session the next day would afford a detailed look at the piece. The work was recorded in sections, with tonmeister Christoph Franke at the desk. We now had complete coverage but the plan was to record both the dress rehearsal and the concert. The opening concert was to be in the Sporthalle at Darmstadt, a roofed venue but quite open. The sound was what one might expect from a space used for sporting events: reflections, reverberations, and, as an added treat, birds roosting in the rafters.

I held my breath during the performance. I find it much easier to be on stage making my own mistakes than watching an orchestra playing my work, aware that any problems will be blamed on the composer. Adding an antic touch to the event was the first chair of the second violins, a gentleman showing a marked antipathy to dissonance and sudden loud dynamics. Claren's score was more continuously textural, but both Rihm's work and my own gave ample opportunity for this clown to telegraph his reactions measures before the offending event. As the passage approached, he would scrunch down in his chair, violin in his lap, fingers jammed tightly in his ears and a cartoonish display of pain on his face and in his eyes. He repeated this pantomime a number of times throughout the concert. Despite the presence of this buffoon, I was able to listen and be satisfied with what Rundel drew from the orchestra. In the finale, there are silent sections ranging from five to twelve seconds, each punctuated by huge chords (or, as I prefer to call them, vertical simultaneities). The roosting birds would then make their presence felt in clouds of chirping. The audience response was mostly quite enthusiastic but there was also plenty of booing. Afterwards, Bernd Leukert was gleeful: "You broke all the rules of Darmstadt!"

March of 2003 saw the buildup to "Iraq War II" on fabricated justifications by the unholy axis of Bush-Cheney-Rumsfeld-Halliburton-Feith-Perle-Wolfowitz, a war for which the world is still paying a huge price as I write. At the same time, the Sirius String Quartet was preparing an evening at Roulette, one of the best performance spaces in greater New York, and asked me for a new piece in which I would process the sound of the musicians. The result was *Dispersion of Seeds*, with a title based on a newly discovered natural-history work by Henry David Thoreau dealing with the mechanism of reforestation and the propagation of plant species, which I saw as a ripe metaphor for the possibility of positive memes thriving and spreading in a time of crass stupidity, fear, and militarism.

The score to *Dispersion of Seeds* is extremely simple, with just a few instructions and a structure comprising nine measures with one chord in each organized in three systems of three, five, and eight minutes in duration. In each system, the musicians begin arpeggiating their written chord very slowly and quietly, speeding up to a loud and vicious blur about two thirds of the way through the system, and then slowing down again to nearly nothing to move on to the next system. The fingerings are such that players always have two open strings in play and bow position moves freely between *sul tasto* and *sul ponticello*. The result is a complex skein of overtones and split tones giving the effect of many more than four players. For the Roulette premiere, the sound of the quartet was vastly expanded using electronic processing: ring modulation and pitch transposition, granulated walls of noise, the entire field verging on harmonic feedback through the use of tuned resonators. Later, we recorded an acoustic version of *Dispersion of Seeds* at my studio using close microphone techniques. I processed the tracks after the recording to create three different versions. The electronic processing yielded results that were engaging, even sometimes astounding. Ultimately, though, I found the sonic manifestations purely in the acoustic realm more compelling.

The laptop running Ableton Live and Max/MSP became my default processing rig both for studio work and in concert, whether working with string quartet, brass (*Beyond the Curve* for Meridian Art Ensemble), piano (*Suberrebus* for Jenny Lin) or my own solo electro-acoustic guitar concerts. With the recording of *Dispersion of Seeds*, I began to feel an increasing sense that the electronic sounds weren't always an enhancement. By the turn of this last century, extreme sounds were quite easy to achieve with only a mouse-click. I was missing the "sweat equity" generated by more labor intensive strategies. More important, acoustic instruments pushed to their limits with extended techniques possess a tactility, immediacy, and complexity of timbre that is unmatched by electronics, at least for now. When the means of audio production is a physically excited vibrating string, column of air, membrane, or reed, one has a greater sensation of the movement of molecules in a space, a greater perception of the initial transient within which so much of the identity of a sound resides. In a live performance situation, this sensation is reduced when the sound ultimately emerges from a speaker. The nadir seemed to be the proliferation of "laptop concerts" in the mid-1990s. Though the music could be quite wonderful, attending a typical event of this kind was akin to witnessing an internet cafe in action, with a group of nerds, eyes glazed, sitting behind their screens. Missing was the pheromonal handshaking and the stink of creativity.

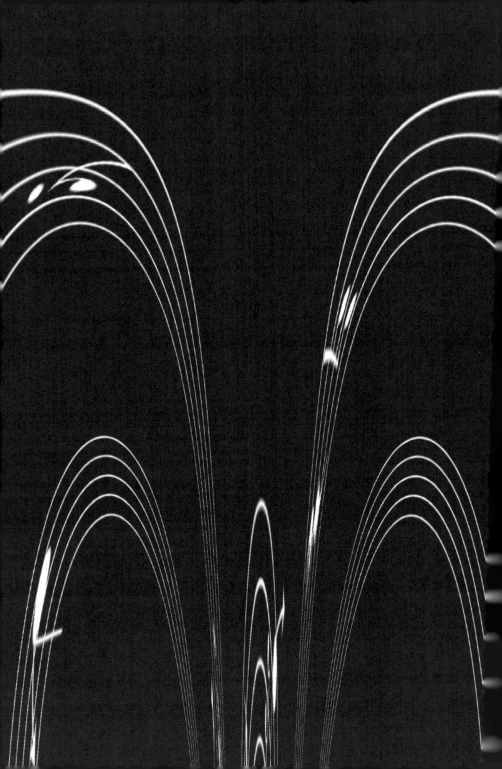

XIII.

Octal, Twins, Foliage

Developments in technology and aesthetics are often inextricably linked, each enabling the other in a feedback loop. I had been hearing new guitar music in the Void and dreaming of a semi-acoustic eight-string guitarbass with which to realize it. In 2003, I contacted luthier Saul Koll of Portland, Oregon and after a number of exchanges by email and telephone over the next two years, in July 2005 I received this incredible instrument designed to open new wormholes to the Inner Ear. Compact and headless, the guitar not only was fully hollow but sported a fanned-fret fingerboard allowing for longer scale lengths for the bass strings graduating to the shortest length for the highest treble, thus optimizing both string tension and sound. I'd requested an oval soundhole to pay homage to the Selmer Maccaferri and Favino guitars favored by Django Reinhardt and other gypsy jazz players. The instrument looked to be grown rather than carved, attesting to Saul's incredible artistry. Completing the picture was a "Realist" piezo pickup from David Gage, allowing a semi-acoustic sound to be added to the mix. I immediately began work on a series of pieces that would make full use of the instrument's potentials. Eventually comprising three books, *Octal* was a mix of through-composed, algorithmic, and graphic scores with improvisation. The first two books of *Octal* were directly inspired by concepts from physicist Lisa Randall's encyclopedic study of post-quantum physics, *Warped Passages*. How does one play the music of string theory (outside of the obvious puns)? Reading the descriptions of the theoretical states and processes triggered a palpable sound, a complex interaction of fingers on the guitar combined with sonic potentialities, an abstraction of structure and action, a waking dream state codified into score and playing. Essentially, this was how I always approached composition: the feedback loop between Mind and Sound. After the *Octal* premiere at Issue Project Room, I was asked by an audience member how I could write music about theoretical physics. My answer was that it was no more (or less) difficult than writing music about love.

Can one discern a direct causal chain between events in one's life and one's art? Probably one can, though nothing so simple as a one-to-one correspondence. For Janene and me, profound changes began in September of 2005 with the birth of our twins, Lila and Kai. Of course, we had been preparing for the birth in many ways, but once the reality hit we entered a different state of being, one outside our control. I felt a window opening into a dimension of life that I hadn't realized existed. Deep challenges and deeper joy. Did the music I was composing change as I did? Was my hearing, especially in the Inner Ear, now operating in a new way? Can I be objective enough to easily answer these questions?

One thing I can say with certainty: the constant sleep deprivation yielded an altered state of consciousness, a shift in the spectrum of my sensitivity to sound and light. Time at the studio was much reduced, forcing me to find a new strategy for composing: a memory game where work in the Inner Ear would pass through a process of filtering and evolution and eventually, when time at the studio was found, transcription of the results. The Inner Ear was honed and sharpened.

One of the greatest "video games" ever is the software Photoshop. Since getting a Mac in 1991, I'd spent many an hour immersed in its operations, both out of functional necessity for various projects and for the sheer joy of it. As a seventh grader, even though I had a solo show of my prints and paintings in the window of the local Macy's department store, the teacher awarded me a "D" in art because I lacked classroom discipline. Apparently, my desire to make art trumped her instructions: "Let's draw a house. Make a square..." With my devotion to the visual thus derailed, I continued painting and drawing only in the shadows, with forays into graphic notation once I was at Bard College and on a few other occasions.

I tend towards insomnia. Rather than see it as an affliction, I've happily used my time on the living room couch at 3 a.m. as an opportunity for reading and writing. On one such occasion in 2006, I experimented with importing into Photoshop a page of notation from one of my scores, which I then began to manipulate. Some of the application's plug-ins were analogous to the processing strategies I favored when manipulating sound. The images could be inverted, stretched, filtered, modulated with various waveforms and feedback, layered, and otherwise distorted to create images that retained a resemblance to musical notation while manifesting their own visual identity. The results evoked clear sonic images outside of any notation system and felt like a direct translation from Inner Ear to printed page. I was anxious to see how some of my colleagues would react to this work. A new generation of musicians raised on sonics, texture, densities, personal sound editing, and graphic notation of all types should, I thought, be able to easily transform these images into sound.

With a Roulette concert looming and another request from Sirius for a piece, I assembled a number of these graphic experiments into a score, *Seize Seas Seethes Seen*. We rehearsed a variety of strategies: having each musician play selected systems; all read through the systems in unison; all use stopwatches to time individual trajectories. For the premiere concert in 2007 and the subsequent recording, the quartet was divided, with two of the musicians playing the systems in one direction while the other two played in the reverse order—all this over a thirteen-minute arc, with movement between modules cued.

A simultaneous request for a score from Gunnar Geisse for his Munich-based electric guitar trio led to the creation of *Volapuk*, a concentrated dose of ten pages, some of which directly represented waveforms, some musical references, some iconic abstractions. Performance operations included having all players play one page at a time, in unison, with assigned timelines corresponding to the changing of the pages; giving players different pages to be played simultaneously; making mosaic patterns of timelines with each player having different sequences of pages but with some overlapping and unisons. Ultimately, for the concert performance of *Volapuk*, we played a mix that combined all of the above options over a strict timeline.

In 2009, I was provided with an incredible opportunity: a commission to compose a duo for the virtuoso violinist Hilary Hahn and her equally brilliant pianist Cory Smythe. Though I felt that a graphic work or one

based on algorithms would be inappropriate, I allowed my current
work in those realms to shape the music. The plan was to create a fully
notated score that would be true to what I was hearing in my Inner Ear
and seeing in my mind's eye. *Storm of the Eye* flowed effortlessly onto the
page, written during a teaching residency at Atlantic Center for the Arts in
Florida. The piece is meant to be an abstract narrative without a script: a
series of episodes each unfolding from its predecessor and then returning
to unfold again, but seen and heard from a different angle. Topological!
It also tips its hat to both Paganini and Xenakis in that it functions as an
étude—demonstrating some of the sounds and techniques I'd developed
over the years—yet exists in its own narrative.

Storm of the Eye is very much a fixed work, meant to sound the same
in every performance; specific sounds and psychoacoustic effects require
this exactitude for their proper manifestation. Hilary and I rehearsed via
Skype during 2011, then in person in December of 2012. Though she
sent me recordings from the Deutsche Grammophon studios in Berlin
and from a concert performance in Paris, they didn't prepare me for
hearing *Storm of the Eye* live. This would happen at a 2013 benefit for the
Kaufman Music Center, where Hilary and Cory performed a few of the
commissioned works from *In 27 Pieces*. Hilary is a force of nature, with
a ravishing tone, ferocious attack, deep groove, and the ability to render
complex and cerebral music passionate and exciting. She and Cory nearly
brought me to tears with their realization of *Storm of the Eye*.

Late in 2010, I asked Zach Layton at Issue Project Room about
observing my upcoming 60th birthday with a gig. In answer, Zach
and Luke DuBois told me they were already working on the idea with
development director Michelle Amador, and had come up with a plan
to combine my birthday concert with a fundraiser for Issue at their
new space (where construction had just begun) at 110 Livingston Street
in downtown Brooklyn. This would be followed, on the next night,
with a marathon of my work at their space in Gowanus. At Gowanus,
the documentary *Doing the don't* by Bert Shapiro would be presented,
along with *Octal* solo; Butch Morris conducting Orchestra Carbon in
a performance of *Flexagons;* Jenny Lin performing *Oligosono;* a version
of Bootstrappers with a band comprising computer-music pioneer Carl
Stone, pianist Anthony Coleman, laptop artist JG Thirlwell (a.k.a. Foetus
and other identities), Melvin Gibbs on electric bass, and Don McKenzie
on drums; Marco Cappelli performing *Amygdala;* and to cap the event, a
performance of *SyndaKit* by twelve electric guitars.

Issue commissioned a new composition for the benefit, *Occam's Razor* for double string quartet, to be performed by JACK and Sirius. In addition, I would do a solo guitar performance; short sets with Tracie Morris and Jack Womack, who would read from their work with my guitar accompaniment; and a set with actor Steve Buscemi and his wife, filmmaker and choreographer Jo Andres. During the 1980s, I had composed a number of pieces for Jo's visionary productions, which combined movement with light and projections on smoke, scrim, gauze, water spray, and bodies to create striking simulations of holograms. Steve and Jo were on Issue's board and we'd all been part of a close-knit performance scene in the East Village. It would be a pleasure to work with them both on Jo's short film *Trinity*, with text read by Steve and my live score.

The new Issue space was in a Beaux-Arts building from 1926, with grand if decayed marble interiors providing a six-second reverb time. In *Occam's Razor*, microtonal strategies would exploit difference-tone effects enhanced by the room's acoustics. The two quartets would be set up in opposite corners of the space, with the audience in the middle. Sections would start with a sustained initial pitch for each of the players, with a target pitch also delineated. The musicians would alternate between the initial pitch and a brief grace note of the target. This would be repeated, with the initial pitch decreasing in length and the target pitch increasing to create a gradual shift from an initial dronality to the subsequent one. Sections would add target notes until, at the music's peak, the two quartets would be generating a dense array of flashing pitches that would blend and refract, bend and transform, manifesting ghost instruments and impossible melodies. The rehearsals in the empty space went exceedingly well, the musicians' skills and openness bringing the music to life and the room's acoustics kicking it into another dimension.

At 5:30 p.m. on the day of the event at Livingston Street, I arrived by subway from my East Village studio with the Godin electroacoustic guitar over my shoulder in its gig bag. Entering Issue through the revolving doors, I noticed a brief and slight sense of obstruction but thought nothing of it and began setting up the mixer. Steve arrived soon after and we tested the microphone for his narration. With that out of the way, I fetched my guitar. Running my hand on the neck, I felt sharp edges, a strange roughness. I couldn't believe my eyes: the neck of the guitar was broken in the middle, revealing the metal of the truss rod. It was as if, in a waking dream, I were staring into my own arm, ripped apart and displaying the bones within.

I looked away, then back again, as if I could reboot my eyes. It was now 6:15 and the audience would be entering at 7. I had a spare Godin neck back at my studio but to return there at rush hour, replace the neck and tuners, and get back to Issue in time for my first set at 7:30 would be beyond impossible. The sound engineer, Philip White (a fine composer and musical thinker), was dispatched to a nearby hardware store for Crazy Glue and a C-clamp. His mission was successful and I poured the container of glue into the gaping opening, then clamped it shut. Amazingly, the neck repair held when I removed the clamp 30 minutes later and I was able to play my solo and the pieces with Steve and Jo, Tracie, and Jack. The guitar felt a little off but neither musical colleagues nor audience members seemed to notice that anything was amiss.

It was with deep relief that I completed my playing for the evening. I could now relax, listening as the double string quartet ran down *Occam's Razor*. The packed house absorbed a lot of the reverberation, damping resonances and difference tones and making for a different listening experience than intended, though I believe the sonic integrity of the piece came through nonetheless. Fortunately, we had recorded the work when the hall was empty. When Janene and I returned home that night, I pulled the guitar from its case and found that the neck had opened up again, returning to its flayed state. It hangs on the wall of Studio zOaR.

As I continued to use Photoshop and Gimp to manipulate my scores, I became more and more enthusiastic about the process. In 2012 I often found my 3 a.m. living-room-couch time devoted to generating pages, *leaves*, and thus *Foliage*. Some 250 pages were created, with the idea of editing them down to produce a book or boxed set of prints from which musicians might play. In its primary function, *Foliage* is a graphic score open to interpretation and realization by any instrumentalist or ensemble of any size; for an extended duration or a succinct hit; as a concert performance or an installation. Much of my composed work uses traditional notation, often the most efficient way to convey instructions to such ensembles as a symphony orchestra. Improvisation, too, has been vital, the best way to create social music. But there is another path— between composed and improvised—that is often best represented with graphics. *Foliage* is the closest I've come to presenting the "look" of what I'm hearing when I compose in my Inner Ear, a visual manifestation of sonic processes. The pages show implied movement, process, transformation.

With *Foliage*, players may "read" through the score sequentially or randomize the elements, focus on one page or encompass the whole. Various simultaneous verticalities may be created by players each using different combinations of pages to create unisons or separated parts. For ensemble performances, the pages of the score may be projected, or they may be enlarged, printed and displayed. As musicians move between the various stations, their sounds will be choreographed in a suite of movements that will both manifest the music spatially and develop its narrative arc through the cumulative effect of the iterations, superimpositions, and transformations. There is never a notion of "correct" or "incorrect" in *Foliage*—I welcome all realizations and hope that the reader, player, and listener may hear it as they see it.

As I plunged into *Foliage* and its process, old questions were revived. Mere "pretty pictures" at their worst, graphic scores at their best can serve as highly specific catalysts to music making. As someone who, from an early age, has loved both making and looking at visual art, and who has studied the work of John Cage, Morton Feldman, Anthony Braxton, Iannis Xenakis, and others, I've found that graphic approaches may open up very fruitful channels that might not otherwise have been explored. The same visual input will elicit a different sonic output from each interpreter, producing a unique manifestation of the material provided. As a composer, one must acknowledge this essential activity of the interpreter and how these actions are often the final arbiter of the music, even in through-composed pieces. If one is to claim the mantle of "composer," the sonic vocabulary and syntax of a given piece then must be defined to the extent that the identity of the composition will be clear and distinct even though the internal detail of the music may vary from performance to performance.

Desiring to rely more on acoustic instruments, in scores such as *Tessalation Row* (1986) and *Hammer Anvil Stirrup* (1988) I tried to devise means of evoking extreme sounds from the musicians without necessarily giving them minutely detailed instructions. The former piece uses a graphic tablature notation that orders events exactly in time but is open with respect to internal details. The latter combines computer-generated images with text instructions, traditionally notated rhythms, and pitch maps to strike a balance between explicit instructions on the one hand and poetic ambiguity and a sense of ongoing process on the other. A score such as *Hammer Anvil Stirrup* dwells in the realm of oblique narrative, catalyzing the sounds in an arc of time rather than linking them with precise instruction sets. In this way, it makes heavy demands on the performer's power of creative interpretation.

In helping to prepare a performance of any of these graphic pieces, I might discuss with the players why a certain image appears as it does and what it evokes for me in terms of the evolution of sound over time. I might ask the players to begin with a single sound and imagine how that sound would be modified when applying the processes implied by the image— an exercise designed to plumb the depths of the Inner Ear. Parameters might include smooth versus rough tones, varieties of modulation, randomness versus deep control. No sound exists in isolation, though, and the decisions of any player will be modified by the sonic actions of the others in an ensemble feedback loop. These scores are dynamic, never fixed: the music will be different with each and every manifestation.

When quickly scrolling the sequences and sub-sequences of *Foliage*, I found that the work took on the look of an animation. This led to the creation of a "movie" version of the piece, made by crossfading a sequence of the images, varying both the durations of the images and the fade. To tailor the work for different situations, versions were made ranging in length from fiteen minutes to an hour. In a show of *Foliage* at Reverse Space in Brooklyn in 2012, 80 pages were chosen and Risograph prints were made, framed, and hung in a circle around the gallery space. Invited performers could walk the periphery and work with the prints as they saw fit. In addition, for a performance series at the gallery during the run of the show, I invited Tracie Morris, Luke DuBois, the electric guitar quartet Dither, Darius Jones, Lea Bertucci, the Mivos Quartet, the Barry Weisblat/ Andrew Lafkas duo, Shelley Burgon, and the Mary Halvorson/Jessica Pavone duo to each interpret the 40-minute movie version of *Foliage*. I was extremely gratified at the intensity of commitment displayed by all the performers, each finding a way into the score and producing a realization that felt simultaneously true to each of their own personal languages and to the score itself.

Ulimately, *Foliage* is a piece of retinal art as much as it is an instruction set for sound. Form and function are interlocked. The pages of *Foliage* were created through multiple layers of processing upon the image of a specific musical instruction set. The result is a manifestation of the internal synaesthesia that is, for me, inherent to the translation of thought, emotion, and process from one set of frequencies to another.

Following *Foliage*, other works were composed using these same techniques, though specializing the focus for each. *Mare Undarum* used only modulation by sine waves on the source score to create the final output. *Liquidity* was made from hand-drawn distortions of the TIF image, using various plug-ins with a stylus and tablet interface. *Flare* was composed by zooming and magnifying regions of a processed page and then applying further processing with each iteration. This last piece is realized as an installation and performance with movement artists as well as sound; the images are either projected or printed on large sheets of clear acetate to be suspended in the performance space in sequenced layers.

The compelling nature of the animated pages of *Foliage* led to work on a composition that was intended from its inception to be an animation, a sequence of 250 cells derived from eight pages of composed musical gestures. Inspiration came from Sir Francis Bacon's *Sylva Sylvarum; or, A natural history, in ten centuries.* One interpretation of the title may be "the forest of the forest"—an ur-wilderness, a meta-history of life on this planet, source of all that is organic. Processes similar to those used in *Foliage* were employed in creating the individual pages: modulating, filtering, layering, inverting, distorting, sequencing. In this case, the pages were designed to be animated and were composed to create a flowing sequence, which was then layered with appropriated clips of time-lapse movies of flowering plants and of satellite imagery of such locations as the Amazon rainforest, the Arctic and Antarctic ice shelves, and Himalayan glaciers. Versions of the piece range in duration from 30 to 60 minutes.

SysOrk—the name derived from "systems orchestra"—is situational, a fluid aggregation dedicated to graphic and algorithmic scores. After performances of *Foliage* in Tokyo and Nagoya in 2012, New York City's SysOrk debuted at Roulette in 2014 with the premiere of *Sylva Sylvarum,* and appeared the following year at The Stone with a performance of *Mare Undarum.* The players in SysOrk were chosen for their wide range of extended techniques, their openness to new and challenging performance parameters, and their ability to inject personal creative interpretations into the sonic flux. Many of the NYC SysOrk players had taken part in Orchestra Carbon concerts and their collective experience extended across contemporary and classical music to jazz and free improvisation. Subsequent performances of *Sylva Sylvarum* were booked in Europe, the forces ranging from large ensembles to myself solo and in duos with such intrepid and virtuosic players as Italian guitarist Alessandra Novaga and bass clarinetist Gareth Davis.

Informed by my work in graphics in this period were compositions that used a combination of precise notation with algorithmic sections. Though the music was scored in a traditional manner, the act of composing, of translating from the Inner Ear, followed my nonlinear and synesthetic predilections. A clump of metal ball chain, a spring, an aluminum tube—all led to sound and music. Commissoned by Harry Vogt of the WDR in Cologne and premiered by JACK at the Witten Days for New Chamber Music festival in 2009, *The Boreal* inhabits a sound world of hocketed grooves, difference tone effects, and non-pitched materials generated by the use of alternate bows made from ball chain and metal springs. The title itself is an array of references, all serving to inspire the arc of the piece: Boreas, the Greek god of the North Wind; the ecosystems of sub-arctic & sub-antarctic climates; the Boreal period of our Holocene era (approximately 9,000 to 8,000 years before the present); and finally the Boreal Sea, a Mesozoic body of water bounding the north of the supercontinent Laurasia, one half (with Gondwanaland) of the supercontinent Pangaea. The spring-bows are simply metal springs of various lengths and thicknesses purchased at hardware stores or plucked from trashed desk lamps. For decades, I'd used them on guitar for their ability to create the ripping and tearing sounds of a chainsaw by lightly grazing the strings. The ball chain bows, which produce a more delicate sound, are made by stretching a length of ball chain on an armature made of a section of wooden dowel, bent to tension the material and keep it taut. These bows can excite the string on a specific pitch, but can also excite the two individual lengths of string on either side of the touch point. They may produce pitched glissandi, coarse growls, or gritty percussive attacks, but all in a quiet range.

Tranzience was composed in 2013 and premiered by JACK the following year. In addition to spring bows, *Tranzience* made use of tube bows constructed from one-half-inch aluminum conduit cut into appropriate lengths. The rough side, *col grezzo*, is hand-carved with aperiodic grooves to generate non-repetitive microrhythms and textures. The smooth side, *col liscio*, is polished to produce glissandi and multiphonics.

The transient is the short burst of harmonics and noise at the beginning of any sound. Extreme in dynamics, rich, full of nonperiodic components and high frequencies, transients are the bow sounds, the spit sounds, the scrapes—the sounds that casual listeners tend to unconsciously filter out of their perception of the "musical." From working with samplers and digital sound editors, I'd found that when these sounds are slowed down, they reveal landscapes, textures, and rhythms unheard and unpredicted in the original sound. An imagined transient and its expansion served as the source for the counterfactual musical arc of *Tranzience*. JACK is a fearless ensemble and took to the alternate bows with great enthusiasm, tearing into their valuable instruments with abandon to yield the beautifully vicious sounds that I envisioned—post-industrial, rich in spiky overtones and vocalised textures. Pieces such as *The Boreal* and *Tranzience* are no less visual for me than a projected graphic score, with the drama of the musicians' actions and the striking appearance of their tools contributing to the extramusical experience.

XIV.

Acts and Spectacle

I saw my first opera when I was eleven years old, on a school field trip to the Met: Wagner's *Flying Dutchman*. Though the music did not overwhelm me, the set and staging did. Until then, my notions of opera had been defined by Bugs Bunny cartoons. Seeing the real thing, I was astounded at how the scale of the ritual dwarfed any other performance I had experienced. The air in the hall was thick with a palpable sense of occasion, even a hint of magic, far beyond the intrinsic value of the content. When I left the theater, the world seemed different.

As I continued to participate in music ensembles and plays in school, I began to understand how a performance could be far more than the sum of its parts, how it could have a transformative power. Coming of age in the 60s, I took multimedia art as the norm. To play in a rock band meant, at its best, transporting the sonic moment to another dimension, with the music enhanced, even completed, by light shows, film loops, strobes, dancers. Concerts at the Fillmore East were a total immersion in this alternate reality of sound, visuals, and the pheromonal crowd. The culmination was attendance at the Woodstock Festival of 1969, where the totality of group participation created a spectacle transcending its content.

Arriving in New York City in 1979, I was plunged into endless, passionate discussions of performance and its framing. Events were generally analyzed in terms of the Debordian view of the spectacle. Simultaneously, we sought the anti-spectacle, that which affirmed the visceral, the real. Seeing as many shows as possible in my first weeks in the City, I noticed the care with which performances were staged to maximize the drama and hyperreality of the event, notwithstanding the often banal character of the work and grittiness of the surroundings. Much that I saw was overly self-conscious, directly opposing a more functional ethos that valued content over packaging. Believing the two could not be separated, I wanted to strike a balance. Given the apocalyptic dread in the air with Reagan as President, it was difficult to make any art that did not in some way confront political reality. Thinking about the thinking about the work: a recursive chain of framing. This led me to conceive of an opera about nothing but the dread itself, a post-apocalyptic witnessing that might be more real than any of the events we were experiencing—or might be pure delusion. Though I would call it an opera, my plan was to strip it down as much as possible by eliminating singers, plot, libretto, and staging. It would be a spectacle created with less-than-spectacular resources, a transmission from my life in a dump in a decayed and dangerous neighborhood.

Innosense received its premiere in November of 1981 at Studio P.A.S.S. on West 22nd Street. Set in a basement in the Lower East Side, it treats of catastrophic events that are never revealed or explicitly discussed, but are manifested only in fragments of sound from the main (but virtual) characters: Bio/logicals, The State, and Myth. These parts were prerecorded and played back from stereo cassettes, one for each of the performers, who used foot-operated volume pedals to bring sounds into the mix. The materials for these characters included voices from television and radio news and advertisements; bird and animal sounds from various recorded libraries; texts sung or read by Victoria Vesna or Felipe Orrego that I had written or appropriated from such sources as natural-history works and political tracts; and my own throat-singing. The three "live" characters are the Three Improvisers. For this premier event we were Charles K. Noyes on percussion, Lesli Dalaba on trumpet, and myself on fretless electric guitar, soprano sax, and bass clarinet. Finally, the GeoClock is a prerecorded percussion track made with a stainless steel pot half-filled with water and struck with a hard mallet. It plays back continuously throughout the 45-minute work, with beats derived from Fibonacci numbers. The work had only one specifically visual aspect: the office that hosted Studio P.A.S.S. was bathed in deep red light from two incandescent fixtures.

After the premiere of *Innosense*, the nature of opera and musical theater grew even more ambiguous for me as I spent time performing and hanging out in such venues as the Mudd Club, Tier 3, Hurrah, Darinka, A's, 8BC, Limbo Lounge, Club 57, Danceteria, Experimental Intermedia, and other semi-underground zones, with occasional forays to more legitimized spaces such as The Kitchen, Dance Theater Workshop, the Joyce Theater, and P.S. 122. The feedback loop between the various operative elements worked to create an overheated and exaggerated set of gestures encapsulated in a compact and densely packed unit. How to rise up over the ambient noise and interference? Louder! Faster! Weirder! I found inspiration in Japanese Butoh and the operas of Robert Ashley. I composed for and performed with such artists as Fiona Templeton, Yoshiko Chuma, and Kinematix. For the most part, though, my theatrical tendencies were satisfied by participating in band projects and composing formal works such as *Crowds and Power*.

Involved in explorations of sampling and the digital reconstruction of music, I began work in 1992 on an opera that, incorporating these elements, would be nonlinear and focused more on cultural commentary and sonic crosstalk than on song structures or a master narrative. *ArePopEra* would make use of a number of independent audio channels, one for each singer or instrumentalist. The performers would be fed fragments of melodic material, some composed for the work, some culled from popular songs and commercials. For the libretto, there would be newly written text as well as speech taken from radio and television, transcribed and then transformed. This seed material might be sent to the players in real time from a sound library for true random access, or prepared in advance as a multitrack master. At the time, I was unable to find a producer or venue willing to present the work. Since *ArePopEra* is not tied to any particular content or time frame, I'm hoping it might still be realized in a newer version, accommodating any source material input to the translation channels.

Working on music for Dael Orlandersmith's play *Yellowman* brought me back into the theatrical realm, but it wasn't until 2004 that I found my way into a more personal involvement. I had been primarily focused on work for orchestra and self-organizing systems when author Lauri Bortz asked if I might be interested in composing a short opera. After reading her darkly hilarious and absurdist one-act play *A Modicum of Passion*, I agreed. The story takes place in a dystopic future where women may only be housemaids or babymakers while men comport themselves as they will and raise male children to power. *A Modicum of Passion* premiered at the Bowery Poetry Club in September 2004 with a cast consisting of Eric Mingus, Benjamin Miller, Devorah Day, and Becca Schack, and with the Yellin String Quartet playing the score. Lauri requested "Shaker-like" music and I composed a score shaped by that concept, rhythmically simple and mostly tonal. Setting the lyrics required that the vocal lines be suspended over and across the instrumental accompaniment. Tonality formed only a set of suggestions; the verticalities were the result of counterpoint, not harmony, and sometimes led pitches astray. The score included a Cajun-inspired waltz and sporadic gestural tributes to Bernard Herrmann. The concentrated act of setting text to music was refreshing and inspiring and opened the door to an invitation to present a project at the 2005 Howl Festival, a Lower East Side arts extravaganza directed by Two Boots Pizza mogul Phil Hartman.

Here, at last, was an opportunity to manifest *Binibon*, a work that had been gestating since the morning after the events in question in 1981. I asked Jack Womack, a friend and brilliant writer, if he might be interested in creating a libretto. The result was both a murder ballad and a capsule history of the Lower East Side's transformation from drug-ridden slum to trendoid playground and inflated market for art and real estate. With Jack playing The Writer and a cast including Mike Lubik, Latarsha Rose, and Deian McBryde, we premiered the work over a four-night run at the upstairs performance space at Hartman's new restaurant Mo Pitkin's. I'd prepared soundfiles for playback in Ableton as part of the underscore. These included textures and grooves composed using sampled loops, electronic drum programming, Korg MS-20 analog synthesizer, and acoustic instruments transformed in Pro Tools with various plug-ins. I performed the top layer of the score live, using tenor sax, bass clarinet, and electric guitar to comment spontaneously on the drama. *Binibon* was presented again in 2006 at Roulette, with further refinements in structure and score. This, in turn, led to an invitation from Deb Singer at The Kitchen to present a fully staged version.

My original concept for staging was simple and used little in the way of props or costumes: the actors would be seated at tables and might don headgear to accentuate the identity of their characters. Video would have a vital role in providing setting, subtext, and commentary. Here I would rely on Janene's video work, which is charged with a great sense of drama in contrast and movement, yet is painterly and subtle, its secrets revealed with reserve and mystery. I had a strong and clear idea of directorial strategies for the work and what my approach would be to the relationship between text, staging, and music. Unfortunately, Deb told me that The Kitchen had seen too many operas ruined by allowing the composer to direct; I could choose to simply do a music concert, but if *Binibon* was my priority I would have to work with a producer and director. Even though I knew how I wanted the work to be, I was also interested in gaining experience working with expert, creative professionals in this realm. Beth Morrison was brought in to produce and our discussions were frank and constructive. When we discussed bringing in a director, I understood it to mean hiring a technical director to help me realize my vision for *Binibon*, not substituting another's vision for my own. Our choice was a recent Yale graduate, talented and knowledgeable; I liked her reel and very much enjoyed our first meeting.

Our first conflicts were in casting. We agreed completely on most of the actors: Jedadiah Schultz as the murderous author Jack Henry Abbott; Ryan Quinn in multiple roles including Johnny, the junkie writer, and Fabuluscious the drag queen; and Sonja Perryman as Suzie the waitress and Contessa the graffiti artist. One of the most crucial roles, though, was that of Ted, the jazz musician, who also provides narration, laconic commentary, and wisecracks. My librettist, Jack Womack, had read this role in our previous productions, channeling himself, and the character very much inhabited his vocal rhythms. I was, however, outvoted when it came to this role and the job fell to a professional actor, who played it more as a Las Vegas Rat Pack pseudo-hipster. A bad beginning, but I deferred to expertise; I believed we all shared a common aesthetic vision of *Binibon* and the proper sense of give and take to make it all work. Zane Pihlström's mockups for the sets were brilliant and Janene had begun work on the video with results that were dark, evocative, and visually stunning.

A 1981 photograph by Andreas Sterzing of the corner of Fourth Street and Avenue B was the image that would open *Binibon*. The lofty midtown Manhattan skyline loomed in the distance, making the rubble from the destroyed buildings and the empty lots in the foreground all the more striking. Seemingly unaware of recent history in the East Village, the Yale crew, young and green, asked if Janene had created this image in Photoshop!

PS1 Contemporary Art Center graciously donated rehearsal space and we were able to spend a solid month working there before heading to

The Kitchen. Our director took a very textual approach, spending days analyzing the libretto word by word and line by line. Yet much of Jack's libretto, though deeply nuanced, was straightforward in the manner of a classic *noir* and I felt we would gain more by first getting a sense of the overall narrative arc and then digging in to clarify textual details. As the piece slowly began to fall into place, more conflicts arose, especially over the ratio of music to text. This was an opera, after all! I wanted sections where there would be just sound or just video, with the actors either frozen or barely seen. The response: "If there is any time an actor is not doing or saying something, people will say I'm not doing my job!" We even battled over the presence of a fifteen-second clarinet solo in the middle of a background story about the Jewish "Rialto" of Second Avenue at the turn of the century. There were more fights over the role of video, tensions escalating. As we edged closer to the opening, the conflicts increased to the point where the drama in rehearsal far eclipsed what was happening on stage. Fortunately the cast was solidly professional and kept their cool throughout.

While this was not the *Binibon* I had conceived, it ended up being a tight and entertaining work. The house was sold out for the first two nights and there were lines down 19th Street for the final two shows. The multitrack audio recorded at The Kitchen formed the basis of a CD release which was then completed at Studio zOaR. For the CD, I had Jack Womack reprise his role as the narrator, restoring it to its proper sensibility. I also vowed that I would be the undisputed director of all of my future operas.

After The Kitchen, *Binibon* lay dormant until 2016 when a conversation with Juan Puntes, director of the White Box art center and a longtime friend and collaborator, led to his inviting me to present *Binibon* as a weeklong workshop with open rehearsals and three performances in October of that year. Fortunately, Jedadiah and Ryan were available and enthusiastic. Sonja had moved to Los Angeles so I engaged the singer Julie Brown for the roles of Suzy and Contessa. Jack would continue as the narrator. I could now present *Binibon* as originally intended, with the video functioning as intended.

Another operatic challenge was presented to me in 2007 by the soprano Donella Del Monaco, a committed interpreter of classical opera and early music and a passionate improviser. Donella commissioned a work from me to be performed at the upcoming Venice Biennale and written for her ensemble of players from Venice and Padua, an ensemble that performed both compositions and improvisations. Given the wide range of abilities of her musicians, I wanted to come up with a structure that would feature her vocal talents, allow her players to easily navigate the various elements, and have a coherent (albeit abstract) story. This work would be titled *EmPyre*. With W's Iraq War in full shambles, I thought to draw parallels and contrasts between New York City and the city-state of Venice during the Crusades. NYC seemed to be an island of resistance in the current American political climate yet Wall Street was funding the war, reaping its benefits, and preying upon the American populace through a number of unsavory strategies. Venice from the 12th to the 14th century retained a fair amount of independence and was a haven for refugees and free-thinkers, yet also practiced ruthless trading policies with both European and Byzantine entities.

I had no desire to create an information-packed historical pastiche, but rather a series of interrelated abstractions to be presented within the confines of a 40-minute set, the story completed by their cumulative effect. My old friend Steve Piccolo, living in Italy since 1981, was drafted to create the libretto and to sing the bass-baritone part. A structure was quickly devised, the music mixing through-composed elements with seed material for algorithmic processes for the players. Donella would superimpose her written parts over these processes or, in some sections, be free to take off in improvisational flights. The text mingled historical allusions with subjective nuggets, as well as sections of vocalized gibberish derived from internet spam.

One of the fringe benefits of this project was meeting bass-baritone Nicholas Isherwood at a post-concert dinner with various friends, including producer Massimo Ongaro, musicologist Veniero Rizzardi, and composer Stefano Bassanese. Nicholas had performed a stunning realization of Maurizio Kagel's *Phonophonie* and a beautiful work of Stefano's. After hearing him sing, I knew I had to compose for him. I asked if he would like to sing the Walter Benjamin role in my opera *Port Bou*. He readily agreed. *Meraviglioso!* All that was left to do now was to create the music and libretto, design the production, and book the premiere. Simple.

I thrive on doing things that I haven't done before, and the Bayerische Staatsoper in Munich gave me an incredible opportunity: to create an opera for all-teenage performers, to be premiered at the Pavillon 21 MINI Opera Space as part of their Summer Festival in July of 2010. The work would be titled *About Us* and my initial idea was to have the teens make the work about crucial events in their own lives. The participants, aged thirteen to eighteen, were found through an open call put out through the Munich school system. There were no minimum requirements for acting or musical abilities: the project was open to all who applied, none of whom had any major theatrical experience. Through a series of workshops at the beginning of the project, participants who proved to have musical or dramatic strengths would be steered towards more important roles. Parts had to be found for everyone, with some participating only in group scenes or in support roles in stagecraft such as costumes, lighting, and props. Initially there were 75 kids participating, but the production required a major commitment of time and energy and by the time of the performances only 35 remained. A production team from the Bayerischer Rundfunk wanted to make a television documentary about the development and presentation of the work and so they, too, became part of the process.

The first sessions were in December 2009. I flew in from NYC and, after a nap and double espresso, had a last-minute strategy meeting with our wonderfully talented and easy-going team before facing 75 teenagers from all around the Munich metropolitan area. I would be working closely with a German assistant director, Natascha Ursuliak; a dramaturge from the Opera, Rainer Karlitschek; Ursula Gessat, the educational outreach person; costume designer Herold Falko; and set designer Marie Pons. Fortunately, everyone spoke English far better than I spoke German so we were able to conduct our work together quite easily. We had the kids divide up into small groups and spent the first two days introducing ourselves to one another, which included telling something about our lives or art. By the end of that week, I requested stories from all about life-changing events. From these, we hoped to create a libretto. As the team read through the tales, we were dismayed to find that most of the stories were about getting too drunk or forgetting to do homework. Concluding that we'd have to take another tack, I decided to sketch a framework on which the kids could build their own variations.

In this story, Earth passes through a singularity. As a result, creatures from a parallel universe coinhabit our space. They are visible only to teenagers within urban aggregations large enough to generate hormonal clouds. These creatures, nicknamed Schrödingers, catalyze spontaneous acts of creativity and empathy. Naturally, the forces of civil and religious authority deem this a threat and prepare to detain and even euthanize all those affected. After many tensions, the situation is resolved when the planet passes through a second singularity.

With this narrative in place, we could now workshop scenes with the young actors and have them place their own imprints on the story. Though cases of bad behavior, self-indulgence, and unnecessary egoism were not unknown, most of those continuing with the project took it quite seriously. We found some very talented individuals, some of whom had never performed before. A shy but charismatic young woman was cast as Dr. Bhik and her *Sprechstimme* aria became a high point of the performance. Others revealed their power as they became comfortable with the notion of performing. Steadily, we built the production.

By late in April, I had finished composing the music to be recorded by the Bayerische Staatsoper Orchestra for playback in the production. Most of the music did not employ anything that I would deem radical, whether in sound or technique. The conductor, Christopher Ward, told me that he had no problem with any of it personally but that some of the players did, and he conveyed their feedback. One cellist said that he would only play "under protest." The brass section as a whole claimed that the music written for two short interludes was "impossible to play" and they would not even attempt it. I was furious. My first impulse was to tell Christopher to tell them that if we were recording in New York, I could just call any of the brass players in my book and not only would they sight-read the parts, but they would then improvise in the style of my writing. But I restrained myself. Fortunately, once we were all face to face, the musicians ended up being much more genial (except for the brass players!) and we were able to get master takes quite quickly on almost all of the cues. For the brass interludes in question, I ended up having to use samples triggered from my score in Sibelius.

Some of these recordings were then processed using a variety of software and hardware strategies, as well as by layering multiple takes and overdubbing analog synthesizers. These tracks would be played back over a four-channel system during performances of the piece, sometimes layered with live playing by the teenage participants.

For the kids, musical workshops in gestural improvisation, rhythm, choral singing, and songwriting were conducted, with mixed results. Some of the most sensitive and enthusiastic work was emerging from those who had no musical or instrumental training. A number of the participants became part of the "pit orchestra," which used percussion and "found percussion" instruments as well as violins, piano, and flute. This ensemble accompanied dramatic actions, sometimes with worked-out parts, sometimes with greater freedom to create something spontaneous. Simple scores were developed for each scene, mostly using verbal descriptions as many of the kids had only rudimentary skills in reading music. I was extremely happy with this ensemble, which created very vital and often surprising music.

The greater portion of the script was spoken but some parts used *Sprechstimme*, with individual words or short phrases sung. A number of songs were also written for the production. Some were for soloists but most were chantlike and intended for interlocked solo voices or choruses. None required virtuosic vocal abilities; gesturally, they resembled contemporary rock and hip-hop music and were sung over prerecorded electronic grooves.

For the aftermath of the climax of the third act, I composed a simple process piece, *After the Second Event*, in which the actors are divided into five groups, each assigned one of the syllables "ah", "bh", "ow", "tt", and "ss". Beginning at a very slow tempo, these syllable groups are looped without any synchronization, growing faster and louder with each cycle. At a certain point, the group sounds as if it's singing a granulated version of "about us." As the process continues, the ensemble sound drifts out of the recognizable lyrics and into a percussive rhythm, leading to the final song, *The End and the Beginning*.

About Us was finally coming into focus. Once we began using Herold's brilliant costumes in our rehearsals, the energy of the kids perked up considerably. We moved into the Pavillion one week before the premiere. Marie Pons and her crew did a fantastic job creating a simulacrum of a Munich underground metro station for the starting point of our set. Through the use of plexiglass panels and creative lighting, many wonderful effects were presented, greatly transforming the stage. For the climax of the work—the encounter with the second singularity—I wanted something both sonically and visually overpowering. The solution was two large tympani, heads covered with thin reflective plastic and angled to catch the high-intensity spotlights aimed at them. Perched on an elevated platform, they were hidden by tarpaulins during the previous scenes. At the climactic moment, the tarps were removed and the young drummers pounded out an intense and rapid figure, the reflective surfaces filling the hall with shards of brilliant light. Strobes were also employed and the amplified sound of the drums was augmented with prerecorded analog synthesizer sounds.

Port Bou was first conceived in 1989 as I was reflecting on Walter Benjamin's life and texts. Especially vital for me remain "The Task of the Translator," "The Work of Art in the Age of Mechanical Reproduction," *The Origin of German Tragic Drama,* and the *Arcades Project. Port Bou* presents Benjamin's last moments as he was fleeing Nazi-occupied France in 1940. What might we surmise about the internal state of a man deciding that life is no longer liveable, especially when that man is Walter Benjamin in that place and time, attempting a radical departure of whatever form? As the Second World War was increasing in magnitude it was not uncommon for Jewish writers, artists, and professionals to carry the means of suicide with them, believing it to be preferable to internment and torture at the hands of the Nazis. This was a time of desperation and *Götterdämmerung* was in the air, whether global or personal. And Benjamin's story had special resonance because of the tales my mother had told of her family's survival of the Nazi occupation of France.

Benjamin was unafraid to delve into the myriad philosophies and modes of living presented to him but could never fully give himself to any of them, no matter who demanded it of him. Domestic tranquility, the mysteries of the Kabbala, political Zionism, the erotic, pure Communism, academic abstraction: all offered seductions and enticements but never enough for a complete commitment. Benjamin was solipsistic and sybaritic, sufficently fulfilled by his solitary obsessions and interests to remain an autonomous free agent. His strengths were of the aesthetic, the cerebral, not those of a man who might suffer and fight for his ideals, or for someone elses's.

While attempting to reach Lisbon and from there, ship's passage to America, Benjamin was detained with a few fellow refugees in the Pyrenean border town of Portbou. Denied entry into Spain and informed that he and his companions would be turned over to the Vichy authorities, Benjamin concluded that the obstacles to his salvation were insurmountable. Then and there, he chose to remove himself by the obvious means at hand from conflicts both internal and external. We might see this as an act of exhaustion, not a willful exit but a collapse of will. In *Port Bou* I attempt to manifest this state as it plays out in Benjamin's last few minutes of life. As composer and author, I tried to act as an antenna for the emanations of his distress and translate them to the frequencies of music and drama. Benjamin was heroic in his thoughts but I made no attempt to make a hero of the man. He was yet another innocent casualty of a great tragedy, one in which he might never have imagined himself a protagonist.

Sections of *Port Bou* would be revealed to me in fragments: sounds, images, words, melodies. How to put them together? Sometimes a deadline is the best impetus to creative work, but none was in sight. Fortunately, Issue Project Room came to the rescue. I'd been involved with Issue since its earliest days in 2003 as a side project for a fashion magazine operating out of a finished garage on East 6th Street. Suzanne Fiol nurtured the idea of an artist-directed multipurpose venue. She garnered support from many quarters and Issue continued to develop, finding a long-term home in downtown Brooklyn in the sepulchral former offices of the Board of Education. At a meeting in 2011, Issue director Laurence Kumpf and business manager Matthew Walker expressed their enthusiasm for *Port Bou* and the process of planning and fundraising began, with a target of Fall of 2014 for the premiere. In February of 2014, we received news of a modest grant from the New York State Council of the Arts that would allow the production to proceed.

My original idea was to have *Port Bou* take the form of a monodrama featuring Nicholas Isherwood, with a chamber ensemble of twelve instrumentalists. Accordion would be prominent because of its associations with Middle Europe and with the "boulevard music" of Paris. Piano would likewise have an important role and the ensemble would be filled out with B♭ and bass clarinets, trombone, classical guitar, strings, and percussion. Electroacoustic sounds, to be played back from soundfiles, would complete the score. Sadly, as we examined our operating budget it became clear that the instrumental forces that I desired would be unaffordable. Instead, the accordion and piano would be played live and the other instruments would be recorded in advance. Fortunately, I had two virtuoso players in accordionist William Schimmel and pianist Jenny Lin, who would play their parts with both passion and technical perfection.

The entire opera would take place in the hotel room where Benjamin found himself on the night of his suicide in 1940, in the small town of Port Bou (one word in Catalan, two in French) on the Spanish side of the French border. Superimposed on that bare hotel room, video by Janene Higgins would provide a larger set and setting, offering visual commentary and counterpoint to the music and sound. The video would present shifting physical and mental states, memories, visions, fears, desires, and harsh realities. Using video in this way would allow us to stage the opera in almost any space, from small gallery to large concert hall.

Because of a grueling touring schedule throughout the spring and early summer, work on *Port Bou* was intermittent, though I did manage to complete the overture and the libretto. Once unencumbered by gigging, I could concentrate and constructed the score in the two weeks straddling July and August. I'd been living with the work for so long that the writing felt like transcribing from the Inner Ear.

Port Bou is divided into eight acts: *Overture, A Room, Sh, Words, Ajsa, Creation, Reproduction,* and *Translation.* Melodic and textural fragments reappear throughout the piece. An altered version of John 1:1— "In beginning was the Word, and the Word was with...and was the Word"— and an isorhythm derived from it is one key motif; I removed the reference to God from the phrase to better correspond with Benjamin's notions of word, text, and religion. Act III, *Sh,* is about Benjamin's relationship with Judaism: not a mannered discourse but a guttural sonic wrestling match with the ancient prayer *Shema Yisrael* created by recording Nicholas reciting the through-composed syllables and sounds, which were then processed using a variety of strategies. In performance, Nicholas would sing along with this seething miasma, amplifying or contradicting. Electroacoustic transformation of voice was also the basis of Act V, *Ajsa,* referencing Benjamin's relationship with the Latvian actress Ajsa Lacis, who'd brought Benjamin to Moscow and introduced him to Marxism. Again, Nicholas recorded a through-composed melody which I then time-stretched, looped, and convolved with a sample of a soprano singer to provide a female foil for Benjamin in an erotic duet of longing and mourning.

In constructing a virtual chamber orchestra in the studio, I had to make use of my skills on clarinet and bass clarinet, trombone, classical guitar, and percussion. I would use enhancement techniques on viola and cello, my abilities on both instruments being extremely modest. For the relevant string passages, I would render lines using samples of these instruments from my Sibelius score, yielding an accurate but lifeless version of the part. I would then record myself playing the part on the real instrument along with the soundfile, capturing all of the attendant flaws in intonation and articulation. Convolution is a technique of cross-synthesis in which the characteristics of two audio files are imposed on each other, creating a third that displays characteristics of both. By using convolution of the sample with the sound of the actual instrument, the line would then be played correctly but with the attack transients and spectrum of my physical viola and cello. Once layered and mixed in with other parts and processed for ambience, the result was quite realistic.

With the October premiere of *Port Bou* looming, there were many details to be attended to: staging, lighting design, changes in the score, logistical issues with both soundfile and video playback. These were all worked on in the gaps between instrumental rehearsals, the main focus of the moment. Once Nicholas arrived from Rome we went into overdrive, with two long days of work putting everything together before the dress rehearsal in front of a packed, invited audience of friends, supporters, and colleagues. Over the three performances, the work became tighter in its structure and looser (in a good way) in its feeling, much as a band on the road might hone its interactions. The audience response was extremely positive and we were all pleased at what we had produced in so short a time.

In January 2015, I moved to Berlin with my family for a Berlin Prize residency at the American Academy. For six months we lived in a luxurious environment in Wannsee with an incredible cast of Fellows for company: Mary Jo Bang, Sean Wilentz, Sanford Biggers, Bruce Ackerman, William Urrichio, Christopher Johnson, Tom Drury, Jeffrey Goldberg, Siyen Fei, Tomas Venclova, Evgeny Morozov, Nathaniel Levtow, and Karen Hagemann. The twins attended The John F. Kennedy School and Janene worked on various of her own projects.

As part of my fellowship, the Academy produced *Port Bou* at the Konzerthaus Berlin, a majestic 18th-century edifice in Mitte designed by Karl Friedrich Schinkel. With Jenny and Bill flying in from New York and Nicholas from Paris, schedules only allowed for one long day of rehearsal and then a dress rehearsal on the day of the concert. Still, this was more than enough as everyone tore into the score with passionate abandon, tempered by meticulous attention to detail. We were honored to have Volker Schlöndorf, director of *The Tin Drum* and other great films, give a spoken introduction to the performance.

The project I had proposed to the Academy was to begin research for an opera to be titled *Substance*, about the life and thought of Baruch Spinoza. When, as a child, I first came into contact with the ideas of Spinoza, I was deeply affected. In addition to my regular studies, I'd been attending Hebrew School since age eight; though I had no great desire to do so, both my mother, a Holocaust survivor, and my father, a son of immigrants who escaped the pogroms in the Ukraine in 1905, were determined that I should have a sound knowledge of my heritage. For the most part, I took my Jewishness for granted, but reading world history and hearing the first-hand stories of miraculous survival, I tried to contextualize being a Jew in modern America. Biblical tales I placed in the realm of fantasy. Going through the motions of prayer at religious services never filled me with any sense of spirit; I felt more of this essence when drawing and painting, reading, or riding my bicycle, a vehicle that could transport me into vast and uncharted alternate realities. When I was eleven, our Jewish-history teacher introduced us to a simplified version of Spinoza's ideas, presented as one of the many "wrong turns" Judaism had taken over the milennia. Tarring him as a heretic who tried to destroy Judaism, he lumped Spinoza's philosophy with the rash of false Messiah cults beginning in the Middle Ages. Yet even as a two-dimensional caricature, Spinoza's ideas excited me. Projecting a sense of the infinite in both macroscopic and microscopic realms, his logical rationalism made perfect sense and resonated deeply. I felt that if "God" was as universal and infinite as usually depicted, then the essence or substance of "God" had to be contained in all matter and energy.

The notion that Spinoza should be punished for his ideas was horrifying, yet led me to consider the various ways one might simultaneously resonate with the Void and defy unjust authority, not at all mutually exclusive states. I was drawn to the writings of Gandhi, Laozi, Martin Buber, Jean-Paul Sartre, William Burroughs—a direction of thinking that would serve me well in the '60s struggles for free speech and civil rights and against the Vietnam War. Already counting myself an atheist, I had endless debates with my school friends about the existence of "God" and what "God" and religion meant in modern life.

Decades later, rereading Spinoza's texts and Gilles Deleuze's reflections on his *Ethics*, I was moved to consider the creation of an opera, *Substance*, to explore and present my own sonic meditations on these matters. Both Spinoza and Deleuze would be characters in this opera, refracting each other's visions and dancing around the opposition of "substance" and "process." Providing commentary would be the Collegiants, a network of progressive thinkers (a female choir), and the Edifice, the combined Jewish and Christian religious hierarchies that censured Spinoza (a male choir). *Substance* will be written for a full orchestra with electronic augmentation.

More than historical pastiche or a dramatization of the *cherem*, the excommunication of Spinoza, *Substance* will be a meditation on Spinoza and his legacy. The text will be extrapolations on writings of Spinoza. Though *Substance* will be sung primarily in English, key passages will be written in Portuguese, Ladino, Yiddish, German, Latin, French, and Dutch. The vocal writing will draw on the melismatic ornamentation of Sephardic music, a feature of Spinoza's Portuguese heritage.

Spinoza's vocation as a lensmaker will be an important factor in the staging and sound design of *Substance*. Acoustic "lenses" will be used to process the voices, adding layers of meaning both positive and negative. The vocalists might be singing along with their own voices, prerecorded and manipulated. At other times, their voices might be altered in real time using both hardware and software processing. Lenses (whether physical or virtual, using video with computer manipulation) will also be used to manipulate the perception of macroscopic and microscopic magnification, the sense of looking deep within or out into the universe.

Substance is now in suspension until a presenting structure is found. In the meantime, there are a number of projects in the stage of research and development that overlap the boundaries of theater and installation, all operating with the idea of nonlinear narrative and with the audience not fixed in position or point of view. Farthest along in its conception is an opera/installation titled *Filiseti Mekidesi: In Search of Sanctuary*. This is a commission from the Ruhrtriennale to be premiered in September of 2018 with personnel including the Palestinian singer Kamilya Jubran, vocal group Voxnova Italia, the Cologne-based instrumental ensemble MusikFabrik, movement artists under the direction of Junko Wada, and video by Janene Higgins. Migration and sanctuary have been crucial to humanity since our first steps out of Africa thousands of years ago. Today, issues of refuge and free movement are as critical as ever, and highly charged politically. I hope to be able to translate some of what's in the air these days into sound, motion, light.

The other work within sight of production is *A Passionate Journey*, based on the (nearly) eponymous 1919 book by Belgian artist Frans Masereel, a pioneer of the graphic novel. A pacifist and social critic, he created allegorical Expressionist woodcuts, affecting and visceral, that became favorites of mine in the late '70s and remain relevant to all denizens of the industrial world. The libretto will make use of short phrases expanded in a virtuosic manner by the singers to emphasize phonemes and sung in a modernized version of the *bel canto* style. The few words chosen will be packed with meaning, both textual and allusive. *A Passionate Journey* is scored for six singers, three female and three male, plus chamber orchestra, as well as prerecorded soundfiles and an unspecified number of movement artists. Constructed in the form of a series of *tableaux vivants* in different locations at the performance site, the work may be experienced by visitors in any order. Stark lighting will play an important role in the staging, evoking Masereel's woodcuts. Intermittent video segments, both in the performance areas and in between, will provide expansion and commentary.

XV.

Room Tone

Along with my explorations of sound in time and action, I've long been intrigued by the sometimes ambiguous notions of sound with light and sound in space, divorced from traditional modes of listening. Sound with light means movies, and here inspiration abounded: Bernard Herrmann, Bebe and Louis Barron, Stanley Friedman, Ennio Morricone, Elmer Bernstein, and Jerry Goldsmith were a select few, not to mention the use of Györgi Ligeti's music in *2001: A Space Odyssey*. As for sound in space, Charles Ives, Xenakis, Henry Brant, and Alvin Lucier all explored the ways in which location and acoustic space affect the perception of music. Playing saxophone by a stream is a very different experience from doing so in a practice room, or on a stage, or accompanying dancers, or when underscoring a scene in a film. During my student days, we tried many strategies to shake up our audience's and our own process of hearing: placing musicians in balconies or in corners of the hall, under stairwells, in storage closets and bathrooms. Sometimes the musicians were asked to spin around to generate Doppler effects. *Innosense* completely eliminated stage and staging, suspending the performers in negative space. In contrast, by surrounding the audience with the musicians, *Crowds and Power* erased the safety of the distance between audience and performer.

As a fledgling composer for film, I had to learn some tough lessons. Rarely does one face a blank canvas on which to paint at will. The composer can function like an actor, donning costume or accent, channeling historical or geographical references. Always to be remembered, though, is that the filmmaker is the artist and you, the composer, are there to help them manifest their vision—a reality that at first can be difficult to accept.

On my first major scoring project, Amy Greenfield's film *Antigone* in 1985, there were disagreements between us over the very form the music would take. She insisted that I give her "stems," individual tracks with specific instruments and sounds: all percussion, all guitars, all saxophones. These would be mixed later by her sound editor, using the elements in whatever way worked for the film. Somewhat arrogantly, and without much understanding of the process of making a film, I felt that the mixing and placement of sounds in time was very much the composition of the music itself, and that I should create the finished music for each scene. Luckily, Amy was patient with my inexperience. With Roma Baran producing, we ended up recording some bass clarinet tracks for the film. In the final mix, the sound editor overdubbed separate percussion performed by David Van Tieghem. I was unpleasantly surprised on hearing the results at the screening. But after mulling over this seeming affront to my artistic integrity, I learned an important lesson about the process and how it differs from composing music for its own sake. Music for cinema should be composed with intensity and passion; once recorded, though, it no longer belongs to the composer, but to the filmmaker and sound editor for them to use as they wish.

My next scoring gigs went more smoothly. For *The Salt Mines*, a 1989 documentary by Susanna Aikin and Carlos Aparicio, my sonic ideas melded perfectly with theirs. They had me prepare tracks synchronized to the picture, and my finished mixes were used in the film unchanged. *Daddy and the Muscle Academy*, by Finnish filmmaker Ilppo Pohjola, is a documentary about Tom of Finland, the graphic artist who created iconic gay images with costumes echoing exaggerated roles in society (along with exaggerated genitalia). Ilppo gave me a few vague guidelines and suggestions but left me great latitude. The score was composed and recorded in 1991 over a period of a few months with a mix of music synchronized to picture and abstractions that might be used anywhere in the film, creations based on mood and shades of light and dark. Electronically processed guitar played a major role in these fragments.

Over the next few years, a number of small scores were commissioned for video and film, with budget limitations defining my instrumentation and approach. Beginning with *Daddy and the Muscle Academy*, I had begun to put aside funds to purchase equipment with which to build up a personal studio. The studio would serve not only for realizing finished productions, but for capturing ideas on the fly and creating tracks that could be used in live performance. Soon enough, I was producing finished masters.

The next major score was for Toni Dove's *Spectropia*, a sci-fi *noir* involving time travel and taking place in London in the future—with images of a spectacularly drowned New York City—and in New York itself in 1931. *Spectropia* would be a single-channel feature film, as well as an interactive sound installation that Toni created with Luke DuBois. For the score, Toni and I worked closely together on spotting cues. The future would be portrayed with broken drum machines and heavily distorted guitars. For 1931, I imagined the "jungle band" of Duke Ellington as orchestrated by Edgard Varèse. I was able to assemble a fantastic collection of players for a group that I dubbed The '31 Band: Duane Eubanks on trumpet; Art Baron, Curtis Fowlkes, and Steve Swell on trombones; Rudresh Mahanthappa on alto sax; Anthony Coleman on piano; Dave Hofstra on bass and tuba; Danny Tunick on vibraphone; and Don McKenzie on drums. The '31 Band was joined by the Sirius String Quartet led by Ron Lawrence; I myself would play B♭ and bass clarinets, tenor sax, drum machine, and guitars.

Toni asked that I compose a song for the film that would be both futuristic and nostalgic. She supplied me with keywords from the script, which I adapted and assembled into lyrics to create "This Time That Place." We contacted Blondie vocalist Debbie Harry to sing the song. I had long been a fan of her voice, a rare and compelling combination of ice and sensuality, and knew from Roy Nathanson that she possessed excellent musicianship. Basic tracks of The '31 Band were recorded at a studio in Brooklyn; I conducted using either a stop watch or metronome to match timings. The tracks were imported into Pro Tools at my own Studio zOaR, where I overdubbed my guitar and reed parts as well as the string quartet. Debbie came in to do her vocals, an exciting session in which she nailed the parts in two takes with just a few inserts. Debbie Harry at Studio zOaR! Hard to believe… Finally, I mixed and assembled master versions of the tracks, as well as stems that Toni and her sound editor could use as desired.

.

As part of Roulette's *Mixology* festival in 2012, Toni and Luke would present a demonstration of the *Spectropia* installation, after which I would bring The '31 Band on stage to perform the score. We had appeared at the 2007 International Jazz Festival Saalfelden, so the music was road-tested—though I'd sung "This Time That Place," offering a poor substitute for Debbie Harry. For the Roulette performance, the wonderful actress and vocalist Barbara Sukowa sang a haunting version of the song, a different flavor of the fire and ice demanded by the music.

Early in 1996, as internet speeds became faster and browser capabilities increased, I began to think about creating work that was not linear, neither narrative nor following an arc in time, but random access, interactive. The first plan was for *Sonome*, a web-based sonic installation inspired by the ongoing Human Genome Project. *Sonome* was somewhere between interactive sound installation, algorithmic radio station, and audio collage and would generate a continuous stream of sound based on contributions by the members of its online community. *Sonome* would be open to anyone and everyone, requiring only that the participant upload a six-second audio sample that would reveal something about their physical location: music, environmental soundscape, local radio or television broadcast. The sample need only be long enough to establish identity, but might define some rhythmic elements as well. The *Sonome* software would mix and crossfade the contributed audio in a continuously updating queue, flowing seamlessly between the samples in an ever-morphing stream. A visual interface on the *Sonome* website would display on a global projection where each sound originated. Casual listeners might log on to *Sonome* at any time to listen to the stream and view the results. As this was beyond my own programming capabilities, I floated proposals to various institutions to sponsor the creation of *Sonome* but met with no success. Given advances in both audio streaming and web software, it might be much easier to manifest *Sonome* now.

In parallel with these activities, Janene and I began to produce and present collaborative work. She would spontaneously mix and process live video that she had previously shot and edited, while I improvised the music, usually on eight-string guitarbass and various electronics. A live camera might also be brought into the mix. These performances had an easy flow—each of our roles freely shifting from foreground to background—and the special pleasure of working with one's life partner.

Thanks to Alanna Heiss and the Clocktower Gallery, I was given an opportunity to create a work not at all meant for focused listening but rather to function as ambience, what Erik Satie called "furniture music." *Distressed Vivaldi* was composed to be the soundtrack for the exhibition *Model Home*, opening on October 20, 1996; it played continuously at low level in the gallery. In this piece, two minutes of Vivaldi's *The Four Seasons*—30 seconds from each movement—were sampled into the computer and then manipulated using both software and hardware processing to generate a 60-minute piece in four sections. With its obvious imagery, *The Four Seasons* is one of the best known examples of program music and lends itself well to the notion of bourgeois comfort, especially given the trendy architectural practice in the 1990s of making a space look as if it had been ever-so-artfully damaged by the ages. The repetitive nature of *The Four Seasons* (as of other works by Vivaldi and his contemporaries) might also be seen as a precursor to Minimalism. Extreme time-stretching and pitch-shifting were my basic strategies, the resultant aliasing and other distortions contributing to the work's signature sound.

Tag was an interactive audio installation created for the Clocktower's next exhibition, *Departure Lounge*, opening on March 9, 1997. *Tag* was designed to allow visitors to the exhibition to leave their own temporary contribution to the ambient underscore. Four microphones in small metal boxes with grill openings were placed around the exhibition space, clearly labeled and height-accessible to a wide range of the public. Signal from the mics was fed to a mixer and routed to a hardware vocoder, the venerable Roland VP-70, along with a rhythmic pattern programmed on a Roland TR-505 drum machine using a detuned and softened cowbell patch. The MIDI output of the TR-505 modulated the vocoder's carrier signal, thereby tranforming any audio input to the vocoder. This combined signal was fed to an eight-second digital delay with a moderate amount of feedback, allowing signals in the system to last approximately 45 seconds. The final output was fed to a number of speakers situated around the gallery. Through signage, the public was encouraged to enter their "tag" (any verbal utterance, whether speech, singing, or some other sound) which then, modulated and recycled, became part of the gallery's soundspace. The continual refreshing of input information, combined with the relaxed groove of the 505, created an ever-shifting sonic environment reflective of the changing population of the show—simple music transformed by the vocal contributions of the visitors. The opening of *Departure Lounge* was packed, as Clocktower openings usually were, and the heat of the moment contributed to the manic underscore. I was thrilled that visitors to the gallery quickly picked up on the nature of *Tag* and pitched right in.

In 2000, Alanna asked me to join her in curating a comprehensive survey of sound art at PS1. I wanted to title it *Volume*, a word with many definitions and appropriate allusions to the context. During a series of brainstorming sessions to determine the content and presentation, Klaus Biesenbach came up with the idea of building a giant futon, the "Bed of Sound." Now titled *Volume: Bed of Sound*, the show would feature not one, but two giant futons, each in its own gallery. The first gallery presented 57 individual headphone stations mounted around the futon, each streaming a single artist. The other had a two-hour cycle of tracks from the entire collection of artists, played over a high-resolution speaker system so that visitors could lie on the futon and take in the sound.

The sound company supplying the huge, state-of-the-art speaker columns had brought in an acoustician to tune the devices to the room, and they were very precisely placed. When Maryanne Amacher (she whom my boss at the Buffalo electronic-music studio had warned me I'd one day meet and never forget) brought us the CD with her track, she insisted that during the playback of her piece, the speakers would have to be moved! Impossible. In the cafe there would be a Sound Art Jukebox, a two-hour streamed set of "classics" of sound art. Finally, two of the smaller galleries each featured individual work by Christian Marclay and Jonathan Bepler.

One of the highlights of curating the exhibition was a telephone conversation with Walter Murch, the brilliant sound designer and polymath, whom I'd invited to contribute a piece. To my delight and amazement, Walter sent a copy of the digital eight-track master for the infamous helicopter scene from Francis Ford Coppola's *Apocalypse Now*. After receiving the tape, I set up eight guitar and bass amplifiers in a ring in the live room of Studio zOaR on 30th Street, with the output of the DA88 digital tape deck routed through the mixing board and then to the amps through eight sends. I could barely contain my excitement as I prepared to hit "Play" on the deck. The sound was earth-shaking, beautiful in its massive monstrosity.

Volume: Bed of Sound opened on July 2, 2000. I had flown in that day from my residency at the Civitella Rainieri Foundation in Italy and went directly to PS1. Fortunately, like most PS1 openings, this one was packed and the atmosphere was galvanic. We'd wondered if New York City strangers would relax their guard enough to lie down near each other in public; in the event, they jumped without hesitation right onto the futon and into the headphone stations, the phones offering just enough separation between bodies. People took a little longer to discover and make use of the speaker room but it, too, was always crowded. Very satisfied, I headed back to JFK that night for my Italian sojourn: five weeks in Umbria, where I could compose and read undisturbed when I chose, but also enjoy the fantastic food and commune with such fellow Fellows as pianist Andrew Hill, painter Bhupen Khakhar, photographer Abelardo Morell, installation artist Sabrina Mezzaqui, and sculptor Sandile Zulu.

That autumn, I was brought to the School of the Museum of Fine Arts in Boston to do a series of lectures and workshops with students in the Time Arts department. As part of the gig, I was to create an audio work for the Dangerous Waves exhibition at the school's gallery, with an opening on January 24, 2001. Perusing the spaces in the gallery, I was drawn to a small sub-gallery, approximately fifteen by eight feet, and decided to use it for *Chromatine*—both musical instrument and sculpture. Four lengths of eighteen-foot piano wire, tuned in ratios of small whole numbers (1/1, 3/2, 5/3, 8/5, where 1/1 = 16 Hz) were mounted on the walls of the room and excited into vibration using the guts taken from Ebows, yielding a thick drone that would subtly change as the strings moved. The bridges for the strings were mounted on a wooden sub-assembly that also held a magnetic pickup for each string and the exciters. The output of each string's pickup went to a mixer and was there routed to its own amplified speaker, with a subwoofer reproducing a mix of all the low-frequency info. The sound from each string was also fed into a computer, with Max/MSP software running a patch written by Luke DuBois that analyzed the sound and both triggered and filtered prerecorded samples of long-string sounds made from the installation. Visitors to the installation might pluck, touch, tap, or rub the vibrating strings at any point to produce a variety of sonic effects. Certain points on the string—nodes— would produce distinct tones that would cause the samples to be triggered and played back in the room.

Volume: Bed of Sound was to be brought to the Henry Gallery in Seattle in 2001 in a somewhat reduced form. There would only be the one giant futon with headphone stations, along with a room featuring works by selected Seattle-area artists. For the opening, I was to give a short talk and concert. In the spirit of the exhibition, rather than perform an instrumental work I decided to premiere *Living Room,* a performance using mechanics, feedback, and room resonance as resources. The work is also a small tribute to Alvin Lucier's seminal *I am sitting in a room,* in which his text about room resonance is read, recorded, played back, and rerecorded over a number of iterations with surprising and beautiful results. For *Living Room*, a small microphone is swung overhead continuously for the 45-minute duration of the piece, picking up any sounds occurring in the space—including the sound of its own movements, "seed material" consisting of my fragmented spoken texts and vocal sounds, and, finally, acoustic feedback. These sounds are processed through filtering and delay plug-ins in a laptop to orchestrate the results into a symphonic mass of sound. *Living Room* has been performed in a variety of spaces, from small galleries to large theaters and lecture halls. Perhaps the strangest venue for the piece was poolside at the PoMo-glitzy Delano Hotel in South Beach, Miami, for Art Basel in 2005, where I joined the Art On Air staff as a DJ, organizer, performer, and creator of a sound installation, *Wet*, consisting of a playlist of aquatic-themed tracks played back through the swimming pool's underwater sound system. Up on dry concrete, I would play classic tracks of sound art and pioneering new music, and twice daily perform *Living Room*.

XVI.

Pursuing the IrRational

The process continues, asymptotic. The channels of my activities seem to be more clearly defined than ever before but by design they must allow for quick change, parallel realities, translation of state. They strive to balance the conceptual and the concrete, the abstract and the material, the direct narrative and the nonlinear, art and survival. Recorded music has been sorely devalued of late but now I find the concert experience to be charged up, hotter than ever. "IrRational Music" is still the best way to describe what I do in all of these channels. I can't separate its pursuit from my desire not just to make art, but to understand how and why I do what I do and thereby find newer and deeper ways to do it. As my understanding of the Inner Ear grows, I ask if it can be separated from the Mind itself.

We believe that our minds define our selves, not just in the everchanging present, but delving back into our complete past and projecting forward into our still-incomplete future. Minds transmit and receive data in a feedback loop, constantly updating our state of being and inputting new information into our perceptual systems, a process essential to our survival (and perhaps the source of our consciousness). The search for the nature of this Mind of ours has been a puzzle and inspiration for both reflection and generation, extending back to the dawn of self-awareness. A signal is sent out, then received again at its source, but with the ever-so-tiny delay caused by the gap in the synapse. The receptor recognizes the original signal, perhaps with some hormonal stamp. In this transaction, this recognition, awareness of self could form, then consciousness.

With daily discoveries stretching boundaries, our minds have become plastic, mutable in function, digesting and accepting new definitions and generalizations. We may find these elements contradictory; we may find them enlightening and clarifying. With every advance in knowledge of the physical and chemical workings of the brain, humans remain—in a paradox worthy of Zeno—woefully distant from complete knowledge of the nature of their own consciousness. Gödelian concepts apply as well to our self-awareness: with self-perception nested in self-perception, are we doomed to perpetuate self-deception? Can we break out of the frame and actually know Mind? As we verge on a time when Turing tests will be aced by AI toddlers, how will we recognize the Mind of the Other when we're still not absolutely clear as to its nature in ourselves?

We might say that our craniocentrism blinds us and deafens us. Certainly our very anthropocentrism has limited our outlook. Only in recent decades have modern Westerners (as opposed to their pre-Cartesian ancestors) graciously admitted that other creatures might indeed possess consciousness. The common belief has been that consciousness and memory reside in the brain, are solely a function of its chemistry. Are we so sure that Mind can be divorced from organs and muscles, from viscera, from our bubbling neurotransmitter stews that drift out into the very air around us? Witness the octopus! It might be said that every sight we see, every sound we make or hear, every move or shift, every pheromonal handshake, is part of the free-floating and expanding consensual reality that is Mind. Even though our hardware has been running for many thousands of years without a major update, our software is continually transforming to accomodate new modes of data transfer and processing, environments, definitions and frameworks.

It's no longer a radical notion that our individual memories have been externalized in something very like a cloud. And if memories can be external to the person, then could Identity itself, the individual consciousness, also be externalized? Would a conscious entity with no physical locus conceive of itself in the same way as an embodied one? How would the perceptual systems function in a disembodied Mind? What are the possible input and output devices? What would the mechanism of internal feedback be? If a disembodied Mind is to interact with a physical world, then what would the interface feel like, both to that Mind and to anyone encountering it? What would music be to such an entity?

Both concepts and technologies of Artificial Intelligence have advanced in recent years to the point that interaction with AI's is considered a normal part of daily life. But is the "I" in AI the same "I" that we think of as intelligence, the "I" that is truly a sense of self? Mechanical processes, even when happening millions of times per second, even with a heavy feedback component, are not the same as intelligence and certainly not the same as consciousness. Will a digital zero/one on/off mind feel the same, both internally and externally, as a slippery-slope chemical mind? Where is the all-important porosity that makes our intelligence what it is? Could it be embedded in a process of knowing and deciding that is based upon the continuous polling of tendencies, analogous to quantum states? Explicit expression, but with vast amounts of background processing contributing to the flux? A meat-machine hybrid brain (that concept so beloved of modern sci-fi)? I'm waiting for the day that an AI can experience synesthesia and express it. And what about AS, Artificial Stupidity—might that be closer to human consciousness? Will an AI ever compose music that rends your heart and soul, or is this reserved for those whose language can't be boiled down to just two states? Is the transcendent mystery of art somehow linked to the roots of its generation?

There's much in the air these days about how our local universe is undergoing a "singularity," how humanity must prepare itself for massive transformations. I contend that we've already been deeply into the singularity for quite a few years. A singularity isn't built in a flash or even a day! Whether this is seen as glorious or apocalyptic depends on the teller, and there are as many definitions of the nature of this singularity as there are tellers. The development of "self-awareness" in computers is often cited as a primary sign of this cusp-point. Contact with an alien civilization is another. How will humanity find a commonality of expression to communicate with an intelligence conceivably so different from our own that there is no recognition? Again, the question of interface and who controls it. What will the emergent power relationships be? In science fiction, the superior alien intelligence often adopts anthropic form and speaks English. Will a truly emergent AI condescend to speak to us as equals or might it demand true peer-to-peer contact and insist that humans rise to the occasion? Could music be the medium by which we measure cosmic intelligence and consciousness? Will music allow us to morph into fully realized beings able to meet an unfamiliar modality halfway? Can we learn to communicate, perhaps even sing songs using airborne molecular polymers, chains of regenerated RNA? Flashes of color? Qubit packets? Modulated sine waves? Will that achievement equal a willingness to let go of our traditional assumptions of mind grounded in physicality, of music grounded in sound? By abandoning these moorings, do we abandon the very core of our humanity? If that is indeed the case, then we might finally ask "Is this a good thing or a bad thing?" and have reasonable expectations of getting a clear answer. Psychoacoustic chemical change remains the prime motive for my work: translation from the Inner Ear, source of the IrRational.

Elliott Sharp
Selected Discography

Solo and Leader

Aggregat, Dialectrical (Clean Feed, 2016)
Momentum Anomaly (New Atlantis, 2013)
Aggregat (Clean Feed, 2012)
Octal, Books I-III (Clean Feed, 2007-2012)
Sharp? Monk? Sharp! Monk! (Clean Feed, 2005)
Quadrature (zOaR, 2004)
The Yahoos Trilogy (zOaR, 1985-2004)
The Velocity of Hue (zOaR, 2003)
Tectonics, Errata (Neos, 1998)
Tectonics, Field & Stream (zOaR, 1996)
Cryptid Fragments (zOaR, 1992)

Orchestra Carbon and Carbon

Transmigration at the Solar Max (Intakt, 2018)
Void Coordinates (Intakt, 2009)
Radiolaria (zOaR, 1999)
SyndaKit (Neos, 1998)
Rheo~Umbra (Neos, 1996)
The Age of Carbon (Intakt, 1984-1996)
Interference (Atavistic, 1995)
Amusia (Atavistic, 1994)
Serrate (zOaR, 1992)
Larynx (Neos, 1988)

Orchestral and Chamber Music

Oceanus Procellarum (Cavity Search, 2017)
Tranzience (New World, 2016)
The Boreal (Starkland, 2015)
Oneirika (Zeitkratzer, 2014)
Storm of the Eye, on Hilary Hahn: In 27 Pieces (Deutsche Grammophon, 2013)
String Quartets, Vol. 2 (Tzadik, 2002-2008)
Racing Hearts-Tessalation Row-Calling (HR Media, 2003)
String Quartets, Vol. 1 (Tzadik, 1986-1996)

Opera

Port Bou (Infrequent Seams, 2016)
Binibon (Henceforth, 2011)
Em/Pyre (Opus 10, 2008)
A Modicum of Passion (Abaton, 2004)
Innosense (zOaR, 1982)

Soundtracks

Room Tone (zOaR, 2019)
Calling All Earthlings (Cavity Search, 2018)
Incident (zOaR, 2016)
Q-Mix (zOaR, 2016)
Spectropia Suite (Neos, 2010)
Commune (zOaR, 2005)
Yellowman (zOaR, 2002)
Suspension of Disbelief (Tzadik, 2001)
Figure Ground (Tzadik, 1997)

Terraplane

4am Always (Yellowbird, 2014)
Sky Road Songs (Yellowbird, 2012)
Forgery (Intuition, 2008)
Secret Life (Intuition, 2006)
Do the Don't (zOaR, 2003)
Blues for Next (zOaR, 2000)
Terraplane (zOaR, 1994)

Collaborations

Chansons du Crepuscule w/ Hélène Breschand (Public Eyesore, 2017)
Rub Out The Word w/ Steve Buscemi (Infrequent Seams, 2016)
Tectonics, Fourth Blood Moon w/ Eric Mingus (Yellowbird, 2016)
Crossing the Waters w/ Melvin Gibbs/Luca Niggli (Intakt, 2013)
Let Her In w/ Nels Cline (Public Eyesore, 2013)
Electric Willie w/ Henry Kaiser, Glenn Philips, Eric Mingus, Melvin Gibbs
    (Yellowbird, 2010)
Scharfefelder w/ Scott Fields (Clean Feed, 2008)
The Prisoner's Dilemma w/ Bobby Previte (Grob, 2002)
Anostalgia w/ Reinhold Friedl (Grob, 2002)
High Noon w/ Christian Marclay (Intakt, 2000)
GTR OBLQ w/ Vernon Reid & David Torn (Knitmedia, 1998)
Blackburst w/ Zeena Parkins (Victo, 1996)
Jajouka New York w/ Bachir Attar (zOaR, 1990)
Bone of Contention w/ Semantics (SST, 1987)
Hara w/ David Fulton (zOaR, 1978)

Compilation Producer

I Never Metaguitar, Vol. I-IV (Cleanfeed, 2010-2015)
Secular Steel (Gaff Music, 2004)
State of the Union 2.001 (zOaR, EMF) 2001
Volume, Bed Of Sound (PS1, 2001)
State of the Union III (Atavistic, 1999)
State of the Union II (MuWorks, 1992)
Real Estate (Ear-Rational, 1990)
Island of Sanity (No Man's Land, 1986)
State of the Union I (zOaR, 1982)
Peripheral Vision (zOaR, 1981)

Acknowledgments

This entire volume could be considered an expression of thanks to the many artists, teachers, thinkers, doers, friends, and colleagues who have inspired and aided me on my path. My wish here is to convey that appreciation more directly.

For the initial impulse that catalyzed this book, I thank Lennart Stähle, a fine musician and web innovator who reached out to me in 1992 with Datacide, a comprehensive site he had created for my work, and then again in 1997 with the suggestion that I create a "weblog," an online diary of my activities on tour. That diary grew and expanded and its DNA infuses this book.

John Palmer, composer, pianist, and author, interviewed me in 2014 for his excellent *Conversations* and promptly invited me to publish a collection of my writings with his imprint Vision Editions. As that project metamorphosed into this one, John's feedback and focused suggestions were instrumental in helping me transform a Proustian mountain of text (in size if nothing else) into something approaching a readable book.

At that point, David Rothenberg of Terra Nova Press, species-breaching musician and philosopher, stepped in. With relentless enthusiasm and generosity, he both broadened and honed the outlook of this work. I am further indebted to David for introducing me to the esteemed author and savant Evan Eisenberg, who would become my editor at Terra Nova. I thank Evan for his punnery and for guiding me in ways both subtle and direct towards finding my authorial voice. Ed McKeon's generosity as a reader and magnifying glass was also key to my refining the text. I'm grateful, as well, to Kyla-Rose Smith and Chris Marianetti of Found Sound Nation for the ideas and energy they applied to both the architecture and the nuts and bolts of this edifice.

Since childhood I've been fascinated with the art of writing—the magic that allows a sequence of letters to inform, affect, and transform reality—and over the years have counted a number of authors and poets as friends, collaborators, and creative instigators. Some I've pestered with questions about the craft, some I've worked with, and with others I've just been content to exchange a few words. In addition to the aforementioned, they include Jack Womack, Tracie Morris, Jonathan Lethem, Lucius Shepherd, Dael Orlandersmith, Barbara Barg, Pat Cadigan, Peter Cherches, George Lewis, Jen Sacks, Ed Keller, William Gibson, Edwin Torres, Allen Ginsberg, Michael Benson, Veniero Rizzardi, Maggie Estep, Eric Bogosian, Lisa Randall, Benoit Mandelbrot, Eric Mingus, Dan Kaufman, Charlie Keil, John Kruth, Tom Drury, Nathaniel Levtov, Christopher Johnson, Sean Wilentz, Lynne Tillman, Wolf Kampmann, Eric Bogosian, Ronny Someck, and Lauri Bortz.

Here's to all the musicians, bandmates, players, and ensembles with whom, over the decades, I've exchanged sounds, thoughts, and emotions beyond words. Special thanks to the core—those metaphysicians who, in the extended hangs of our wonder years, furnished so much of the foundation: David Fulton, Steve Piccolo, Joel Eckhaus, Steve Cohan, Mari Jensen, Chris Vine, Jim Whittemore, David Goessling, Al Kaatz, Bobby Previte, Tom Bussoletti, Marla Cade, Paul Diamond, Greg Ketchum, Mark E. Miller, Charles K. Noyes, Christian Marclay, and Butch Morris. And to my fellow travelers Frances-Marie Uitti, Anthony Coleman, Henry Kaiser, Rhys Chatham, Michiyo Yagi, Carl Stone, Melvin Gibbs, Joe Mardin, Zeena Parkins, Dave Hofstra, Marc Ribot, Vernon Reid, David Torn, Brandon Ross, Jamie Lowry, Wayne Horvitz, Reinhold Friedl, Nels Cline, Robin Holcomb, John Zorn, and Glenn Branca, I say "Yo!" in the fullest sense of the word.

Alanna Heiss has been a supporter, mentor, and synergist since the 1980s and, together with Fred Sherman, a prime mover in the genesis of this work. Whether in collaboration or conversation, Toni Dove has likewise been the perfect radical stimulant. Bernd Leukert and Clair Lüdenbach have long extended their hospitality, opening doors to new realms in E-Musik. Karl and Isabella Bruckmaier opened to me their house and the windows of Hörspiel. Matthias Osterwold continues to define for me the meaning of "Freunde guter Musik." To Bert and Charlotte Shapiro, I am indebted for their vision, wisdom, and garden; to Andreas Sterzing, for the decades-long loan of his keen eyes.

Substantial portions of *IrRational Music* were written during my Berlin Prize Fellowship at the American Academy in Berlin in 2015, and I continue to appreciate the warmth and generosity of that institution and its staff.

Thanks to my parents, who brought me into this plane and offered love and encouragement, criticism and discipline, a deep sense of appreciation for science, art, music, knowledge, justice, compassion. Thanks to my siblings, aunts, and uncles for being there (and a special shout-out to my uncle Charles who, since my childhood, was always a "bad example" in the best way).

To my life partner, Janene, my deepest gratitude for her conservation of angular momentum, which keeps my often erratic gyroscope always in the groove. Without the love from her and our children Lila and Kai, this book could not have been written. They keep it real and make it all possible.

–Elliott Sharp, New York City, July 2018

Many thanks to all of our Kickstarter supporters and especially

Christopher Allis
Anthony B. Creamer III
Joe Dizney
Howard Eisenberg
Charlotte Freeman
Ed Keller
Fred Kendrick
Rainer Koch-Koelsch
Matteo Liberatore
Katy Luo
Barry Magid
Harvey Nosowitz
Charles K. Noyes
Katie O'Looney
Markus Reuter
Bert Shapiro
Victor Shargai
Lennart Stahle
Taylor Van Horne

Illustration Credits

p. 107: In Cleveland, 1954, photo by Bernard Sharp.

p. 108: At Cornell University, 1970, photographer unknown.

p. 109: Excerpt from graphic score for *Yugen*, 1973, by Elliott Sharp.

p. 110: With Buffy, Williamsburg, MA, 1978, photo by Cletha Francis.

p. 111: Active bows, 1982, photo by Catherine Ceresole.

p. 112: With triple-course bass pantar, 1991, photo by Janene Higgins.

p. 113: Coffee with Hubert Sumlin, 1994, photo by Alex Kahane.

p. 114: With Muhammad Abu Ajaj, 2000, photo by Ze'ev Schlik.

p. 115: With Janene backstage in Porto, 2004, photo by Elliott Sharp.

p. 116: Conducting *Quarks Swim Free*, 2006, photo by Janene Higgins.

p. 117: With Godin guitar, 2007, photo by Sascha Rheker.

p. 118: At Shinjuku Pit Inn, Tokyo, 2012, photo by Mark Rappaport.

p. 119: With Lila, Kai, and Janene, 2012, photo by Merri Cyr.

p. 120: With Koll eight-string, 2013, photo by Scott Friedlander.

p. 121: With Bachir and Mustapha Attar, 2014, photo by Cherie Nutting.

p. 122: With Cecil Taylor, 2014, photo by Don McKenzie.

Chapter opening illustrations all from
Elliott Sharp, *Foliage* (2012), a series of 250 graphic scores.

Cover photo by Andreas Sterzing.

Index